CRITICAL ELT IN ACTION

Uniquely bridging theory and practice, this text introduces and overviews the various domains associated with the term *critical pedagogy* in the field of TESOL/ELT. Critical pedagogy addresses concepts, values, curriculum, instructional and associated practices involved in language teaching for social justice. Bringing critical pedagogy to classroom practitioners in a practical and comprehensible way, the text is designed to help teachers get started on critically grounded work in their own teaching.

Features

- Textbook extracts offer direct and quick illustration of what this perspective might look like in practice
- Coverage of feminist and anti-racist pedagogies; sexual identity, oppression and pedagogy; peace and environmental education—and their implications for second-language teaching
- Historical background—shows that critical ELT can be done because it has been done before
- Theoretical background on language and learning—provides confidence that critical ELT pedagogy is well grounded
- Consideration of applicability of critical/radical educational concepts and traditions to non-Western cultural contexts (critical English as a foreign language)
- A focus on issues of compromise and resistance—what can a teacher do in contexts where the institutional or social context is not favorable?

This original, timely, and informative text is ideal for any course on methods and approaches in TESOL.

Graham V. Crookes is Professor, Department of Second Language Studies, University of Hawai'i at Mānoa, USA.

CRITICAL ELT IN ACTION

Foundations, Promises, Praxis

Graham V. Crookes

Routledge
Taylor & Francis Group

NEW YORK AND LONDON

First published 2013
by Routledge
711 Third Avenue, New York, NY 10017

Simultaneously published in the UK
by Routledge
2 Park Square, Milton Park, Abingdon, Oxon OX14 4RN

Routledge is an imprint of the Taylor & Francis Group, an informa business

Library of Congress Cataloging in Publication Data
Crookes, Graham.
Critical ELT in action : foundations, promises, praxis /
by Graham V. Crookes.
    p. cm.
Includes bibliographical references and index.
1. English language – Study and teaching – Foreign speakers.
2. English teachers – Training of. I. Title. II. Title: Critical English
Language Teaching in action.
PE1128.A2C724 2013
428.0071–dc23   2012032643

ISBN: 978-0-415-88348-1 (hbk)
ISBN: 978-0-415-88349-8 (pbk)
ISBN: 978-0-203-88425-0 (ebk)

Typeset in Bembo
by HWA Text and Data Management, London

SUSTAINABLE
FORESTRY
INITIATIVE

Certified Sourcing
www.sfiprogram.org
SFI-00555
The SFI label applies to the text stock.

Printed and bound in the United States of America by
Walsworth Publishing Company, Marceline, MO.

To my family, and to Ikaika's future

BRIEF CONTENTS

CONTENTS

PREFACE

The purpose of this book is to address issues that might face those beginning to explore second language critical pedagogy, including my own questions as a beginner. What are its elements, main points, primary concepts? How might a language teacher start doing critical language pedagogy? Where does it come from? What underpins or supports it? Where is it going? And are there any dangers I face if I try it?

The primary audience is teachers of English as a second or foreign language, partly because that is my primary professional community, and partly because, for now, English is the most powerful language and the language most deeply involved in international lineages of power and privilege. But I draw on some of the (small) literature of critical language pedagogy of languages other than English, and I believe that large portions of the work are not language-specific, so that teachers of other powerful (sometimes imperial?) languages such as Spanish, or Chinese, or any language that is potentially a tool of emancipation as well as a device of oppression, could draw from what is here.

A distinctive feature of the book is the opening chapters, with their focus on sample materials. Teaching materials have received less emphasis than they deserve, within the large literatures of critical pedagogy generally. Another distinctive feature is in the last chapter, where I turn from critical language teaching and learning to critical forms of social organization, a topic which is a logical implication of the thrust of critical pedagogy, yet nevertheless another topic underexplored by those writing about critical pedagogy.

Overview

Chapter 1 introduces the material and content of critical language pedagogy in a substantive way. In Chapter 2 I review some classic textbook materials exemplifying key aspects of this perspective.

In Chapter 3 I break things down into a set of elements of curriculum that I see as implied by and contained in critical language pedagogy. My idea here is that we could develop our first steps in critical pedagogy by taking up one or another of them; or perhaps some at the same time, but maybe not all at once.

In Chapter 4 I go back to the histories of this tradition and discuss where this line comes from (now that we have some better idea concerning the practicalities).

In Chapter 5 I take a more academic approach, trying to answer the questions of those who would ask about whether the approach is based on theories of language and of second language learning.

Chapter 6 opens things out by looking at different domains of critical pedagogy. There is a range of different things which need to be addressed if social justice, in one form or another, is to be fostered through our practice as language teachers.

Chapter 7 responds to the fact that you don't just get into a classroom without somebody setting things up and administering things, usually. It suggests, first, the importance of institutional contexts and options, and second, that critical language pedagogy has to include educators who administer as well as teach.

Chapter 8 tackles a couple of difficult questions that you'd probably want to hear an answer to—like, "is it ok to do this"? It also asks about actions and outcomes of this work. And Chapter 9 says, where's this all leading to, anyway?

And at that point, of course, you won't know all there is to know about this critical ELT pedagogy. No one does, not even the many specialists whose work I cite. I provide plenty of references to their work throughout this book. On the other hand, you have to become your own specialist, in that each one of us has different local conditions to contend with. So, through your own work, explorations, and reflections, you will become your own specialist. Stay in touch, tell others, even write your own book—please.

ACKNOWLEDGMENTS

I am happy to acknowledge the support and encouragement of my editor, Naomi Silverman. A substantial part of the writing was done during a sabbatical at the School of Languages, Universidad de Antioquia, Medellín; I would like to thank Dr. Doris Correa and her colleagues there for their particularly patient support during my time with them.

My wife helped me press forward with the work, for which also many thanks. And finally, in a way this book is partly thanks to Dr. Steven Talmy, except that it arrives about a decade after he might have expected it. Better late than never …

1

INTRODUCTION

Teachers have been doing something called "critical pedagogy" for fifty years (using that term), and for hundreds of years, or perhaps always, under a range of related terms. In a general sense, a pedagogy which can use the term "critical" is a perspective on teaching, learning, and curriculum that doesn't take for granted the status quo, but subjects it to critique, creates alternative forms of practice, and does so on the basis of radical theories of language, the individual, and society that take seriously our hopes for improvement in the direction of goals such as liberty, equality, and justice for all. In this book, I hope to address the practical questions that any language teacher starting out to engage with this viewpoint might ask. My primary group of language teachers are teachers of English as an additional language, but teachers of other languages, indeed any language of power, or any language associated with an oppressed group or culture as well, might benefit.

Variants of this tradition were in place during my time as a high school student and implicit in the widespread counter-culture taken for granted by many young people in those days. But it was not part of my education as a teacher, and though some elements of it were visible on the margins of my upbringing as a language specialist, it took a long time for it to come in to applied linguistics and language teaching generally. Thus even for those of us who (like me) have the time and conditions to reflect in writing on this topic, many beginner and beginning questions concerning critical pedagogy and its practices have still to be worked out. Many language teachers have an apprenticeship of observation that spans decades even before they come to take on the role of teacher; but almost none of us has a period of apprenticeship in which to observe critical language pedagogy. Thus many of us have to tackle the question of "how to begin" without any models, external or internal, to guide us. My goal in this book is to start to fill this gap.

And my goal in the next lighthearted section is to begin in as rapid a way as I can. I wrote the book to answer questions that I asked myself, that I asked specialists, and that I was myself asked. So I think I can still hear some of those questions, and I imagine some potential readers asking me them now. Should they really have to wade through the whole book—could I give them a quick preliminary answer now? I would like to do so in a way that suggests that the people involved in critical language pedagogy are real, talk, and engage in dialogue, and are in a hurry to get on with things, important things (like critical language pedagogy itself, a form of action above all else). So here follows a little imaginary exercise in something that's almost the opposite of academic prose, for once!

Voices

Voice 1 I came to critical pedagogy because I didn't have the means to back up what I wanted to do. I wanted the chairs in a circle, the principal said I couldn't, I didn't have an argument to give him. But just a few days earlier, someone had given me a copy of Freire's *Pedagogy of the Oppressed*. I went home, I stayed up the whole night, and I was hooked.
(Henry Giroux, http://www.youtube.com/watch?v=UvCs6XkT3-o)

Voice 2 What happens, then, when a young teacher meets for the first time the hypothesis of changing his or her behavior in the classroom? What happens when the young teacher meets the possibility of changing her or his teaching practice? Maybe she or he read some text and thinks for the first time to become a critical educator, a new way of simultaneously reading the word and reading the world. What happens?

He or she comes to the classroom with a new conviction, but this new teacher was already shaped into the dichotomy between text and context. Then, it is hard to overcome the old dichotomy and integrate words and world. The teacher has a hard time giving witness in overcoming the rupture of intellectual study from the experience of the world. Dialectically connecting the two which have been separated so far and for so long is opposite to the teacher's official training.
(Paulo Freire in Shor & Freire, 1987, p. 136)

Voice 3 [A] quote on my wall reminds me every day why I teach. I want to think and learn along with my students, so that they can feel the excitement of lifelong learning. I appreciate their insights, their abilities to synthesize and question, to struggle for truth and reason. I want my students to pursue questions that don't have easy answers …

"1   The purpose of education in an unjust society is to bring about equality and justice.

2   Students must play an active part in the learning process.

3   Teachers and students are both simultaneously learners and producers of knowledge.

—Paulo Freire"
(Mary Cowhey, 2006, p. 124)

Voice 4   I have to admit this course was the most direct and enlightening teaching experience that I have had, although it had some contradictory effects on me. First of all, I felt isolated, destitute, and high and dry; since my colleagues were quite reluctant to even share their ideas (the course was radical and dealt with taboos and forbidden topics). Ignorance is not a blessing, but critical reflection made me dissatisfied and skeptical about everything. Every text seemed to be biased and served a particular group interest. I saw power, dominance and social inequality more clearly than before, and I felt futile and incompetent to change the world around me. But there was something else: I changed myself a lot and when a person changes, there is a chance for the world to change too!

(Sima Sadeghi, EFL teacher, Iran; see Sadeghi, 2009, p. 359)

Voice 5   I started teaching in the mid-seventies when … negotiating the curriculum [was an] element of a familiar educational discourse in my home state of South Australia … Being "radical", as we understood it at that time, was almost the norm amongst my cohort of newly appointed English teachers …

(Barbara Comber, in Cooper & White, 2006, p. 51)

Three imaginary dialogues

[The first speaker could be you, or one of you, the readers of this book. The second speaker is me; I'll introduce myself after the dialogues. The dialogues are here to give you a quick sense of what this book offers you, some of you, depending on who you are …]

Dialogue 1

– I'm a young English language teacher—people say I'm enthusiastic, energetic, and eager. I want to try out critical language pedagogy. How do I start?

– OK, you are currently teaching a class, right?

- Yes.
- Adults, high school kids or elementary?
- Can we talk about all of them?
- Sure, and there are plenty of finer divisions that are relevant. I think I'd deal with elementary separately. In fact, why don't we talk about them first. OK, it seems to me that there's a lot of focus on literacy (not to mention basic math skills) within the core of the elementary curriculum. And besides basals and phonics, lots of teachers read to their kids. Rug time read-alouds are absolutely standard practice. So what kind of books should be read? Those that simply reestablish mainstream dominant culture positions, or those that might lead to some questioning?
- The second kind, of course.
- So without disrupting the rest of your lessons, your scope and sequence, or any of your other activities, one thing you could do—if you could just put your hands on some different, critical literacy content—you could use them in your read-aloud time, then carefully engage the kids in some discussion afterwards. If you try this, I believe you would be on your way. There's lots more that could gradually be moved towards.
- But I'm in an EFL situation.
- OK, the EFL context is more difficult. There is a lot more elementary EFL than there used to be, and in developed countries it has picked up a lot of the general elementary curricular practices, which means activities-based, games, songs, and so on. So simple picture-book read-alouds aren't out of the question; the question is, at what level? And here I think you might have to make your own materials, adapting some of the stuff I've already mentioned.
- OK, what about adults?
- Much depends on the nature of the course. But one option is, without disrupting the rest of your lesson or the week's activities, ask for some oral—or better, written—feedback on their interests and the reasons they're taking the course, even if you think you already know. Basically I think a relatively simple, not too disruptive line is to move towards participatory curriculum development.
- What's that?
- It's students having substantial input into the content of the course.
- Sounds difficult. What if they just want to talk about rock stars, hobbies, boring stuff like that.
- You have to go at it a bit at a time. But you're entitled to state your views and if you can develop the language you and they need, then you can have a discussion. But ethically, you also have to know why your students are there.

- Usually it's because they have to be.
- What could be done about that?
- Not much, not all at once.
- Exactly. Getting this to work often involves very small steps. But even if they have to be there, wouldn't they be better off if they had a say in what was going on in the class?
- Yes, that makes sense. And high school kids?
- Equally, I think we should be moving towards a critical needs analysis (huh?)—finding out what they really need or want. But it could also be that you could identify what bugs them most about their class. If it's exams, for example, there's lots to be said and done about "democratic assessment."
- What's that?
- Well, answering questions like that is why you picked up this book …
- Yeah. But I think I've got the main points now. I'll get started and read the rest of this later.
- No, no! You can't go off half-cocked. Lots of people have tried critical pedagogy with only half an idea about what it is, had a bad experience, and then said that it doesn't work. Do me the favor of reading the whole book first before you try anything at all! Or another one. There's plenty on the shelf next to this one. Look, lots of people have been working on this for fifty years or more and you may as well take advantage. Let me say a bit more before you drop this back on the shelf: This perspective is not for the faint-hearted; it's not even for the absolute novice in language teaching. It needs a language teacher with energy, experience, and a vision of social change. And she still needs to read this book, or another like it, and for that matter get in touch with people really trying out these ideas.

Dialogue 2

- I'm an experienced, cautious, proficient English teacher in an EFL high school. I am confident of my ability to plan and introduce new material, but I am wondering, how politically dangerous is this critical pedagogy—and what about student and parent resistance?
- Good questions! Well, people *have* been trying out this sort of thing in a range of EFL contexts, and I can provide you with some summaries. Student and parent resistance, however, can only be tackled gradually and might still be overwhelming in some cases, such as upper level classes which have traditionally been devoted to exam prep. It is a matter of choosing your sites. If you're a very experienced teacher and you want to extend your professional skills, maybe you must ask to be assigned a junior class!

Dialogue 3

- Never mind the theory and the history—where's the textbook?
- You put your finger on a sore point. Do you like your textbooks?
- No, not really, they never get at students' real needs and worries.
- Well then, what do you think about developing your own?
- That might be really hard; not to mention time-consuming. Have you got any examples?
- Yes, we do … and with them in hand, you and your students might be able to make your own …

And who is this person writing this …?

I'm a teacher educator and researcher in English Language Teaching. I'm a white middle class man, married with one child, and I've been working as a language teacher and teacher educator for a long time now, more than thirty years. A large part of it has been in the role of a professor in a department of the University of Hawai'i. I've worked on and investigated a large range of aspects of language learning and teaching. Over the last decade or so, I've begun to explore the ideas of critical pedagogy, working almost entirely with young teachers who, like myself, don't have a lot of pre-existing relevant experience to draw upon. This was because of a variety of reasons. I became increasingly concerned that the research that academics engage in doesn't fully get transformed into improved second language learning for all. One possible reason for this is that the resources needed for good education, for advanced forms of second language teaching and learning that are research-based, are extremely unequally distributed. I noticed that even those curricula and syllabuses which were supposed to be motivating and reflect the needs of learners, didn't in many cases respond to what were their more important needs, that reflected their position in a society where resources were unequally distributed and opportunities and daily life concerns vary so much. That is to say, we were missing a "critical" needs analysis. This is only one point of concern; more will become evident in the chapters that follow. And more personally, I was looking for ways in which my values and my view of society could be better integrated in my work, my teaching and research. As I have a critical view of society, I would like to see things improve, in particular directions or in respect to particular limitations of present forms of society; thus I need critical forms of educational practice (not to mention critical forms of second language research and teaching). I have been a perpetual beginner in this area, trying out one or another angle in this arena, and always trying to provide reasonable answers to the questions the teachers I work with (some of whom are quite experienced language teachers, some not) have been asking me about this area, this approach, this perspective. If you value basic ideals such as equality, democracy, freedom, and solidarity and are looking for a way to bring those fully to bear in your professional practice as a language teacher, critical language pedagogy may be for you.

Questions for discussion

1 Although it may be a bit early to consider this, how do your personal values as a teacher manifest in your teaching? As a professional (*if* you are accorded professional working conditions) you presumably have professional values, and a sense of what is ethically appropriate in language teaching. What are some of those values? Do they concern only the individual student and the teacher, or do they have wider (even societal) features?

2 Alternatively, some say that teachers must be neutral. This is a position particularly transmitted in contexts where a teacher is primarily a civil servant or a public worker. As you will see later in this book, that is not a position that is consistent with the idea of an active citizen or the idea that professionals necessarily have an active role in the development of society. What are your present views about this?

2

GETTING STARTED

Materials and curriculum content

Preliminary definitions

Critical language pedagogy emerges from the interaction of theories and practices of language teaching that foster language learning, development, and action on the part of students, directed towards improving problematic aspects of their lives, as seen from a critical perspective on society. It applies both immediately (that is, it could address learners' current situation, in or outside of school) and in the long term (that is, it should foster learners' active citizen participation in democratic processes for social change in the direction of equity and justice for all).

Critical pedagogy is teaching for social justice, in ways that support the development of active, engaged citizens who will, as circumstances permit, critically inquire into why the lives of so many human beings, perhaps including their own, are materially, psychologically, socially, and spiritually inadequate—citizens who will be prepared to seek out solutions to the problems they define and encounter, and take action accordingly. Second language professionals within the project of critical pedagogy focus on language and culture—matters which, to a large extent, make human beings what they are. Such second language teachers are creating the subfield of critical language pedagogy, as some specialists and practitioners have been doing off and on for some thirty years now.

Critical traditions in education and language teaching go back a long way (for details see Chapter 4), but for now suffice to say that during the 1980s they showed up in the field of second language (L2) studies in a very small way in foreign language teaching, and slightly more substantially in second language ESL-related immigrant education (in places like the USA and the UK), under the heading of critical pedagogy. They also surfaced under the heading *critical language awareness* at that time. (Critical pedagogy and critical language awareness are two central terms for the discussion here.) Since the 1980s many other variants as well, such as critical literacy, critical whole language, and critical multicultural education, and second language related versions of them have appeared and will be explored further on in this book.[1]

Getting started: The utility of sample materials

This chapter focuses on certain selected materials samples and lesson plans, and also notes some specifications of content.[2] Teaching materials in particular are important because they may provide, to language teachers new to the topic, a concrete sense of where a teacher could start and also an idea of what *some* critical language pedagogy classrooms have looked like. Of course, language classrooms vary enormously. Even mainstream language teaching perspectives wouldn't suggest using materials designed for one context in another. However, like others before me, I think that materials examples are a pretty good place to start learning about what a particular way of teaching looks like, if you can't turn to videos and you haven't got actual classrooms of the type of interest to visit. Listening to teachers talk, or reading their accounts of critical language pedagogy are also good. As Edelsky and Johnson (2004, p. 123) say,

> a multitude of situated examples are needed to make it easier to adapt, improvise, and invent for other contexts, to make critical education more readily imaginable.

In critical language pedagogy we don't actually have as many of these accounts and examples as exist in other areas of second language curriculum (or of critical curriculum, for that matter). So in addressing language teachers new to this area, I'm going to say, "Let's start by looking at some sample materials," then, in the next chapter, "break them down" into options and things to try to see if you can figure out which you want to tackle first.

Very few language classes are started in a complete vacuum. Teachers often have some idea what was taught before, what the previous or a related scope and sequence or syllabus was, even if a needs analysis has not been done. In developing or taking on a class or course, language teachers naturally ask for or look for such things, and in particular, are curious about what materials have been developed or used before, or are available. The availability of a good textbook or locally developed materials will make a considerable difference to the confidence of a teacher taking on a new course.

Relatedly, when teachers of any kind, and of course language teachers, hear about or are curious about critical or radical pedagogies, in the back of

---

TASK: REFLECT

Think about a course you have taught. Did you start with a textbook, or with some indication of what had been done before, or with a needs analysis? In general, how dependent are you on materials? How obliged are you to use existing materials?

---

their minds, and perhaps in the front of their minds as urgent and important questions would be, "What kind of materials could I use to teach in this way or with this perspective? Are the materials going to be difficult or challenging for me? Where will I get them from?"[3] Such teachers may be surprised when they hear that a classic tenet of critical pedagogy is that, to a fair extent, students and teachers make, or bring in, "the materials."

Back in 1978, Linda Crawford was perhaps the first foreign language specialist[4] to systematize the critical pedagogy of Paulo Freire, presenting it in a reworked version for foreign language teaching. Consider point #12 of Crawford's 20 principles of Freirean critical pedagogy (1978, pp. 90–91, 99; Crawford-Lange, 1981): "[12] ... the learners produce their own learning materials."[5] This point could be quite challenging to the beginning teacher in this area, but it can be diminished by access to fully worked out sample materials, including ones which demonstrate how understandings of language play out in critical L2 pedagogy classrooms. Actually, samples of materials are to be found in Freire's early writings. His initial publications in English included a conceptually important set of illustrations that he had used to stimulate the first round of instruction in his L1 literacy "culture circles" (Freire, 1973; originally published in 1969).[6] These were scene-setting pictures intended to induce student reflection and discussion of a theory of literacy that would include the idea that reading the word provided the potential for changing the world. Subsequent phases of instruction were based on (a) core word lists; and (b) locally relevant terms and issues that were brought up in specific courses. These of course varied from location to location, though Freire reproduced some of the word lists in more than one of his books.

Publications which largely constitute materials used in critical pedagogy are few in number compared with those describing critical pedagogy practices, and much fewer yet again than those that develop the theory of critical pedagogy.[7] There are *descriptions* of pedagogy, which may be accompanied by approximate lesson plans (a good early non-L2 example is Shor, 1980; a more recent ESL example is Morgan, 1998[8]). Because of their length it is hard to summarize the narratives. And indeed, many of these do refer to things students brought in, or things that teachers developed on site with students[9] rather than presenting items and formats and materials that teachers could use "straight out of the box." But still, Morgan (1998, p. 129) reports after presentation of his accounts of practice at a conference, "Many ... teachers enthusiastically approached me afterwards for copies of my lesson plans and with requests for more 'practical' materials." This is the point I am exploring here for a moment, the need for more practical materials.

Before we go on, note that when formal content material is necessary in a class (particularly in areas closer to the sciences, or engineering), standard content textbook materials could be used. Shor writes (1992, p. 35),

> [It is not the case that] students have nothing to learn from biology or mathematics or engineering as they now exist. Neither does it mean that students reinvent subject matter each time they study it or that the academic expertise of the teacher has no role in the classroom. Formal bodies of knowledge, standard usage, and the teacher's academic background all belong in critical classrooms. As long as existing knowledge is not presented as facts and doctrines to be absorbed without question, as long as existing bodies of knowledge are critiqued and balanced from a multicultural perspective, and as long as the students' own themes and idioms are valued along with standard usage, existing canons are part of critical education. What students and teachers reinvent in problem-posing is their relationship to learning and authority. They redefine their relationships to each other, to education, and to expertise ...

In these cases, standard content textbook materials could be used, but they would be subject to the same problematizing and critique that any other brought-in object or materials would be. Which doesn't directly answer the question, "What would core critical language materials look like?"

A few critical pedagogy specialists have published sample curriculum guides, frameworks, and lesson plans. These can be quite helpful (though they are not particularly well-known or easily accessible). Because of the tenet I mentioned earlier concerning student-made materials, those who have described or outlined materials have sometimes prefaced them defensively (e.g., Kanpol, 1999, ch. 6). That said, it should also be mentioned that quite a lot of critical pedagogy specialists, including some in language areas, have produced narrative works, both articles and books, in which they describe at length their teaching procedures. These are often very stimulating, though lengthy for the busy teacher. In many cases one is obliged to acknowledge that the circumstances described were rather favorable; or indeed not initially favorable but as the result of many years of work, were made favorable by very dedicated teachers (e.g., Cowhey, 2006). These accounts though are sometimes a bit daunting by the degree of dedication they indicate, and at the same time they don't necessarily offer an immediate way in to trying out the ideas of critical language pedagogy (precisely because they are accounts by very experienced, gifted, and committed teachers working in favorable circumstances). Also, being extended narratives they do not constitute or offer an immediate handout or lesson plan for use "on Monday morning." And then there is the academic literature of theoretical critical pedagogy, which is probably what Kanpol (1999, p. 138) has in mind as one reason why he presents materials outlines:

> If critical pedagogues are to make inroads into schools of education at the higher education level and in public schools, something must be done about making critical pedagogy's ideas at least pragmatically accessible. Of course, this is not a call to simply lay out a formula of how to "do it." This is totally against the tradition of critical pedagogy and would simply be an act of deskilling. But what must finally be realized by critical pedagogists is the necessity to find alternatives to a stultified and standardized curriculum. There is a need to attempt a critical platform in some operational manner if we are to begin to grasp any sense of a democratic dream that critical pedagogists strive for.

He continues, a little defensively, saying that he doesn't need to defend this.[10] His unit plan is a useful description of a unit in critical multicultural education, intended to cover one semester or fifteen weeks' work, and based in the specific needs of a specific class consisting of "eighteen white, six African American, three Hispanic; and three Asian." It reads like a retrospective syllabus, and was actually designed by his students for a specific teaching context. In concluding remarks he comments simply "I did not want to provide lessons but just provide some examples" (p. 156).

But similar to what I am outlining in the rest of the chapter, preprepared materials do fly in the face of some key positions in critical pedagogy. Torres (1994, p. 86) is dismissive of an actual literacy program for immigrants that had a "pre-determined list of 'generative themes'" and thereby was acting "antithetical to the methods and spirit of critical teaching." However, as presented by Kanpol, and through analysis of descriptions by Shor, and more explicitly through the fully worked-out sample materials of Auerbach, Wallerstein, and Janks (to be discussed in some detail shortly), through Auerbach's descriptions of teachers working together to create curriculum, and through the retrospective account by Wallace of a critical reading course, and so on, such materials and reports of materials in practice can serve a critical teacher's pedagogy, rather than replace the procedures of critical pedagogy. This suggestion is consistent with the views of Edge and Wharton (1998; cf. Hutchinson & Torres, 1994; Waters, 2009[11]), who state (p. 299) that a carefully designed course book can *in itself* encourage development: it can carry the seeds of its own creative adaptation. Far from making the skills of decision making and pedagogical reasoning redundant, it can assist teachers to develop these skills further.

So I regularly turn to the handful of fully worked-out examples of critical language pedagogy embodied in published textbooks. They should not be followed just as they stand, in most contexts where beginning critical language teachers operate. The authors themselves would certainly never suggest that their materials (written for fairly specific contexts, in some cases decades ago) be used now in different contexts in ways other than to stimulate reflection and action.[12]

In the following section, I will discuss some of these examples. As I do so, please bear in mind that this whole area (of materials for L2 critical/radical language pedagogy) is rather under-developed, for various reasons. One surely is the strong commitment to student- and teacher-made lesson plans and to the use of local, immediately relevant realia (as opposed to long-lasting, generally applicable textbooks). But another is that it's usually difficult to get the large mainstream commercial publishers who dominate the international TESOL field to produce materials of this orientation (cf. Gray, 2002, 2010)[13]. Furthermore, the small amount of sample critical materials tends to address the intermediate (or advanced) second language learner, or the false beginner, in primarily ESL contexts. We have almost nothing for beginner levels and EFL contexts. I will address these points after I have discussed some of the most prominent actual samples we have, to which I now turn, drawing on three lines of work all dating back to the 1980s: first, classic ESL materials and practice from North America; second, L1 language arts work with a more direct connection with Freire; and third, work associated with English language learning in the context of the political struggles of South Africa.

Classic ESL materials and practice from North America

Nina Wallerstein and Elsa Auerbach: Early L2 adult education work

One of the earliest examples in this literature is Wallerstein (1983a), which could be seen as a Mark 1 version of later textbooks (Auerbach & Wallerstein, 1987a; Wallerstein & Auerbach, 2004). Nina Wallerstein writes that the material in her 1983 book,

> had [its] beginnings in 1973, when I helped organize a community education project in a Spanish-speaking neighborhood of San Jose, California. Under the auspices of the Metropolitan Adult Education District, we had

> a year-long state education grant to develop an adult education program
> with residents of this underserved community ... When I started I knew
> very little about the educational method called problem-posing ... I was
> not sure, however, how a "Freire" approach could apply to low-income
> adult education students in the United States. True to a Freire approach,
> we started the program by listening. Our team of five to seven persons
> conducted research for two months on the needs of "themes" of the
> community ...
>
> (Wallerstein, 1983a, p. iii)

The themes which eventually appeared in her 1983a text were autobiography,
family, culture and conflict, neighborhood, immigration, health, work, and
money.

Wallerstein's development of this line of work began in 1973, and so was
extremely close to the initial appearances of Freire's work on the US scene.
At the same time, it is not clear how direct the transmission was. One point
of difference concerns the structure of her course as it appears in her 1983
textbook. Freire reports that his literacy courses had a two-part format, with an
initial presentation of what might be called a critical theory of literacy by way
of "codes" in the form of pictures and associated-led discussion. This element
does not appear in Wallerstein's (1983a) published material. The use of pictures,
or "codes," as projective devices central to materials is certainly there, but the
emphasis on students as cultural workers using literacy to change their culture
is not so explicit.

The basic structure of a textbook unit as developed by Wallerstein, and then
by Auerbach and Wallerstein usually begins with a core element—we find a
code, usually in the form of a dialogue with at least one illustration, usually quite
carefully composed and capable of being mined for implications, or drawn upon
as a projective device by the teacher. Then there is a phase ("tools for dialogue") in
which the code is used, first to establish initial levels of comprehension, then for
the students to tell the teacher (and each other) what they think about the situation
and whether it is relevant to them. After this, "Suggested Activities," particularly
in Wallerstein (1983a), include quite brief instructions for role-plays that address
aspects of the problem situation. On this, Wallerstein (1983a, pp. 28ff) provides
some guidelines for teachers. The role-plays can be worked out in detailed
written form, with students acting out the dialogue and she notes, this "leads to
improvisations and unexpected, humorous twists to the role-plays" (p. 28; on
p. 34 she amplifies this to include "role-plays with alternative endings"[14]).

There are also "Stories" in Wallerstein (1983a), though not in Auerbach and
Wallerstein (1987a). These are codes "which teachers can produce after listening
to their students" (Wallerstein, 1983a, p. 29) and are primarily autobiographical
or deal with students' actual personal experience of problem situations.

Other stories and reading matter can come from newspaper articles, school bulletins, community leaflets, or signs. They can also come from phone books, welfare or food stamp forms, advertisements [and] letters from their children's teachers ... The result is a class which continually develops its own curriculum.

(p. 29)

This is the category of "materials" (that is, realia) which presents a challenge for the use of this approach in EFL contexts. Wallerstein goes on to identify and detail the use of pictures (slides, photographs, drawings, collages, photo- and strip-stories) and even puppets.[15]

Codes are followed by "Tools for Dialogue," which go through five problem-posing steps:

1   Describe *what* you see
2   Define the problem
3   Apply the problem to your lives: tell *how* you feel about it
4   Discuss the social/economic reasons: tell *why* there is a problem
5   Ask *what* you can do about it.

This is one of the few explicit occasions in which the critical social theory behind Wallerstein's work appears, in the early materials. The idea that there inevitably are "socio/economic reasons," rather than a personal/individual reason behind these problems, is noteworthy. Other phases in the material include practice, which includes systematic teaching of grammar, which Wallerstein saw as a requirement, though one that should be contextualized; conversation circles; reading comprehension skills; writing exercises; and what she calls "active techniques" (including Total Physical Response, flash cards, communication games, etc.).

Some years later,[16] a larger-format textbook appeared by Wallerstein and her collaborator Elsa Auerbach. This was a two-book set (student book and teacher book), used the common 8.5 inches x 11 inches format of many ESL textbooks, and had more illustrations and slightly more substantially worked-out units of materials. Like its predecessor, it was written for use in US adult immigrant L2 classes. In introductory comments, Auerbach and Wallerstein expressed some concerns about pre-made materials:

In one sense, working from a published student text is antithetical to genuine problem-posing; lessons are best generated from stories and issues from members of a particular class. Teaching time constraints and similar workplace issues, however, make a text an appropriate starting place for classroom interaction—and student-produced materials. In this spirit of inspiring student "ownership" of their learning, we offer the Student Book as a model of problem-posing for teaching English in worksite settings, i.e., pre-vocational or vocational classes, employee or employer-sponsored programs, community ESL or labor classes. We hope our examples will support teachers and will stimulate curriculum-writing by students.

(Auerbach & Wallerstein, 1987a, p. viii)

Most of the main elements for unit structure were carried over from Wallerstein (1983a), though there was little reference to the use of role-plays explicitly. The teacher handbook included material that had been presented in the first couple of chapters of Wallerstein (1983a) but added treatment of teacher education for critical language pedagogy.

In the Auerbach and Wallerstein (1987a) materials, the following unit headings are used:

- Introductions
- Getting a job
- Starting work
- Making money
- Getting through the day
- Acting for health and safety
- Moving toward equality
- Participating in a union
- Looking ahead.

Some of these are self-evident, but let me describe some of them in a bit more detail.[17]

First, the *Introductions* unit. (Much of the first unit is copied in the Appendix, Part 1.) This is a classic. Doing introductions is indeed very often a "unit 1" of many a textbook, often a merely instrumental and in no way interesting one. But not in this case. Here, after an initial phase that is student-run (assuming students with something like low-level false beginner proficiency), the code dialogue is one in which an introduction goes wrong. The participants are a Vietnamese immigrant worker who is starting a job and his co-worker, presumably an American woman. She can't pronounce his name and takes the unilateral step of assigning him a name in English; he can't pronounce her name, and she spells it out for him; the code is ambiguous as to whether she does so patiently though it's possible she does it with an aggressive tone or at least high volume (marked by capitals in the code). In my reading of the code, a power imbalance is suggested by the co-worker's taking the unnegotiated step of renaming the Vietnamese worker. In the next phase, the materials ask the students to investigate naming practices among themselves, modeling questions the students should use, such as "Have you ever experienced this?", "What do you say when …?" And eventually they lead students to consider ways of dealing with this problem, allowing for them also to say whether or not they have had this sort of experience, or other problems with their names in the US or English-using contexts they have come to.

Now consider the unit *Getting a job*. The code here is a job placement interview. The Vietnamese immigrant is being offered a menial job when he was a professional in his home country. The US placement officer shows no interest in his previous career. After the "questions for discussion," which allow development of background information that the students may have about the matter, as well as a focusing on comprehension of details, the materials go on to "thinking activities" which prompts the class to discuss the options available to this individual—options that the students themselves may have faced upon coming to the US, and may face again in their lives as adult immigrants. There then follows a grammar section. Next is "action activities," which helps the students to actively review their actual experiences and realize the skills that they do have. "Student action research" follows, in which actual job applications are sought out and brought in, people with a job a student might like are interviewed, and the teacher is to bring in a resume and help the students write their own. Several pages of more difficult text providing the history of immigrants and the work they did in the history of the US is then provided as a close to this part of Unit 2.

Almost all of the units and their topics are very close to matters of employment, which makes sense as getting, keeping and not suffering from mainly low-wage employment was (and is) a crucial concern of adult immigrants. In addition, the content of many of the units clearly draws on Auerbach's experience as a union organizer. The codes often present the interactors as discussing an issue within the workplace.

The second set of units includes *Acting for health and safety* (about safety on the shop floor); *Moving toward equality* (against discrimination at the workplace) and *Participating in a union*. Reflecting the union orientation, the action phase of the units is typically not "write to your congressman" but, at most, write a letter to the Office of Safety and Health Administration (OSHA) and, more likely, talk to the union representative. There is little or nothing, for example, about dealing with landlords, schools, or doctors, or voting or civic participation.

We cannot know how many teachers may have drawn on these units of materials, though the original versions were in print for many years. There are just a few critical materials-related reports in the years following their publication. In the following decade, Schleppegrell and Bowman (1995), working in a Peace Corps operation in Africa, shared their materials and made it clear they had drawn on the Wallerstein/Auerbach and Crawford traditions. Auerbach went on to grant-funded work for immigrant L2 development and published materials and curriculum-related work in teacher-friendly formats—including the grant-funded work that resulted in both *Making meaning, making change* and its companion volume, *Talking shop* (Nash et al., 1992).

During the 1990s, Auerbach occasionally commented in print in more general terms about the processes and concepts she had used on the various projects she'd been involved in (for example, Auerbach, 1995, which has further helpful comments about materials). And in 2004, Wallerstein and Auerbach saw the reprint of a slightly updated and extended version of their joint 1987 books, now under the imprint of a small immigrant-oriented Canadian publisher, Grassroots Press (Wallerstein & Auerbach, 2004; Auerbach & Wallerstein, 2004). It is clear that this work is still in demand and still in use, and continues to be influential (though its move from a major multinational publisher to a minor alternative Canadian publisher may be significant). They are one of the most extended concrete examples of what critical pedagogy means in practice for adult language learning contexts.

Ira Shor: Early L1 work oriented to materials and curriculum

One of the specialists in critical pedagogy (though not a L2 specialist) who has provided useful guidance about materials over a long period of time is Ira Shor. Besides works co-authored with Paulo Freire, several of Shor's books are among the most practical descriptions of critical pedagogy in action, and are based on his many years of teaching English as a first language, including "freshman composition" in a US community college with a mainly working-class student body (e.g., Shor, 1980, 1992, 1996). Shor's writing in this area is mainly in the form of accounts or narratives of his teaching, in some cases supported by lesson plans and student work. This is one step away from the fully worked-out textbook-style materials of Auerbach and Wallerstein, but still far more practically explicit and detailed than much critical pedagogy writing.

It is in his early (1980) book *Critical teaching and everyday life* more than his later works that Shor most simply and explicitly addressed materials and curriculum, as opposed to narrating pedagogical practices. In this book he presented his practice as a teacher as partly based on the study, by his students, of their own lives as working-class community college students[18] in the economically depressed period of the 1970s ("from the Open Admissions years of the City University of New York, 1971–1977"; Shor, 1980, p. 127). This content provided the base for the development of writing skills in low-level post-secondary English or language arts classes, through "literacy projects" or "language projects."[19] After excerpting below his initial summary of the content, I will then use his descriptions to consider the implications of this work for the topic of this chapter.

Shor describes several units of curriculum that he developed with his students, addressing a range of themes.[20] He goes into considerable detail on how this material was worked out in practice and includes sample student products.

> Some examples of literacy, conceptual and aesthetic courses will be presented. … In a number of my classes, we studied hamburgers or made video plays from our experience or investigated family life through the writing of marriage contracts. Each class began with a very familiar feature of experience—what Freire would call the "codification," or representation of an ordinary piece of reality, abstracted from its habitual place in society, as a theme for class study. We studied each object or situation structurally, using writing, reading, speaking and analysis to unveil the meaning of this event in our lives and in the totality of social life. In the case of the hamburger we recreated the largely invisible commodity relations which deliver a fried piece of dead beef to our palates. I brought hamburgers to class so that the familiar object would be as close at hand as possible, for the launching of unfamiliar analysis. The separation and re-entry from this exercise was rewarding, as the dialogue moved to consider "junk food" versus "health food," and the need to cooperatize the school cafeteria. … The final teaching example involves a class which examined sexist dimensions of family life through the writing of marriage contracts. The contracts were literate documents which exercised numerous skills writing, reading, organizing, editing, group and individual composing, etc. This project facilitated critical awareness because the emerging goal became the writing of a contract for an egalitarian marriage.
>
> (Shor, 1980, p. 106)

Backing up a bit, Shor then takes the reader through a course, starting from his introductory activities on the first day. Because he started his course with introductions and an overview that included the class instructional methodology itself, he was then able to move directly to having the students do some initial writing on bad and good teaching methodology, classes, and teachers, which, Shor says, helped students get their "anti-school feelings" and "teacher repulsion" out into the open. They began an autobiographical process intended to validate their lives (which, in Shor's view, had been ground down by the realities of working-class life in the depressed US East Coast 1970s).

Shor's initial theme is "work." (He doesn't seem to describe whether this is negotiatedly selected.) He asks the students to write on the worst jobs they've had (or can imagine). He leads the class in an analysis of features of these (after initial writings). Through analysis and reflection he is seeking to build possibilities for what he calls "transcendent" thinking.[21] Getting students to reflect on their lives and to analyze them, somewhat from a distance, seems like a good way to get some useful thinking going (as well as prompting good freshman composition). Perhaps this could be called problematization; Freire's whole idea of the code is also intended to allow distance, a necessary precursor to analysis, which in turn presumably should precede action.

On the basis of the analysis, Shor then brings in readings (a reasonable move, given that it's an English class) keyed to the analysis and perspective that has developed so far. Discussing the text samples or readings, Shor comments as follows:

> In deciding what kinds of materials to introduce, I look for a few things. The selections should be in a reasonably colloquial idiom. If the language is jargonish, technical, abstract or formal, then it will alienate the attention of my students. Richly critical ideas and debate can be started from accessible language, so I scour the mass media, books, etc., for articles on the problem theme of work. I like engagingly written things, but they must also suggest a problem, a critique or an idea of transition, for the class discussion to gain transcendent qualities. The readings have been selections from longer pieces or small articles ...[22]
>
> (1980, p. 142)

After this theme of "work" has been used to get the class started, Shor uses the theme of "utopia" to allow for further analysis of the real world of the students while at the same time providing opportunities to write and develop literacy skills which are a crucial component of the course or a main rationale for the existence of freshman composition within the central liberal studies element of the first couple of years of most US university and community college curricula.

> In a language project, reading and writing are legitimized as human activities because the class study turns towards daily life in a critical and dialogic fashion. The students are not lectured about the meaning of their reality, but rather engage in a self-regulating project through which they discover and report that meaning to each other. The group nature of the inquiry supports peer relations for a student group largely alienated from each other. The project cannot reach completion without peer cooperation. The degree to which students assume responsibility for the thematic investigation serves again as an internal test of the learning process. I can initiate and animate the program along the way, but I cannot finish it without the class's participation, and I do not know in advance its eventual shape or endpoint.
>
> (1980, p. 196)

At this point in the description, we are well in to the definitely non-mainstream conception of the teacher as facilitator, co-participant, and animateur of the class, with its concurrent risks. Shor says that he usually does not know exactly how things will turn out; from his point of view, some projects (as he reports) were respectable efforts in the practice and development of literacy but did not show evidence of forms of thought or social analysis that transcended mass culture or mainstream perspectives. In any case, this is a good example of where the stimulating narrative writings by critical pedagogy specialists might go beyond what the teacher who is beginning in critical pedagogy might feel comfortable with. Once again, we are talking about materials largely developed on the fly based on proposals made by students that are fielded by a very experienced and unusual teacher; one who, for that matter, has the liberty to engage in instructional practices whose outcome he can't entirely predict. This is certainly not the territory of the tightly controlled, Student Learning Outcomes audit culture of the early twenty-first century of state education. And indeed, later on in Shor's work, in the very stimulating and brave book *When students have power* (1996), Shor writes about failures as well as successes, and times of student resistance that must have given him considerable worry and heartache as a teacher.

The reader will have noticed that Shor arranges his materials in terms of themes (as did early L2 specialist Crawford). He has three main categories or kinds of theme (Shor, 1992, p. 55):

1   generative themes [which] "make up the primary subject matter ...[and] grow out of student culture and express problematic conditions in daily life";
2   topical themes [which relate to] "a social question of key importance locally ... raised in class by the teacher"; and
3   academic themes: "material brought to the discussion by the teacher [with] ... roots in formal bodies of knowledge."

He states that:

> Critical teachers are willing to take the risk of introducing topical themes because student conversation and thought often do not include important issues in society ... A topical theme, to be critical and democratic, cannot be an isolated exercise or unchallenged lecture by the teacher. ... The topical theme is part of a syllabus students can reject or amend as they exercise their democratic rights ... Critical teachers offer students a topical thematic choice which they can accept or reject.
>
> (Shor, 1992, p. 56)

For L2 teaching, it could be that these ideas extend most easily to EAP writing. The content is almost the same: literacy skills, which in terms of the official course content include process writing procedures, idea generation, revising, reading to write, and so on. But any critical teacher can select productive themes for the practice and development of literacy or even oracy skills, and call for analysis of the themes in their social context.

TASK: REFLECT

How does Shor's way of teaching composition in the first year of post-secondary education compare with your own experiences? What do you think about Shor's remarks concerning not knowing how things will turn out?

Early L2 critical language awareness materials from South Africa

During the 1980s, one important social struggle with a substantial language component was the contested transition to democracy of South Africa. The country had suffered under a constitution which explicitly separated citizens on the basis of their racial characteristics, since the 1950s. Many options for protest and change (both non-violent and violent) were eventually taken up, reflecting the fact that the political system was designed to prevent social change rather than channel such impulses. The beginning of the end was associated with massive social disturbances triggered by the government's decision to stop making education available in English to most non-white South Africans (the Soweto riots, 1976). Large numbers of students, teachers, and activist scholars were involved at all levels of the struggle (along with ordinary people, workers, and revolutionaries). Private sector schools (which operated enrolment policies of inclusion) were a major force within education-based initiatives for change (Wieder, 2003), and language itself was an important site of struggle. A few studies and reports, and even materials, surfaced in the international literature of ESL education as a result of this.[23] Here I will provide a brief exposition of some of the publications of two activist scholars, Janks and Pierce, both of whom produced materials-oriented publications dated around 1989.

Bonnie Pierce: A graphic novel with critical content and critical literacy commentary

Pierce's (1989) report begins by providing some background on realities of the South African movements for change, referring to two national conferences held in the mid-1980s establishing commissions on People's Education and People's English, within the responsibilities of an organizing entity called the National Education Crisis Committee. During this time, conventional English teaching in schools was characterized by heavy attention to grammatical analysis, memorization and translation, and very limited and conventional understandings of appropriate forms of reading material and genres for writing (essayist and employment-related literacy). All of which was enforced by a substantial regime of school inspection.

Thus the publication by Ravan Press of what we would now call a "graphic novel" (a novel in comic-book form) while it would not be seen as revolutionary these days, was, at the time, an act of resistance and a challenge to authority. This work, which Pierce discusses, was also a very concrete manifestation of an alternative pedagogy of English, consistent with the values of critical language pedagogy. The work in question (for extracts see Appendix, Part 2) is an autobiography of a famous South African writer, Ezekial Mphahlele (1959). As a graphic novel, its pictures make this material vivid and accessible. The author becomes politically conscious, takes part in early anti-apartheid struggles, and the work concludes when he decides to go into political exile. Pierce highlights crucial aspects of the publication. Probably written with high school students in mind, the comic book itself takes up the first twelve pages; in the remaining ten pages the reader is first exhorted to "Become a writer like Es'kiah Mphahlele" and then encouraged to "brush up on your writing and reading skills," and critical literacy instructional content follows. As Pierce writes (1989, p. 415), quoting the work itself:

> [M]ultiple readings of the text are validated. Consider the following instructions:

> Look carefully at the following pictures. How much information can you get from them? Answer the questions about each one … Compare your answer with a friend's. Pictures can be interpreted in different ways and so your ideas may differ. That is why we have not given you any answers to refer to (South African Council of Higher Education, 1988, p. 15).

> In addition, the text is punctuated with requests for readers to respond: "Did you find this comic interesting and enjoyable? Do you think we should produce more comics like this one? Please send us your comments. You may know of other stories which would make exciting comics. Write to …" (inside cover) … The exercises in the comic enable students to "hear what is said and what is hidden; to create; to explore relationships; to read and write with confidence" (National Education Crisis Committee, 1986/1987, p. 39).

> In addition, they encourage the sharing and pooling of ideas, the collecting and recording of community-based experiences. It is significant that the comic draws attention to the young Mphahlele's developing consciousness:

"At first political debates were just a jumble of words to me. Gradually as I listened I began to put in their proper place the scattered experiences of my life in Pretoria. Poverty, police raids, the curfew bell, humiliation ..." (South African Council of Higher Education, 1988, p. 5).

In addition, as the last part of the quote makes clear, this material had content that provided a model for learners concerning personal identity within a political context. That makes it, in a sense, more didactic and slightly less student-centered than the Auerbach and Wallerstein materials, which have more inductive processes. But there is, as is often said, no one critical pedagogy and context is extremely important. The South African context was one of the most extreme cases in which teachers and language played a very important and active role in a successful social struggle, despite brutal forms of repression and state action. The work received the ultimate accolade from the government—of being banned—but it continued to circulate and aided in the critical literacy education of L2 learners working with the language of power.

This again is one of the early handfuls of examples of published L2 materials that manifest a critical pedagogy. However, this model is not one that can be easily adapted by L2 teachers unless they are well resourced, simply because it requires pre-existing graphic novel material. On the other hand, there is more material of this sort available now than before, for those who have the ability and inclination to seek it out. Moffatt and Norton (2005) continues the story; see Chun (2009) for an extended review of graphic novels in critical ESL, and Templer (2009), extending to EFL contexts as well.

Hilary Janks: Early critical language awareness materials for EFL high school classrooms

During the same period also in South Africa, activist scholar Hilary Janks[24] directed the publication of a six-title series of what she called "workbooks": small English textbooks for use in high schools (esp. Janks, 1993a, b; cf. Janks 1995; see Appendix, Part 3).[25] These were about fifty or so pages long, of a mid-sized format with a mixture of graphics and text, published by the South African branch of Hodder & Stoughton with the support or imprint of Witwatersrand University as well.[26] I mention the publishers (here and earlier in the case of Auerbach and Wallerstein), because a general question is how critical pedagogy materials get published. The end of the apartheid regime seems to be dated to 1990, during which year the white-minority government began the handover of power and changes in laws began. However, many of the attitudes and social structures of oppression persisted, and Janks has said that without the support of the university, no major publisher would have published the books.

Janks's introductions to the books identify the series as in the domain of critical language awareness (CLA). This is a line of work which has a similar critical perspective on language and society as does critical pedagogy; however, it doesn't derive directly from critical pedagogy. Nevertheless, it has been and continues to be very influential, and may be considered a parallel tradition.

Directed to students who already had a substantial competence in their second language and were using it to learn academic material of a high school level, Janks's series presents worked examples, using authentic samples of language from apartheid-era newspapers, to show how language is being used as a tool of mystification and oppression, or in some cases to resist official dogma. It also provides a range of exercises for the students to encourage creative and self-liberating uses of English. These works are much further from the commercial ESL textbook format that Auerbach and Wallerstein use to great effect, and instead are closer to progressive high school materials in a particular subject area (language arts, English studies). Here are quotes from the introduction to one of them (Janks, 1993a, p. iii). Clearly Janks is being quite explicit and instructive to the student and or teacher reader.

From the Foreword:

> This workbook will help you to understand what is meant by position. There are many meanings. It will help you to become critical readers by increasing your awareness of how language is working to position you. It will help you to become oppositional readers, readers who know how to oppose the positions of writers, who know when and how to refuse to think what writers want them to think and who know how to recognise writing that they need to oppose. The workbook will increase your awareness of language so that other people cannot easily use language to disempower you.

From the next page (p. iv), on CLA:

> All the workbooks in the series deal with the relationship between language and power. This relationship is not obvious and so the materials attempt to raise awareness of the way in which language can be used and is used to maintain and to challenge existing forms of power. There can be little doubt that power matters, both to people who have it and to those who do not. ...
>
> In any unequal relation of power there are top dogs and underdogs. How people get to be on top in a society has to do with what that society values. It may be age or maleness or class or cleverness or a white skin. It is easier for those who have power to maintain it if they can persuade everyone in the society that there is nothing unnatural about these arrangements, that things are this way because that is the way they are meant to be.

If people consent to being powerless then the people in power need to use less force (armies, police, punishments) to maintain their power. Convincing and persuading people to consent to society's rules is often the job of families, religions, schools and the media. All these social institutions use language and it is largely in and through language that meaning is mobilised to defend the status quo.

But language is also used to challenge the status quo. By refusing to consent and by working together people can bring about change. What makes CLA "critical" is its concern with the politics of meaning: the ways in which dominant meanings are maintained, challenged and changed. ...

Janks also provides a detailed section, "Suggested methods for teachers," which, along with the exposition of CLA, is a good example of how textbooks can teach teachers explicitly. In a paper presented a couple of years earlier (1991, (p. 191) she summarized her initial pedagogical position:

In a critical approach to the study of language, students come to understand the way in which each linguistic feature in a text contributes to the overall positioning of the reader. These features do not function in isolation from one another. It is possible, however, to work with them one by one in the process of attempting to arrive at an overall interpretation of a text. In this way one is able to ascertain whether different textual features confirm or contradict one another. Each linguistic feature is simply one analytic tool which may or may not have critical significance in any particular piece of discourse. This critical approach to language teaching is cumulative: students learn to use linguistic features one by one for de-constructing texts and the number of features that they can use accumulates.

And on the actual features of materials she says:

Texts and examples should be chosen which illustrate the linguistic feature at work in discourse which is relevant to the students' social and political lives. It is important to avoid the bland, neutral exemplars typical of language text books. ... The advantage of loaded examples is that they are not bland or neutral. If students can perceive the relevance of the examples to their own lives, they are more likely to be motivated to examine the language in which they are written.

(1991, p. 192)

Janks (1991) also provides an illustrative (though not exhaustive) list of teaching points or foci of materials. These are specified as structural, semantic, functional, and discoursal features or categories: modality, voice, the article, and sequencing of information. Her instructions to teachers (Janks, 1993a, p. iv) make it clear that a group-based, cooperative, discussion-oriented perspective was expected. The mother tongue is to be allowed, and "Teachers and students should constantly relate the issues and activities in the workbooks to their own lives and experiences." She advises that

> [t]eachers should facilitate class discussions. The workbooks deal with real and sensitive issues. Teachers need to help students to listen to one another and to try to understand the different histories and positions that other people in the class speak from. We need to hear other people and not try to convert them to our way of thinking.
>
> (Janks, 1993a, p. iv)

Unlike Auerbach and Wallerstein, who used a more or less repeating unit structure, Janks is engaged in an extended logical exposition and development of ideas concerning "position" and how language is involved in that. For each step in the argument (usually a page) there is a short explanation, often supported by a graphic, and often a short, simple example of language that shows or takes a position. There is a gradual progression of language samples, from simple poem, to newspaper samples, to extracts from a history textbook. Janks goes on from "position" to "context" and the beginnings of media literacy ("pictures are part of the context," she points out). As we approach the end of the workbook, we encounter a unit called "Using what we have learnt to read texts critically," which provides a summary and explicit guidance about critical reading, followed by some sample authentic texts to practice on. Finally, there is a unit that tells the reader how to read the workbook itself critically. So this provides some "reflexivity" at the end.

Is this something that can be used as a model or guide by language teachers today? Obviously, most of us are not in the aftermath of a successful near-revolutionary change in government from an authoritarian, explicitly racist regime, to an explicitly multicultural representative social democracy. So we don't have an audience of politicized high school students with direct experience of government oppression based on race and implemented in many cases through language (not to mention state violence) and who have seen successful models of direct action leading to political change, and indeed may have participated in such actions.

On the other hand, these texts target a particular level of L2 student and were trialed extensively in real high school classrooms (Janks provides names of schools and teachers). They are directly pedagogical and their use is clear. This distinguishes them from the many academic discussions of CDA (the successor to CLA) or even narrative expositions of CLA/CDA courses (e.g., Wallace, discussed later). I believe that a motivated teacher could certainly use them as a template, replacing the S. African texts with local, current texts. The material is also instructional for the teacher; it doesn't really assume a teacher with experience and knowledge of CLA (though perhaps many South African language arts teachers would have been sufficiently radicalized by their experiences to be right on top of these concepts). As mentioned, Janks (1995, p. 10) based the need for concrete materials on her knowledge of classroom contexts and cites two studies (Botha, n.d.; Hartshorne, 1992) which document the near total dependence on the textbook in her own context in the 1990s.

TASK: REFLECT

How were you taught your first language, in regard to writing or literacy at school? How explicit (if at all) was your instruction, concerning literacy as a social practice? If you teach in a second culture context, or in a host culture, what do you know about first language instruction there? Can we assume that it is simply non-critical?

Critical literacy

Several terms and traditions for the critical analysis of language either co-exist or have flowed one into another. Janks' Critical Language Awareness is close to Critical Discourse Analysis; the term Critical Whole Language is also often used, and we also have the over-arching term Critical Literacy. These lines of work invite the language user and learner to develop tools for seeing the ways in which language has position, interests, power, and can act to disadvantage those on the lower rungs of a hierarchical society. So though it doesn't necessarily invite an action response, as does critical pedagogy, critical literacy is generally thought to be complementary to or consistent with many of the aims of critical pedagogy. Continuing the theme of this chapter, let me ask now, "What physical and material manifestations does it, or any of these associated traditions, have that can be of use to the L2 teacher with a critical orientation?" The short answer is that far more work seems to have been done in L1 than L2 contexts, so actual published materials are more likely to be found that have a first language orientation.

Elementary level

The use of large format, heavily illustrated "picture story books" in elementary literacy instruction is a long-standing tradition. The 'teacher read-aloud' classroom event is one that young children are quickly socialized into in many schools. Teachers with a critical orientation can find an increasing (perhaps still not large) range of titles, mostly with a US focus perhaps, that have socially critical content. This category of text is "social issue picture books"—picture books for L1 students that address topics such as "adoption, bullying, dealing with new experiences, dealing with trauma, disability, drugs & alcohol... ...."[27] But none of this work is designed specifically with L2 learners in mind, and a large proportion of it is heavily dependent on US culture and history. On the other hand, to the extent that the language is simple, intended for very early L1 grades/ages, extensively illustrated, and can be mediated by the teacher as she reads and entertains questions and encourages comments from the students, perhaps this sort of material may be relevant. Considering its use outside of ESL situations, teachers would face the usual problem of both getting it, and being able to pay for it. Nevertheless, a couple of small studies report its use in small critical literacy initiatives in Taiwan (Falkenstein, 2003; Kuo, 2009) though at college level.

I provide a short illustrative list of publications of this type here, drawing on Cowhey (2006, pp. 30–31, 65). Just the few lines of description should indicate the interesting and challenging nature of the contents. A more extensive list is provided by Leland and Harste (2002); see also McLaughlin and DeVoogd (2004). *Si, se puede!* (Cohn, 2002) relates to a union organizing drive and strike, and is bilingual; *The streets are free* (Karusa, 1995), also a bilingual story, concerns poor Venezuelan kids organizing to obtain a playground in their neighborhood; *Tight times* (Hazen, 1983), doesn't sugar-coat reality: a child wants a dog, adopts a kitten, and in the course of this deals with the anger of a parent who has become unemployed; *The lady in the box* (McGovern, 1997), as the title suggests, is about a homeless woman, with whom two children make friends. *Fly away home* (Bunting, 2004) is a deeply touching book about a homeless boy and his father who live at an airport. (I use this one with teachers particularly because homeless people live, or have lived, at my own local airport in Honolulu.) *I hate English!* (note the title, no sugar-coating again; Levine, 1995) tells the story of a Chinese girl who loves Chinese but hates learning English (eventually seeing a need for it, though); and the last in this list yet again resists a world of imagination where no one is unhappy or angry because of their poor living circumstances: *Angel child, dragon child* (Surat, 1990) is about a Vietnamese girl who fights a boy who teases her. Part of the girl's anger comes from the fact that her mother is still in Vietnam, separated from her family. So these are by no means happy stories; and they are not necessarily middle-class stories. Like many of our students, they do *not* come from the Disney-like world of intact families and white picket fences. They are real and students relate to them accordingly.

Secondary level

An encouraging breakthrough at the national level for L1 critical literacy occurred in Australia during the 1990s. Freebody and Luke's (1990) popular "Four Resource" model for the literate citizen's needs in the area of language had become widely familiar among teachers. Its first three resources (code breaker, meaning maker, and text user) were not too challenging, but their fourth, "text critic," implied the development of "critical competence," and, happily, Australian language arts curriculum and teachers' practices did begin to reflect this fourth resource. Academics and teacher educators with a critical focus (and a theoretical orientation to Systemic Functional Linguistics, a theory hospitable to this perspective) influenced the policy environment. With sympathetic state governments in place, during this period state syllabi began to reflect a critical literacy perspective, beginning in 1993 in the Queensland state language arts syllabus and extending to all or almost all states, including the largest (New South Wales). "What sets Australian approaches to critical literacy apart has been their insistence on direct instruction in a sophisticated technical language for talking about text" (Luke, 2000, p. 13). These perspectives were also supported in textbook form by titles published by Chalkface Press. However, by 1999 (Johnson & McCauslan, 1999) there were signs of a politically motivated movement away from the nation-wide dominance of critical literacy in the school syllabi because of the election of a new, unsympathetic national political administration, which retained power until 2007. This trend continues (Donnelly, 2010) yet state-level curriculum guidelines remain in place which strongly support L1 critical literacy initiatives, including in textbook form.[28]

Critical literacy textbooks for the high school are less obvious in the US environment. One exception is Christensen (2000), which reflects the author's experiences teaching at Jefferson High School, Oregon, and combines short analyses written directly to the teacher, along with lesson plans or "teaching strategies." The latter are lesson plans which combine reflective teacher comments based on having run the "strategy" multiple times. Christensen's students are inner city, black, working class students. Their skills are still basically in English as an L1, and by ESL or EFL standards, they can write and read quite well; the obstacles they face are in the violence and prejudice of minority life and the lack of connection between the established curriculum and their real lives and identities.

Obviously, I think it would be desirable if L2 materials of this narrative, illustrated kind, or indeed any kind, were more widely available. L2 teachers becoming aware of what is possible is presumably a first step.

TASK: EXPLORE RESOURCES

Find an example of a social issues picture book and explore it in detail. How usable is it for your students? Similarly, put your hands on a critical literacy text. What is required to make it usable for a second language classroom?

World languages/languages other than English (LOTE)

The attention given to critical language pedagogy by teachers and researchers of languages other than English is less than that for English. However, it is of interest among other things because it sometimes provides a counterweight of thematic emphasis, looking more at grammar and at culture than do the English-oriented studies and analyses.

The very early treatments of critical "foreign languages" pedagogy by Crawford-Lange (1981) must be acknowledged. But her publications seem to have prompted little follow-up work in what was (in the US) then called the Foreign Languages community. Her papers provide guidance for using existing authentic realia as the basis for lessons not based on published material. A long gap, then, is found in the research publication record. Very much later (and by this time, the field has changed its name to "world languages"), Osborn (2006) provides a contribution to the area of sample materials or curriculum guides. His short chapter on this is noteworthy—first, because it comes out of the area of "world language education" (within which there is even less critical orientation than in ELT); and, perhaps more importantly, because it presents a theoretically grounded set of themes that fit with the implication of language or discourse itself in the construction of reality. That language should itself be the subject of scrutiny in a critical language pedagogy course seems unarguable; it is of interest that he does present his work as in a critical pedagogy tradition, however, rather than a critical language awareness line.

He too (like Kanpol, Auerbach and Wallerstein, and Shor) is wary of allowing it to be thought that previously, separately developed materials are entirely consistent with or sufficient for critical language pedagogy. Stating that he is going to discuss and join together some sample activities, he then explains (Osborn, 2006, p. 57) that his ideas are suggestions, not prescriptions, and illustrate practices so teachers can further explore their own views in relation to them. Osborn's approach is more formally language-oriented than the others I have sketched so far. It is also more directive. This may reflect its context, arising from primarily classroom-based "world language education" in US high schools and colleges. As in EFL, there is still a strong emphasis on the elements of language, and it is with grammar and vocabulary that Osborn is initially concerned. However, he also takes up recent understandings of language, drawing on the work of Kubota (2003, p.60):

> She argues that one needs *descriptive* rather than prescriptive understandings of culture, acknowledgment of *diversity* within culture, a view of culture as *dynamic* rather than permanent, and an exploration of the *discursive* elements in our construction of cultural selves and others. These elements (called the four D's) create a heuristic, not formulaic, backdrop for a discussion of vocabulary themes.

Osborn then takes these concepts and applies them to the idea that central concepts or themes within the social critique that informs critical pedagogy could be directly taught, or at least used to organize curriculum material. This again is much less inductive than, for example, the approach of Auerbach and Wallerstein, and appears to allow less opportunity for student input (at first), and he acknowledges this later in his exposition (saying "I recognize that some teachers may be uncomfortable with an approach that embraces the ideals of critical theories as a starting point for generating a course scope and sequence when introducing an alternative approach"; 2006, p. 68). But in this initial exposition, he suggests focusing on fifteen key themes (p. 61):

- Identity
- Affiliation
- Conflict, struggle, and discrimination
- Socio-economic class
- What we believe: Ideology
- Historical perspectives: To the victors
- Schools and languages: Hidden curricula
- Media: Entertainment
- Beyond manners: Register and political or power relations
- Whose culture is whose? Hybridity
- Media: Journalism and politicians
- Who is in control? Hegemony
- Law
- Rights
- Resistance and marginalization.

He then groups these further in terms of: *identity*, including "conflict, struggle, and discrimination; and socioeconomic class"; *social architecture*, by which he means things like ideology, educational systems, languages, the media, all of which structure society and perceptions; *language choices*, which relate to register, power, culture, hybridity and hegemony; and *activism*. These are then (without empirical support) used to direct the selection of grammar points for individual teaching (p. 62):

> Identity, it would seem, would be similar to much of introductory language coursework as currently practiced. Personal pronouns, present-tense verbs, direct and indirect objects, and similar forms might predominate. Oral forms of language could predominate at this point, though certainly identity issues are not restricted to the oral dimension of language use.
>
> Social architecture would likely rely on past-tense verbs (especially for historical perspectives, etc.). Helping verbs such as *should* and *must* would be relevant, as would passive voice and agency. Entertainment and educational settings would often include communicative styles that are reflective of social relations such as the familiar and formal forms of address. Language choices explore sociolinguistic issues of competence... However, a significant emphasis must also be placed on epistemological issues such as reality and alternative "realities," thus the subjunctive and direct/indirect discourse distinctions would be relevant. ... Finally, activism could stress speaking and writing elements predominantly. The specifics of composition, the mechanics of connected discourse, and letter writing, as examples, would be appropriate. At the same time, grammatical forms such as the imperative would be important for exploring activist stances. In relation to activism, the language skills of persuasion and structures used for argument and debate would be important.

Osborn proposes class discussion in the students' first language as students and teacher review some aspects of these themes and engage in simple research, finding out, for example, about local L2/world-language-using communities in their vicinity, such as Italian-Americans, and exploring how matters of identity play out for them in their maintenance of Italian, and so on. Here he writes more generally, taking for granted a generally understood set of pedagogical practices associated with a mainstream liberal understanding of the university classroom as a place for discussion and student research investigation using easily available library and community resources.

One additional source for a thematically organized critical L2 curriculum is Candlin (1989). Pennycook (1994) summarizes this perhaps little-cited example, identifying it as separate and distinct from Freirean inspired ideas, though there is plenty of implicit reference to Freirean ideas just the same. In this work, prominent curriculum theorist Candlin outlined, in some detail, an approach to structuring a second language curriculum (as a proposal, not an empirical report). Pennycook comments as follows:

Candlin (1989) shows how a curriculum was developed around the relationships among certain *issues* (for instance, questions of race, gender, class, rights), the particular *institutions* in which such issues are salient for the students (family, school, work, etc.), different text types or *expressions* (e.g., stories, cartoons, descriptions, poems), and discoursal orders or *functions* (persuasion, dominance, solidarity, and so on). Methodologically, this curriculum then operates through a sequence of *investigating* (what problems does a particular text pose?); *thinking* (what information needs to be explored?); *codifying* (in what ways is this personally relevant"): *dialoguing* (what resources are needed to explain the text?); *critiquing* (what are the underlying issues?); and *acting* (what out-of-classroom action should be taken?).

Overall, such an approach, Candlin suggests, helps in the relativising, personalising and problematising of experience, the enhancing of skills of intercultural understanding, in particular seeking social and cultural explanations for language use, and the extending of knowledge and awareness gained in the classroom setting to address learners' personal life issues in the wider social context of intercultural behaviour outside the institution.

(1994, p. 22)

A small number of studies of critical pedagogy in languages other than English are accumulating (e.g., Ohara et al., 2001) as well as critically informed studies of world language classrooms (e.g., Kumagai, 2007). These demonstrate that (of course!) critical pedagogy certainly is possible with other languages but equally indicate that the visibility of critical approaches in world languages is distinctly less than that of English.

TASK: EXPLORE RESOURCES

Find any basic first-year university world (foreign) language textbook. How is it structured? How does it compare with the themes suggested by Osborn and Candlin? Could it be modified in their direction?

Adaptation and supplementation

There is a long but thin tradition of materials adaptation in TESOL—long, in that the topic regularly shows up in short chapters in survey handbooks but thin: almost never the subject of research. Stevick (1986) is one of the more thorough treatments, now somewhat dated. The topic continues to be of interest to language teachers and materials specialists of course (cf. McGrath, 2002, ch 4; Yang & Cheung, 2003; Islam & Mares, 2003). That teachers should, and do, systematically adapt published materials is central to why I and others have talked about the materials presented here as samples. So what are some of the options? The mainstream (non-critical) literature in TESOL lists a large range of possibilities to be considered in adapting materials, from which I take the following, mostly interactive things, that could be considered in adapting materials in a critical direction: who takes the initiative (teacher or student); whether to personalize; the use of drama and dramatization; the role of students' inferences and interpretation (prioritized over supposed "right" answers a text may have); and the role of translation.[29] All these apply to using a set text in a somewhat critical way, though the limitations are great. Before we go on to consider going beyond the "set" text, however, note an interesting approach in the area of adaptation made by critical whole language specialists Edelsky and Johnson (2004). Referring to the absolutely rigid, phonics-based reading textbooks mandated in many US states, these authors report using these "Open Court" materials as a text to be interrogated rather than directly taught.

> [Johnson] and her students found there were selections they read, fell in love with, stole from for use in their own writing , or read to learn from. She also began to use Open Court for critical literacy. Rather than pretend Open Court was an innocuous set of stories that the teacher chooses, she started to ask her class why one company would want all teachers to use the same book, why a school district would want everyone doing the same work. When students would find selections in the anthology that seemed like poor writing or that seemed to be promoting a racist or classist agenda, she established a time for them to "talk back". She allowed students to send letters to the publishers … explaining why those suggestions offended their sense of justice.
>
> (Edelsky and Johnson, 2004, pp. 129–130)

Critical non-language materials

There are not many non-language textbooks that are inherently critical or written from a critical pedagogy point of view. Any that exist could, almost by definition, be mined by language specialists as well as used by content teachers. One of the most prominent of these in the US context is *Rethinking globalization* (Bigelow & Peterson, 2002).[30] This large-format, near-400-page work has both strengths and weaknesses for our (language-related) purposes. The many contributions in it are explicitly written from a critical standpoint; the authors describe the work as having a "partisan" character. It intends to inform and even call to action its student readers, concerning the international inequities surrounding globalization. It contains "background readings, lesson plans, teaching articles, role plays and simulations, student handouts, interviews, poems, cartoons, annotated resource lists, and teaching ideas. It is curricular without being a curriculum," say the authors (p. 8). They also comment that

> some articles and activities are aimed at upper elementary students; others are aimed at students who are high school-aged and older ...We did not segregate the book into sections for different grade levels. This is because many, if not most, of the activities and readings ... could be adapted for use with high school-aged and older students, and vice versa.
>
> (Ibid.)

It's good that this exists—it is a mine of resources—but for our purposes, it also has (of course) its limitations. Many of the readings are too difficult for all but university-level advanced ESL/EFL students, though some of the activities could be used for intermediate students. The teacher would have to pick and choose and read the lesson plans carefully, and use a reasonable amount of previous understanding of language teaching and critical pedagogy practice.

The publisher of this work, Rethinking Schools, has also developed similar materials in other curricular areas (history, mathematics). While all curriculum areas can be considered from critical or radical perspective, some are in their initial conception hospitable to critical perspectives, for example, peace and environmental education (addressed in Chapter 6). A related but not very prominent area is "world studies" or "global education." These critical and internationally oriented versions of the social studies curriculum overlap with peace education. At least two textbooks, written for L1 high schools in the UK but adaptable for advanced EFL students, were published in the late 1980s with support from Oxfam and other charities (Fisher & Hicks, 1985; Pike & Selby, 1988; Starkey, 1988).[31] Finally, one might look to citizenship education in some countries for possible resources,[32] depending on how active a conception of citizenship is promoted or considered by a government or the materials publisher.

Adapting non-critical language materials

Critical world languages specialist Osborn addresses the topic of adaptation at the level of content or syllabus. He (p. 66ff) describes what he calls a "transition strategy," Starting with "contemporary themes" that he notes are regularly found in textbooks (particularly the French (etc.) 101 US university textbooks that he and most of his readers are familiar with), he briefly suggests connections that a teacher could make between them and the themes of social critique important for critical pedagogy. So, for example, "numbers, year, and banking" could be connected to discussion of the financial system; "weather, housing, hotel accommodations, and furniture" could be connected to homelessness, social status and class, and privilege; "food, meals, restaurants, and shopping" to "issues such as socioeconomic status, immigrant or overseas labor, consumerism, and the interrelationships of each."[33] I think that most readers would recognize that such connections can be made, particularly by teachers with a critical social outlook, and working with moderately cooperative and motivated students, preferably those with a similar outlook or life experiences as those of the teacher. But at this point we are back to the problem that a teacher setting out on a journey to critical language pedagogy cannot be expected to experience immediate success using just this level of pointing in a direction.

It should not be overlooked that a small minority of L2 textbooks have either an overall tilt towards social criticism, or contain occasional units with a non-mainstream orientation. Although most language teachers are not in a position to go searching for these and they are hard to identify from the outside, I include a brief list of selected items here. Certainly these ought to be usable by those beginning to explore critical pedagogy, because they are relatively or absolutely unchallenging, yet address at the least "sensitive" issues, usually with no particularly strong critical focus. Still one could imagine a critical focus being added on.

One major category here would be what I'll call "Issues discussion texts" intended for advanced L2 students in the private language school sector mainly (e.g., Coelho et al., 1989; Numrich, 2003; Shulman, 2004; and Smith & Mare, 1990). All of these examples in fact have the world "issues" in their titles, and indeed present material on a range of social issues (immigration, women's lives, health care, media) that invite the students to voice their opinions and implicitly challenge both US mainstream positions and/or take a stance on cultural issues from the outside perspective of their home culture(s). Relatedly, there are a number of titles which explicitly address US culture for ESL students (e.g., Shulman, 1988; Fox, 1980). Environmental justice has become such a mainstream matter that this gets through in many newer internationally oriented EFL textbooks (e.g., Jones, 2008; ch. 11B "Protecting our environment"). Adult education-oriented ESL textbooks can slip in a unit on community involvement and action, like "Get involved" (unit 10 of Denman, 2007).

TASK: SHARE MATERIALS

Have you encountered textbooks of the orientation just discussed? Can you find or share examples? If you are working with a group, are these works equally usable by all members? (Are they mainly for advanced learners?) Is there, indeed, any notably critical content, or are they nevertheless mainstream?

Domestic EFL publishers may not experience the same forces that international ELT publishers are under, and perhaps there are some examples to be considered here. The Japan state EFL textbook market offers a range of ministry-approved textbooks, within which at least one—namely, Sanseido's *Crown* and *New Crown* series—treats social issues in its material (cf. Hardy, 2007). For example, book 1 of the Crown English Series has one of its eight units on the Vietnam war, including a famous photo of a naked Vietnamese girl who experienced a napalm attack. (This item would almost certainly not appear in a US or international ELT textbook, as it still carries considerable emotional impact, to say the least.) The same book includes a sympathetic account of minority language maintenance in Hawaii, written by an indigenous Hawaiian language teacher. Of the eight units in *New Crown 3* (2005), one relates to the bombing of Hiroshima and Nagasaki, one to environmental destruction, and one to starvation in the Sudan (including a photo of a starving child threatened by a vulture).

Supplementation

For the beginner in critical language pedagogy, use of supplementary materials of a critical orientation tuned to state-required materials could be a productive strategy. This is the line that Konoeda and Watanabe (2008) have explored, both developing such materials and trialing them in a Japanese EFL high school classroom context. The Japanese high school EFL context is an example of many cases in state high school systems where a limited and conventional set of textbooks is all that is available and indeed are texts which must be used (cf. Yamada, 2011, for recent description of this material). However, teachers are allowed to supplement whichever of the set of mandated texts they or their school have chosen.

In the initial phase of their study, Konoeda and Watanabe analyzed Ministry of Education, Science and Technology (MEXT) guidelines as well as the goals and themes of textbooks that are part of the group of texts from which teachers are supposed to select.

> Our thematic analysis of the Columbus 21 textbooks (1st through 3rd grade) showed that the first and second year textbooks center on friendship issues, followed by family matters. In the third year textbook, more societal concerns, e.g., environment, poverty, are introduced.
>
> (p. 51)

They also conducted a simple survey needs analysis of "27 Japanese first-year junior high school students" which identified four prominent issues for students: "(a) school rules, (b) academic work, (c) friendship (bullying, grouping, etc.) and (d) pressure from parents" (p. 51). The textbooks contain, among other themes, those of friendship. In one case, there is a simple case of a snowball fight that has one student being hit by a snowball and a friend of the student expressing anger at this.

Konoeda and Watanabe analyzed this segment of materials and concluded that it could be adapted to meet Freirean principles concerning a code. They rewrote it in two versions, changing the exposition to a more personal retrospective account (they call it a blog). They then provided more structuring for the phase of the material intended to support a dialogical discussion of the code. Auerbach and Wallerstein, working with ESL students, possibly "false beginners," provide quite a lot of guiding questions for this phase too, but at the same time they were dealing with students who communicate in the target language for real purposes. Konoeda and Watanabe are trying to make an EFL classroom situation, in which students are not accustomed to real communication, be more effective for learning; so they rightly provide more guidance. In doing this, they brought to bear the theoretical framework of Task-Based Language Teaching. This supported a more explicit analysis and perspective on the components of the "problem-posing" lesson than has been provided in any of the critical language pedagogy materials or analysis thus far. Furthermore, it facilitates a much more explicit linkage with second language acquisition theory than has been apparent in any of the materials and perspectives we have discussed so far. (The matter will be taken up further in Chapter 5.)

> Among various focus on form techniques developed by second language acquisition researchers ... we chose to use typological enhancement and input analysis. Input was first processed for meaning, and later guided to focus on form for form-meaning mapping. In Unit 12, the textbook indicated the target form (i.e., I (don't) think ... and adjectives) in the margin. Out of the 157 word text, there were only two occasions using the target form (see Excerpt 5). Therefore, we rewrote and added more incidences of the target form with typographical enhancement (boldfacing and ... to direct learners' attentional resources to the form, while reading for comprehension.
>
> (p. 56)

Konoeda and Watanabe also made use of "input analysis (Wolfe-Quintero & Okazaki, 2004), a deductive analysis and generalization of a grammatical form [through which] learners would discover and reconstruct their understanding of a linguistic form" (p. 57). Thus the approach is capable of focusing on form or having a structural emphasis, while at the same time handling critical material and showing a critical orientation. Overall, this is a very important and striking development. Going further, in the case of Japan, it is also noteworthy that the comparatively low cost of publishing and the strength of the domestic publication industry coupled with the importance of English learning in this EFL country allows the availability of local supplementary textbooks (not just teacher-made materials, as in the case of Watanabe and Konoeda). One example is Kobayashi (1997), a compilation of readings with conventional vocabulary and grammar exercises, but on the theme of Japanese education, with almost all readings having a challenging quality (in many cases taken from English-language newspapers in Japan). These topics include bullying, environmental education, drug education, the politics of history writing, AIDs education, and faults in English language education in Japan. Clearly with this kind of supplemental textbook in hand, a shift to a more critical curriculum content is greatly aided.

Looking forward: Internet support

Critical language pedagogy is applicable to both well-resourced as well as resource-poor contexts. Thus the relevance of internet access and digital technologies should be considered. The brief discussion that follows applies to the logistics of accumulating, maintaining, and developing a collection of thematic critical materials and the role of student input. (Other aspects of internet-related matters are taken up briefly under the heading of informal education in Chapter 7.)

One of the points made at the beginning of this chapter was that the emphasis on student-made materials in classic critical pedagogy presented both a conceptual and also a practical, logistical challenge to teachers beginning to work with this approach. However, given current technological resources, accumulating student-made materials and student revisions of initial teacher-made samples of materials, not to mention teachers quickly obtaining supplementary authentic language samples, has become much more feasible in circumstances with basic web access.[34]

The term "Web 2.0" is regularly invoked to refer to the conceptually simple practices that are relevant here, and in particular the key concept "user-generated content."

> Web 2.0 encompasses a variety of different meanings that include an increased emphasis on user generated content, data and content sharing and collaborative effort, together with the use of various kinds of social software, new ways of interacting with web-based applications, and the use of the web as a platform for generating, re-purposing and consuming content.
>
> The seeds of what is now generally accepted as the read/write or shared content nature of Web 2.0 appeared in 1980 in Tim Berners-Lee's prototype web software (thus in Berners-Lee's view there is nothing new about Web 2.0). However, the content sharing aspects of the web were

lost in the original rollout, and did not reappear until Ward Cunningham wrote the first wiki in 1994–1995. Blogs, another early part of the read/ write phenomenon, were sufficiently developed to gain the name weblogs in 1997. It then took until the summer of 2005 for the term Web 2.0 to appear …

One way of summarising the change to Web 2.0 is by contrasting the former web ("Web 1.0") with Web 2.0. In Web 1.0 a few content authors provided content for a wide audience of relatively passive readers. However, in Web 2.0 everyday users of the web use the web as a platform to generate, re-purpose, and consume shared content. With Web 2.0 data sharing the web also becomes a platform for social software that enables groups of users to socialise, collaborate, and work with each other. This change of use is largely based on existing web data-sharing mechanisms being used to share content, in conjunction with the use of web protocol based interfaces to web applications that allow flexibility in reusing data and the adoption of communications protocols that allow specialised data exchange.

(Franklin and van Harmelen, 2007, p. 3)

With the context of Web 2.0 established, let us focus in a bit more detail on the key point, as outlined by Mason and Rennie (2008). Social networking perspectives support "user-generated content" in online course structure and materials, leading some to talk of "Education 2.0." Mason and Rennie note that "observers speak of a 'gift culture' on the web whereby users contribute as much as they take. … The essence of social networking is that the users generate the content" (ibid., p. 4). They comment that

1. Users have the tools to actively engage in the construction of their experience, rather than passively absorbing existing content.
2. Content will be continually refreshed by the users rather than require expensive expert input.
3. Many of the new tools support collaborative work, thereby allowing users to develop the skills of working in teams.
4. Shared community spaces and inter-group communications are a massive part of what excites young people and therefore should contribute to users' persistence and motivation to learn.

… One of the key lessons of the Web 2.0 era is this: Users add value. But only a small percentage of users will go to the trouble of adding value to your application via explicit means. … Through appropriate course design, we can help learners to pursue their 'selfish interests' of passing the course, while at the same time adding value to the learning of other students.

(Ibid., pp. 4–5)

Finally, one might consider the forms that this user-generated content might take. Besides substituting for the initial text-based sample materials I have been discussing so far, it might venture into narrative forms (learners telling stories about their lives, perhaps; responding to stories). McShay (2010) provides systematic guidance for the generation of "digital stories" in critical contexts. And it is of interest that over the last few years, publishers of books for young adults have extensively taken up the idea of user-generated content (Martens, 2011), particularly to develop the audience and market among teens who themselves contribute content both simple and complex to websites dedicated to specific books or book series ("transmedia" works, whose content exists simultaneously on multiple platforms; Jenkins, 2006; Martens, 2011).

In closing

In analyzing in detail the limited materials offerings available for beginning (or any) critical language pedagogy explorers, I have been trying to pave a way for easy first steps in a difficult arena. Classic Freireans certainly would prefer that a course start not with materials but with listening. Beginners exploring an area, however, would benefit from a map of the territory, however sketchy, incomplete, or out of date; cooks like a list of ingredients and a recipe, though only the least inspired or motivated stick to them rigidly time and again. The materials I have reported on can be seen as something like a map. In the next chapter, I take a preliminary, somewhat recipe-oriented approach to attempt a list of components which exploring critical teachers might try out in various mixes.

Questions for Discussion

1   Accumulating useful materials or knowing where to find them is a little-noticed aspect of teachers' professional expertise. Do you have access to a textbook collection, whether language-specific or general? Do you agree with my comment that textbooks of any kind with a critical orientation are hard to find? Are there any chapters or sections of textbooks that you are familiar with which *do* have such an orientation? Share them if you can.
2   What do you think about materials adaptation and supplementation in general? Do you have conditions in which you can do this? Have you ever come across advice about this? What would be a simple example of how you would supplement an element of your current or recent materials in a critical direction?
3   What aspects of your current internet use or social networking behavior have an educational element or characteristic? Do your students (or do you, when you are in a student role) contribute to the courses you are taking part in? Are you in this sense part of Web 2.0, or Education 2.0?

Notes

1 The increasing prominence of these perspectives in TESOL as a whole has been noted by many observers (e.g., Kumaravadivelu, 2006).

2 "It is essential that critical educators should not ignore the question of practice. That is, we must find ways of speaking to (and learning from) people who labor every day in schools in worsening conditions" (Apple, 2009, p. 37, in Shapiro, 2009).

3 E.g., "I come from an educational system which is firmly grounded in textbooks. 'Give me a book, and I'll do the rest—the teaching, the exercises, and the assessments.' Those were my beliefs. They also constituted my learning and teaching styles. A structured course with an assigned book is considered clear for me in terms of its learning objectives and expectations of the students. For me, the textbook provides the outline for the teacher as to what to teach first, second, third, and so on, and also provide practice materials for the students. This included class work and homework" (Lamey, 2009, p. 223). Relatedly, critical ethnographer Carspecken (1991, p. 17) comments, "Another problem that has faced practitioners [in his study of community education with a critical orientation] has been the lack of practical ideas and appropriate materials available … Teachers tried to make their own materials at first and to plan projects, but found that constraints of time soon greatly curtailed their efforts."

4 Or "world language" specialist, to use a more current term; in any case, she was not an ESL specialist like Wallerstein.

5 This was a position not confined at that time to critical language pedagogy. It was also to be found at that same time in the early CLT movement (Breen et al., 1979, p. 5): "This provision of different routes through some activity not only allows for alternative means to learning. It could initiate the creation by learners—in negotiation with the teacher and/or other learners of *new* units of activity." It was also implied by much earlier progressive and radical pedagogy; see Chapter 4.

6 "The initial meetings are wholly devoted to a group of pictures concerning the distinction between nature and culture. The intent is to raise consciousness about the human power to make culture, as demonstrated in the everyday lives of those people in class. Critical consciousness begins with an encounter between students and their human capacity to transform the world. This dialogue on humans as hunters, farmers, builders, tool-makers, etc., proceeds through a series of ten pictures, the last of which represents the literacy class itself, as the latest act of the students in transforming themselves and their reality, through the activity of learning to read and write" (Shor 1980/1987, p. 126).

7 Apple (1988, p. 200): "[T]here is a highly developed body of metatheory in the area of critical pedagogy, but a seriously underdeveloped tradition of applied, middle-range work. To the extent that critical work in education remains at such an abstract level, we risk cutting ourselves off from the largest part of the educational community."

8 See especially pp. 29–38; 44–50; 73–80; 85–99; and 113–122.

9 For example, Wallerstein's (1983c) description of how teachers developed lesson plans for use by SE Asian refugees in camps in the Philippines.

10 "I will not apologize for presenting a unit plan with general or specific objectives. These objectives may be offensive to some critical pedagogues. I do not apologize for attempting to present a unit with structure and form. I think that critical pedagogy needs structure and form despite its antistructural and more postmodern approach and underlying philosophy of endless deconstruction. I would like the reader to keep in mind that the unit I present here is merely an attempt by myself

with the aid of five graduate students ... to formulate ... a 'language of possibility'" (Kanpol, ibid.).

11 Discussing innovation processes in ELT, Waters (2009, p. 444) says: "[B]y the provision of fully developed teaching materials, teachers are more likely to be equipped with the necessary level of detailed and explicit guidance needed to support their efforts to implement new teaching ideas. ... [This] is in contradistinction to the anti-textbook ... stance which prevails in much of applied linguistics ... notwithstanding reports on the negative consequences of the lack of provision of this resource in ... innovation projects."

12 "Apple's (1985) argument, that pre-packaged materials contribute to deskilling teachers by removing decision-making and control from them, presupposes teachers who have received an adequate professional education in the first place," says Janks (1995, p. 11); and, as Janks continues, presupposes a range of adequate professionally produced materials, or even less smooth alternative materials, as available to be chosen from. These conditions did not exist when she was developing her materials, and in many ESL and EFL contexts still do not exist.

13 Note also Edelsky's scathing comments about the political connections between US publishers, national academic bodies, and major politicians (Edelsky & Johnson, 2004, p. 126).

14 Here she may be anticipating Boal (1974; see Louis, 2005), or Scarcella's (1976) "sociodrama."

15 Lest this be thought strangely childish, it seems that a psychotherapeutic concern is present here, as there is reference to using them to "discharge emotions" in connection with painful experiences or stories.

16 Wallerstein (1983c) also tried out her ideas in Philippines camps for Vietnamese refugees.

17 These are still somewhat similar to issues and topics identified in a 2003 workshop for ESOL learners operating on Freirean principles, in London: "childcare; children's schooling; cross-cultural relations; contact with home ...; cultural identity; employment (recognition of qualifications... employer prejudice); ... gender relations; healthcare; housing; immigration;..." among others (Cardiff et al., 2007, p. 10).

18 "My students have a hard time finding jobs, and a hard time keeping the bad jobs they find. They resent their low wages and menial tasks, but how can you live without an income? So, they fade into and out of a wide variety of jobs below their capabilities, as clerks, helpers, 'gofers,' messengers, typists, loaders, burger pushers, cashiers, pump-jockeys and salespersons. Their experience of work is not happy" Shor (1980, p. 127).

19 "The learning mode I will refer to as a 'language project' is an event lasting several weeks to several months, depending on the group of students and the thematic problem it is shaping through media. The document produced by the process represents their model reconstruction of a part of their reality" (Shor, 1980, p. 196).

20 "For Freire, a theme is a concrete representation of an idea, concept, hope, doubt, value, challenge, or obstacle in interaction with its opposite and implying a task to be performed. For example, Freire considers liberation/domination to be the predominant theme of the present epoch. The initial theme of communication/no communication and the topic of language as a communicative tool are represented to the learners ... During the dialogue around the theme of communication/noncommunication and the use of language as a communicative tool, the teacher points out possible themes or topics for study suggested by the students. Examples of such themes or topics concerning the two cultures under study are:

(1) employment unemployment patterns; (2) predominance of familial/ community ties; (3) male/female roles; (4) healthiness; and (5) the educated/ the uneducated. The teacher reflects these themes back to the students, and the entire study group selects the theme for study. The class selects subsequent themes from those generated in the course of study. ... This extension from one theme into another provides for some continuity and flow along study topics. For example, study of employment patterns may generate questions regarding male/ female roles, which in turn may open to problems with the educational system" (Crawford-Lange, 1981, p. 262–63).

21 This is an important strategy, to which I will return in the very last chapter of this work.

22 At this point I hear the beginning critical language teacher, working under less than favorable conditions, say, "well I don't have time to 'scour the mass media'. I need examples, samples; this is again where the no-textbook position favors the well-resourced teacher—even Shor in a community college has more than me, in a South American high school has."

23 Many more are in domestic South African literature.

24 http://web.wits.ac.za/Academic/Humanities/Education/Staff/JanksHilary.htm

25 Her dissertation was in the same area (Janks, 1995). It is worth commenting that dissertations *can* be done on practical matters and have direct socio-political impact! I look forward to more dissertations on material for critical language pedagogy.

26 Janks, 1993a, b; Granville, 1993; Newfield, 1993; Orlek, 1993; Rule, 1993.

27 http://www.growyourwritingbusiness.com/?p=53

28 See e.g. the Tasmanian state curriculum standards: http://www.education.tas.gov.au/ curriculum/standards/english/english/teachers/critlit

29 Stevick and others in this tradition are not themselves interested in fostering criticality, of course. On the other hand, see S. Wong (2006, pp. 35–36) for a rare consideration of adapting traditional methods in critical or dialogic directions.

30 In-house publishing, of a professional standard, by the Rethinking Schools collective; one of a number of similar large-format texts, extending to critical approaches to mathematics, as well.

31 I have not noticed much in the way of successors, but curriculum headings change and it is possible that there is more material of this kind out there.

32 http://www.niace.org.uk/projects/esolcitizenship/Home-Eng.htm

33 Although Osborn's table of connections and suggestions is comprehensive, the section is not otherwise well-developed and could be read as something of an afterthought. As a reader I also felt that he may have been running into length limits here.

34 And this does cover quite a lot of ground these days; even quite poor students, if they live near a town, even if in a peripheral area of a poor country, may be a relatively short physical distance from a small internet café with three or four computers and a T1 line, with time charged in cents per minute. (Personal observations: Kyrgyzstan during the depths of the post-Soviet decline in the 1990s, provincial Vietnam, and the poorest, violence-racked barrios of urban Colombia.)

3

COMPONENTS OF CRITICAL LANGUAGE PEDAGOGY

This chapter picks up many of the important aspects of critical language pedagogy practice that have been mentioned so far and reviews them one at a time.[1] Though they probably shouldn't be separated, nevertheless I can imagine a teacher who is beginning to explore critical language pedagogy taking up just one of them and experimenting with introducing it into an otherwise fairly conventional classroom, as part of initial explorations in this area. Auerbach (2001, p. 269) comments that teachers' praxis[2]

> evolves through an ongoing process of embracing certain aspects of the approach on one level, attempting to apply this preliminary understanding in practice, bumping into problems that trigger further reflection, then applying this new understanding, bumping into new problems (or the same ones), and so on.

Elsewhere (Auerbach & Wallerstein, 1987b, pp. vi–vii), she and Wallerstein advise us that

> students naturally expect a hierarchical style of education, similar to their previous learning experiences. It is important, therefore, to start with structured activities at the same time that you are creating an environment for student-directed learning.

So this would seem to suggest that baby steps are needed. All of the concepts listed and discussed below provide practical challenges to "mainstream" classroom practices[3], so at a classroom management level, or a lesson planning level, one should not underestimate their demands, and should proceed cautiously. In fact, the literature of critical pedagogy contains a number of unfortunate reports whose structure is: "I attempted to implement a critical pedagogy in my classroom for the first time and did not experience success, therefore Freire is wrong or critical pedagogy is not applicable in my context." At the very least I hope this caution (and this list) will head off the sink or swim approach to critical (language) pedagogy that has generated such reports.

Another caveat I would like to mention here concerns resources. All teaching, I suppose, is easier with more resources. At one level, critical pedagogy (particularly if you focus on the materials end of things) seems to demand the availability of considerable resources, though sometimes the resources are not so much material as the less tangible matters of "time" and "teacher freedom." At any rate, as a language teacher I admit to sometimes feeling worried when I read recent accounts of doing, or of how to do, critical pedagogy; most of which emanate from the first world. Many of them take for granted a well-resourced classroom or school, willing students, a culture of cooperation, good communication skills and willingness on the part of the students, and a bank of excellent library materials (not to mention internet access), so that a teacher can simply ask what is of interest, discuss with the class how it is to be investigated, and "We're off!" (cf. Wink, 1997, p. 124). Accounts of critical pedagogy produced by North writers usually fail to explicitly acknowledge the resource-limit part of the picture, which is extreme in the very places where critical pedagogies are most greatly needed. In the specific area of *language* teaching—besides resource needs, the extra demands when students can barely express themselves in the language of instruction or the target language can be great. Which is not to say there can't be discussion in the L1. But this brings me back to a point made in the previous paragraph: the far greater need for lesson staging (carefully planning, proceeding a step at a time) when initially attempting critical second language pedagogy than in L1 contexts is important to consider.

Given these caveats and frustrations, let's carefully and slowly inspect some of these individual characteristics, taken somewhat out of context just for teacher development purposes, and make plans accordingly. Here's my list.

1   Language organization and classroom management prerequisites.
2   Critical or otherwise oppositional stance by the teacher (e.g., feminist as well as other positions).
3   Critical needs analysis.
4   Negotiated syllabus.
5   Codes.
6   Dialogue.
7   Critical content in materials; participatory material development.

8   Critical (participatory, democratic) assessment.
9   Action orientation.

I'll work through most of these elements as the chapter now goes forward.

Language, organizational and classroom management prerequisites?

Language functions, task-specific needs, teacher planning

The closer we are to a basic beginning level of English among our students, the more need there may be for careful recognition of what language forms and functions, speech events, indeed pedagogical tasks, will need to be pretaught, elicited, presented, and/or made the subject of investigation. (This itself could be the subject of interactive discussion and joint investigation by teacher and students, mainly using the L1.) Core literature and sample materials in our area have been ESL-oriented, and take up without much examination its false beginners (or "intermediates," as Auerbach and Wallerstein describe the students for whom their materials were generally designed). Their default setting concerned learners who were already in a position to engage in basic communication in the target language. Wallerstein (1983a, pp. 35–36) has some specific considerations of the extent to which beginners can handle her material and approach, and options for the teacher in working with beginners, but generally we hear relatively little of the details of working with beginners in the critical language pedagogy literature.

The part of the literature that is more concerned with beginners is the critical literacy literature which often is developed with child learners in mind. Much of this also derives from experience in ESL contexts, so the absolute beginners in a class may be assumed to be assisted by other near-peers, and immersed in the target language. With the rise of interest in "young learners" in applied linguistics, we have more general works of guidance for EFL teachers of children but it is not easy to extrapolate from them to critical language pedagogy for the younger beginner learner.

Let me take up one activity type that acquires much more importance in critical pedagogy than in mainstream classes: "discussion." For critical orientations, this is a form of pedagogical discourse that is particularly important. Then, how should one go about orienting a class to it, that hasn't done discussion in the L2 before (and may not have done it in the L1 either)?[4] If it is very much teacher-fronted and controlled "discussion," then perhaps a class can move into it without much difficulty. If the aim is to also have small group based discussion, that is another matter. My interest in task-based language teaching leads me first to think of video recording authentic discussions (and disputes) conducted by suitable models (could be children, or adults, L1 speakers or better, bilinguals), and presenting them to the class, with associated simple role-plays approximating the authentic task being a major strategy for instruction. This is desirable if you take an analytic perspective on language syllabus design, which seems implied by much critical pedagogy. I have a practical concern, however, that this is just as much a "no-textbook" position, implying a lot of preliminary materials development work, as the one I discussed earlier in this work, and has all the associated discouragement. A less-demanding position would simply be that the teacher must provide direct instruction (in the L1 if possible or necessary) concerning what "discussion" is, how long it is going to take, and then provide explicit or implicit instruction concerning the genre structure and phrases to be used. (And perhaps better, if possible the whole matter of what is discussion could itself be a topic for some initial exploration.) Probably some discussion *on* a simple topic should then follow, with focus on form, or error correction, or, that is, learners' attention being drawn to vocabulary, phrases, and structures, as appropriate to the level of the class in the teacher's professional judgment. Perhaps use might be made of conventional, non-critical textbook material that has relevant language content (e.g., Porter & Grant, 1992; see also Young et al., 2001). And then, and only then, could one set forth on discussion of more challenging topics, it seems to me. Which means considerable planning, and the setting aside of time from regular class topics or activities, is going to be needed.

Freire's culture circles took for granted adults who could talk with one another and with an animateur—could discuss, reflect, and propose solutions to problems; in other words, cooperate. (Though he sometimes found an initial unwillingness to communicate.) Children's classrooms in traditional, large, under-resourced, violence-plagued schools all over the world (but perhaps more so outside of the rich countries) are not normally places where there is group work and an inquiry curriculum. That is to say, students there have been socialized into a different set of classroom events. Thus part of the prerequisites for a critical pedagogy may be to explicitly teach the behaviors of cooperative learning (see, e.g., Jacobs et al., 1997, 2002).

I am not suggesting that the language needed for a critical classroom presents a massive hurdle. I am simply thinking that it has to be planned for, and that in some cases forward movement could be slow—might legitimately be slow. In general, a careful "staging" of lesson plans is necessary so that the challenges presented are not overwhelming (cf. Wong et al., 2006, on fostering critical literacy in low-level high school EFL students in Hong Kong).

Democratic classroom management

For the successful introduction of critical language pedagogy, at both high school and elementary school, a teacher must have a good command of classroom

---

TASK: RESEARCH

Audio record a fragment of discussion among your friends, or from popular media (say, a talk show). What are some of the important language features of this discourse? How close could your students get to this? In your case, would forms etc. need to be pre-taught, or could you simply handle problems as they arose? What would be your students' attitudes to learning (language or content) through discussion?

---

management techniques. A class embarking on inherently interactive, possibly unfamiliar classroom activities needs to be one that is already comfortable with a set of routines that will permit these initiatives (established mainly by the teacher, through use of classroom management techniques).[5] Having said that, however, one must be careful not to fail to subject "classroom management" itself to critique. As Weinstein et al. (2006, p. 26) note, "conventional classroom management is presented as if it were culturally neutral, rather than a White, middle-class construction" (and they chastise the field of multicultural education for ignoring classroom management concerns). Clearly, critical pedagogy calls for highly interactive classroom practices and activities, including, ideally, some out-of-class activities, and teachers might experience difficulties in implementing these unless an element, not of control, but of custom, habit, and shared understanding of why things are done a particular way, is established. This might be particularly the case with younger students. The following quote from Australian educators (who have several decades of experience with some aspects of critical pedagogy, such as negotiating the curriculum) is relevant:

> In considering greater negotiation with students, many teachers worry about potential chaos or loss of structure in the classroom. From what we have experienced, negotiating can be much more purposeful and meaningful if structures, routines and record keeping are tightly in place. Essential skills such as questioning, time-management, self-assessment, decision-making and critical thinking need to be explicitly modelled and discussed. In addition, successful teachers actively work on dispositions that accompany independence— persistence, risk taking, patience and having the confidence to seek assistance and receive feedback.
>
> (Murdoch & Le Mescam, 2009, n.p.)

One prominent writer and consultant on classroom management who has written about it from a critical position is Kohn (e.g., 1996). Following an extended and rightfully negative analysis of the many established packages and approaches to classroom management in the US, his central recommendation is for the teacher to determine, through listening and asking, what are the issues and concerns that children in a class have concerning how the class is to run, what actually constitutes "discipline" (in their view), and what things bring about behavior problems and unsmooth interactions among the students. And then on the basis of inquiry and shared discussion between teacher and students, teachers and students should work to establish discipline through routines and agreements arrived at democratically. Recently, and since his work, there may have been a more general shift (at least in US academic writing) on this topic, as Weinstein et al., (2006, p. 28, referring to Freiberg, 1999) comment that "recent discussions of classroom management … eschew behaviorism in favor of an approach that emphasizes the importance of self-regulation, community building, and social decision making." A valuable resource in this area is the comprehensive approach to "democratic discipline" of Hoover and Kindsvatter (1997). Though Hoover and Kindsvatter do not use the term "critical pedagogy" nor cite Freire, they do draw repeatedly on McLaren and Bowles and Gintis, as well as Dewey. They start from a skeptical position, observing that "[w]here discipline is concerned, control and containment of students are predominant teacher motives, while formative considerations consistent with democratic principles have low priority" (p. 178). Their approach is grounded in the view that "schools should educate for an ethical, reflective, critical, and informed citizenry" and if followed carefully, should enable individual teachers to develop a "discipline plan" that is founded in the teacher's own philosophy of teaching. It would reflect the development of a positive classroom climate through attention to respect, freedom, due process and shared decision-making, supported by considerations of motivation and effective managerial practices, such as establishing routines and continuous monitoring (p. 179).

Related to classroom management is the subject of learners' emotions, and their expression. Learning a language is not easy; opening the door to aspects of life that are in need of improvement means that emotions are more likely to be expressed, but failure to express emotions in a constructive way can lead to unproductive forms of interaction and breakdowns in classroom discipline. Critical pedagogue Cowhey (2006) alludes positively to *Second Step* (Committee for Children, 2002),[6] as providing guidance for teachers of children to assist students in articulating emotions. Cowhey's accounts of her work, though not generally focused on classroom management, remind us that critical pedagogy positions encourage the teacher to have substantial contact with parents and community members. Much good critically oriented teaching and indeed action is thereby possible, for her and her class, and this sort of connection obviously could also have positive payoffs in terms of student behavior.

An afterthought: It can be assumed that introducing a critical pedagogy where the normal instructional arrangements are tightly controlled by government-mandated syllabi and textbooks would be difficult, but is a lack of control thereby desirable? I have recently been in EFL schools where though there are some resources (desks, chairs, pens, paper, and apparently willing and interested students), English teachers have no syllabus, no regular textbooks, and very little training; the teachers themselves may have little English and no understanding of government policy or awareness of the existence of any national curriculum; or they do speak English well and are only hired for that reason, performing several other part-time positions and having no commitment to any one. Moving to a critical pedagogy when there is *no* pedagogy could be difficult. Although this is the kind of situation where if only there were one well-structured self-explanatory textbook, perhaps much could in fact be done.

TASK: REFLECT

How confident are you about your classroom management skills? Have you taught under difficult conditions, with uncooperative or resistant students? Have you experienced "democratic discipline," in any form? Would you agree that the fields of language teaching and applied linguistics have little to offer in the area of classroom management? If so, why do you think that is?

Critical (or oppositional) stance by the teacher

Of course the critical language teacher has critical values, beliefs, and a critical philosophy of teaching—at least to some extent. But let me recognize explicitly that a teacher who is starting to explore the possibilities provided by critical language pedagogy may equally well be exploring what his or her values are. Edelsky and Johnson (2004, p. 134) write:

> In order to teach from a critical stance, the teacher has to have a critical perspective. How does a teacher come to have such a perspective? In Katharine Johnson's case, she came to teaching with experience working with others in struggles for social justice. Her critical perspective was honed by her work with Portland Rethinking Schools. She sought out books and attended national conferences that offered a critical perspective. And she worked with the Portland Writing Project directed by Linda Christensen, whose commitment to social justice and critical teaching sharpened Johnson's. The answer to the question of how to acquire a critical perspective, then, is the same as it is to the question of how teachers gain a whole language perspective: they read texts written from a critical (whole language) perspective. They join with others who have

a critical (whole language) perspective; they try watching events closely, asking "Why is it like *this*?" (i.e., they become event watchers in addition to being kid watchers ...).

Activist experience or orientation outside of, and prior to engaging in teaching, characterizes Auerbach and Cowhey as well. In Edelsky and Johnson's remarks, we can note an apprenticeship of experience in a program with a critical orientation (as opposed to one gained through other work, as in the case of Auerbach and of Cowhey). Conferences and books play a role, too. Here I would like to mention the concept of a philosophy of teaching—an attempt to say (or write down) key values and beliefs as well as their implications for one's practice. Teachers are increasingly asked to produce this sort of thing for practical job-related administrative reasons, but engaging in the effort to produce a philosophy of teaching one truly owns can be part of developing a critical perspective. In an earlier book (Crookes, 2009) I devoted a substantial portion of the work to conceptual resources that could be used by a teacher in developing both a philosophy of teaching and a critical stance, that is, a critical philosophy of language teaching. So I will not dwell on this point here, though I think that Chapter 9 will also provide some perspectives of relevance in developing one's values with a long-term perspective.

TASK: REFLECT; SHARE

If you are reading this alone, this might be a good time to stop and reflect and make a few notes concerning the values you hold, as a member of society and as a language teacher. If you are reading this book with a group or as part of a class, and you are comfortable sharing your values, I believe that your fellow students or teachers would benefit from some sharing and discussing of these thoughts. In particular, you might focus on any key or central events that have led you to identify certain values relevant to the critical stance implied by this work.

Critical needs analysis

Needs analysis—finding out what students "need" to learn—has been a curriculum development practice taken for granted in applied linguistics since the beginnings of the notional-functional era, associated with the development of the field of English for Specific Purposes.[7] Wilkins (1976, pp. 69–70) referred to courses whose design reflected students' needs as having early "cash-in" value, because they would teach the students what they most needed at the front of the course. If a student couldn't complete the whole course they had still got what they most needed already. For that matter, students would be motivated because, of course, they were learning what they needed (learning English for *Specific* Purposes, not English for general purposes, or no particular purpose).

Despite the present-day assumption that all well-designed language courses would reflect some sort of needs analysis, and thus the importance of the matter, there is comparatively little literature on how to conduct needs analyses, and few theoretical or conceptual treatments of the matter. A recent language-teaching oriented collection (Long, 2005) has greatly improved the situation; among the positions it takes are an advocacy of the use of multiple sources and methods, including the judicious use of both inside informants (when expert) as well as outside sources. The collection includes Jasso-Aguilar (1999, 2005), which draws on ethnographic methods and takes up power differentials in a study of the English learning needs of hotel workers in Hawai'i. Jasso-Aguilar found differences in the expectations for the language the hotel workers "need," comparing what her management sources specified against the findings of her own participant observation research. If a conventional needs analysis for the target group of students in this study had been conducted, it would probably have taken management's view, and thus reflected the power differential that existed between workers and management. If the needs analysis had confined itself merely to the instrumental needs arising from the task of cleaning hotel rooms with its minimal interactional requirements, this would have been inadequate too, according to Jasso-Aguilar. She notes (1995, p. 45):

> Although [needs analyses] are usually the result of institutional mandates, and will usually be paid for with institutional money, we must strive for a critical research perspective based on dialogue with—rather than observation and manipulation of people … to create a curriculum that will truly engage them in language learning, so as to allow them to become active and functional members of an English-speaking society … as opposed to just cheap labor who can report cleaning discrepancies in their rooms and greet guests in standard English.

Much earlier, referring to the development of critical pedagogy, Freire describes his own (of course critical) needs analysis procedures, which were clearly ethnographic, and included residence in the community in which the adult literacy program was developed. He refers to

> researching the vocabulary of the groups with which one is working. This research is carried out during informal encounters with the inhabitants of

the area. One selects not only the words most weighted with existential meaning (and thus the greatest emotional content), but also typical sayings, as well as words and expressions linked to the experience of the groups in which the researcher participates. These interviews reveal longings, frustrations, disbeliefs, hopes, and an impetus to participate.

(Freire, 1973, p. 49)

The results address students' needs, considering them in terms of the role of the learner as a potentially active agent in society not merely as a worker performing tasks or a student studying the language; overall the perspective derives from a critical view of society, and has always been part of critical pedagogy (cf. Wallerstein's account, quoted in Chapter 2). Contributions to the topic from a critical point of view have been advanced particularly by Benesch's important work (cf. 1996, p. 723; 1999, 2009):

Critical needs analysis … considers the target situation as a site of possible reform. It takes into account the hierarchical nature of social institutions and treats inequality, both inside and outside the institution, as a central concern.

In her influential 1996 study, she reports working with a group of ESL students in a US university, whose "needs" included not merely the language of academic lectures, but also the language (and task-related knowledge) for obtaining their rights, in this case to a decent education within a university that for at least institutional reasons of resource lacks was disinclined to provide this. In this case, ESL students attending a psychology class found themselves often unable to follow the lecture partly because the instructor felt a need to "cover" the material at a high rate, refused to entertain students' questions, and was reluctant to address the heterogeneity of his class, until, that is, Benesch's students developed collective techniques by which to engineer change in the classroom so that their learning needs could be met. The needs analysis that Benesch developed with her students did not take their regular classroom situation for granted—far from it. It approached that situation as one of power imbalance and inequity, viewing it critically, and then, working with the students, Benesch was able to suggest and co-develop strategies that enabled the students to act on their learning situation to improve it. These were not particularly radical, perhaps, and were principally students working together to develop questions which were put to the instructor in class (at the beginning of class), and also their initiation of a series of visits by the instructor to the students' regular ESL classroom, where they both got to know him as a person and also were able to ask more detailed questions concerning the content of the psychology class and get more substantive answers. Benesch also worked with the students on a module of what might be called feminist psychology, taking up (outside of the regular psychology class) the topic of anorexia, which was not covered in the main psychology curriculum.

Non-language critical pedagogy literature suggests that teachers trying to introduce a critical element into their classes often do so either through discussing some of the students' needs and viewing them in light of a critique of society, or in light of a critique of the institutional context within which the course is located It is not difficult to get at this through some in-class discussion (in L1 or L2, as appropriate). Such discussion is firmed up by asking for writing on topics, themes, and so on (see the earlier discussion of Shor's work). Extending this to our critical language pedagogy, Flowerdew (2005, p. 144) reports on an EAP course which has a critical element (though she explains that this is only part of the course). In this case an additional simple technique for implementing some part of a critical needs analysis derives from the cyclical nature of the course offerings and the archiving of previous versions.

> The critical pedagogy aspect of the course: Why are things the way they are? Who decides? What are the possibilities? has emerged out of some of the project topics chosen by students … First, I present some examples of projects carried out in previous years, which have had a successful outcome. By successful outcome, I am referring to those projects where the university authorities have taken up, and acted on students' suggestions (e.g. the provision of more computer express stations in the academic concourse).

In the work of Konoeda and Watanabe discussed earlier, they report use of a simple problem-oriented interview-based critical needs analysis, which confirmed what the authors were already aware of, and has been identified as a feature of Japanese high schools, namely bullying or teasing in their daily school lives. But note, or course, that a non-critical needs analysis of Japanese high school EFL learners would simply have identified the language needed either for exam-passing or for communication with foreigners, or for reading English literature, or for international travel, and so on. Turning to what could be done to improve the immediate situation, which is viewed with some critical concern or suspicion, is typical of a critical needs analysis.

National language policies can be inspected for potential here, perhaps. With globalization, some ministries may have shifted the goals for EFL instruction from the narrow instrumental ones ("communication with foreigners") to something more like "participation in the global economy" or even "global citizenship." Anything along these lines, when considered from a critical perspective, has potential because a great deal is covered under citizenship.

TASK: REFLECT

Reflect on your needs as a student, either in the past, or now. Which of them could be said to be non-critical, or instrumental? Can you identify any that would only emerge from a critical (as opposed to non-critical) needs analysis?

The negotiated syllabus

The position that the content of curriculum arises out of the concerns of students means that the trajectory of the individual course or curriculum is not fixed, nor is it determined by the instructor alone. This component of critical pedagogy has come to be called (at least in applied linguistics) the "negotiated syllabus," and has been discussed inside our field much more than some of the other elements identified in this chapter. In this section I first note the original Freirean perspective on this, then say a few words about L1 language arts syllabus negotiation in critical literacy in Australia, and conclude with a summary of comparatively substantial work on the topic in applied linguistics syllabus design theory and practice.

In the Freirean tradition, there is a listening phase which provides for an initial, perhaps extensive set of topics, and in due course a list of words and phrases to be taught. At the same time, when issues arise in dialogue among students and with the teacher, they are taken up and incorporated in the course. When students bring in material or raise issues, they are clearly having a major role in shaping the content of instruction. For foreign language critical pedagogy, Crawford-Lange (1981, pp. 260, 261, 262–63) summarizes:

> The Freirean educational purpose necessitates that considerable time be spent in the classroom establishing with the students what will be studied and why it will be studied. … Even though the initiation of language study proper may be delayed by a few days, failure to take the time to establish purpose with the students would violate the intention of an existential/ humanistic curriculum. …
>
> [N]either the thematic nor the skills information content of the curriculum can be defined prior to meeting with the learners. The use of predetermined syllabi, just as the use of predetermined objectives, is nullified. …
>
> Freire insists that while themes are classified according to discipline, tangential themes also be defined; as themes are discussed, input from various disciplines be sought; as thematic codifications are interpreted, the study group have no restraints placed on it with regard to relevant subject matter. In fact, the study group's task is to expand perception to see how

a phenomenon previously perceived as limited to itself actually interacts with other phenomena. For example, students may come to interconnect the racial composition of their school with political gerrymandering of attendance areas and housing patterns governed by regulations, the economy, and social factors.

Neither in Crawford's writing nor in Freire's work from that period is the term "negotiate" or "negotiation" used. But as early as 1978, Boomer in Australia was promoting the idea extensively and successfully (Boomer, 1978) within the state education system. And his edited collections (1982; Boomer et al., 1992) provide practical, vivid and detailed teacher-based accounts of L1 content curriculum or syllabus negotiation. The widespread promotion and acceptance of negotiation in Australian education presumably was an influence on the L2 work of the Australian Migrant Education Service which also developed and reported strategies for curriculum negotiation as a response to the needs of teaching small groups of diverse adult immigrant learners of English. During the 1980s, the Australian government continued and intensified its long-standing policy of supporting ESL instruction for recent immigrants; a learner-centered curriculum was promoted throughout the AMES program. A range of reports of the practicalities and challenges encountered exist (e.g., Parkinson and O'Sullivan, 1990; Nunan, 1985).[8] Shor (1996, p. 59ff) seems to have been influenced by Boomer et al. (1992) when he provides an engaging account of one of his efforts to negotiate the curriculum with community college students who have never done or even heard of this practice before.[9]

Syllabus negotiation in language teaching has been discussed and reported mostly independent of the Freirean tradition. Early manifestations within ELT of the idea of a negotiated syllabus were associated with Littlejohn (who reported experiments with the idea in 1982 and 1983; cf. Breen, 1987). Breen et al. (1979, p. 7) use the term as an implication of students selecting materials:

> This provision of different routes through some activity not only allows for alternative means to learning. It could initiate the creation by learners—in negotiation with the teacher and/or other learners of *new* units of activity. In this way any unit of activity may serve as a potential for further activities which emerge during the teaching-learning process. This ongoing discovery and creation of new directions in the teaching-learning process would be characteristic of a communicative methodology in the classroom.

Littlejohn (1983, p. 601) refers to his experimental work as implementing some of these implied components as follows:

In terms of practical implementation, it was decided that the course would consist of three components: Language Learning Workshops, which would be concerned with developing the students' awareness of the "what" and "how" of language learning; Formal Linguistic Input, concerned with the presentation and practice of linguistic knowledge, such as grammar, functions/notions, and vocabulary; and Activities, which would give the students greater experience in the range of possible classroom methods. Obviously, these components were not discrete categories, since any attempt to develop an awareness of the "what" and "how" of language learning would have to be carried out through some kind of "activity." These components, rather, reflected the concern that the students' progress toward exercising greater control should not be constrained by their lack of experience with possible ways of approaching language learning.

On the syllabus details Breen (1987, p. 169) says:

> The Process syllabus … aims towards the development of underlying communicative competence in a new language; prioritises communicating in a new language and for language learning; and assumes that learners are not only capable of being metacommunicative as a means to help their discovery of a new language, but also capable of making important decisions about their own language learning in a classroom with other learners. The Process syllabus does not merely assume that learners are capable of these things, but implicitly proposes that metacommunication and shared decision-making are necessary conditions of language learning in any classroom. It assumes that these things already take place—when teacher and learners work together in a language class, but that they occur in hidden, indirect, and—sometimes—disfunctional ways.

In Breen and Littlejohn's (2000) book on the subject almost twenty years after those early experiments, they note:

> Candlin argued that any pre-designed syllabus was rendered redundant from the moment teacher and students began working and that the only genuine syllabus would be a retrospective account of what the work had covered and what had been achieved from it (Candlin, 1984). Breen formulated the concept of a process syllabus in order to locate the conventional content syllabus more explicitly within and as mediated *by* the teaching-learning process. In addition, a process syllabus was proposed as a reference point for teachers who wished to engage students explicitly in evolving the actual curriculum of the classroom.
>
> (Breen & Littlejohn, 2000, p. 18)

They reference "humanistic education"[10] as one of the major conceptual sources for this perspective, as well as Dewey and Freire. They also point to work influential in the UK and in the early development of communicative language teaching, namely that of Britton and Barnes (e.g., Britton et al., 1969) which provided much more of a role of the learner:

> This remarkable critique initiated a focus among educators upon language across the whole curriculum and anticipated Britten's assertion of the need to see students as active communicating participants rather than quiet spectators in schooling, and Barnes' exploration of small group processes as a means for genuinely interpretative learning.
>
> (p. 14)

In the second half of their book, they provide a collection of ELT examples of syllabus negotiation. (A political analysis, or even a referencing of the implications for, say, active citizenship, is not part of their account. Besides the individualistic emphasis implied by the term "humanistic education," quite a lot of their support for the negotiated syllabus comes from conceptions of second language learning and of the classroom dynamics of language learning, i.e., that it motivates the individual learner.)

In Breen and Littlejohn (2000) we have at least one current full book of advice and accounts of practice existing in the literature of applied linguistics, providing mostly simple case studies of the implementation of syllabus negotiation in contexts (including six reports of elementary and secondary practice, besides the all-too-often concentrated-upon privileged post-secondary sector). And of all the advice they give, I think the most important is that "a gradualist approach to the introduction of negotiated ways of working may be appropriate" (p. 280).

While there continue to be very few reports of syllabus or curriculum negotiation in the language teaching literature, it was apparently a continuing success and prominent throughout the entire Australian education system (as mentioned earlier in connection with critical literacy)—that is, until recently (Johnson & McCauslan, 1999; Murdoch & Le Mescam, 2009). This is a good example of things that *can* be done, if conditions are favorable, so much so that they become taken for granted. Until, that is, the political tide turns against them. There certainly were some such forces in Australia in recent years, and it is not clear that this previously well-rooted innovation will be rooted out, or remain.

Codes

A characteristic feature of much Freirean material (as mentioned in Chapter 2) is the use of "codes." A code (or codification) is a projective device which

TASK: REFLECT

An obvious task in reviewing and digesting this potentially critical aspect of a curriculum is to ask if you, the reader, have input into the content of courses you have experienced or taught lately. What are some of the logistical problems you face, or that you think a teacher taking this approach might face?

allows learners to articulate their own, somewhat unpredictable interpretation of a potentially problematic situation relevant to their life. The code allows reference without determining content. It may allow material to surface that the teacher is not expecting or is unfamiliar with, and besides being important pedagogically also is important ethically, since it means that the teacher is not totally controlling content. Wallerstein (1983a, pp. 19–20) has this to say:

> [Codes are] concrete physical expressions that combine all the elements of the theme into one representation. They can take many forms: photographs, drawings, collages, stories, written dialogues, movies, songs. Codes are more than visual aids for teaching. They are at the heart of the educational process because they initiate critical thinking. No matter what the form, a code is a projective device that is emotionally laden and identifiable to students. Discussion of the problem will liberate energy that can stimulate creativity and raise motivation for using English. A good code should have these basic characteristics:
>
> 1. It must represent a daily problem situation that is immediately recognizable to students. (They already deeply know what is being talked about.)
> 2. That situation, chosen because it contains personal and social affect, is presented as a problem with inherent contradictions. The code (picture, story, etc.) should illustrate as many sides of the contradiction as possible, yet be simple enough for students to project their own experience.
> 3. The code should focus on one problem at a time, but not in a fragmentary way. It should suggest connections to other themes in people's lives.
> 4. The code should not provide solutions to the problem, but should allow students to develop their own solutions from their experience.
> 5. The problem presented should not be overwhelming to students. There should be room for small actions that address the problem even if they don't solve it. Local community issues usually provide opportunities for students to have an impact with small-scale actions.

In essence, a code sums up or "codifies" into one statement a problem (or contradiction) that people recognize in their lives: need for English vs. loss of native culture, stress at work vs. need for work, disappointment vs. hope from expectations in the U.S. Each problem is complex without narrowly defined good and bad sides. Students can project their own feelings and opinions in an attempt to negotiate solutions.

Morgan (1998) provides an example of how students' experiences can be incorporated into a lesson on intonation. Drawing on a text called *Decisions, decisions* (Bowers & Godfrey, 1985), he presented the predominantly Chinese students with a description of a scenario that addressed gender roles in a Chinese family. He then asked students what advice they would give to the female protagonist, Yuen-Li, who wished to learn English but felt constrained by family obligations. The class considered a number of options available to Yuen-Li, which were then incorporated into a scripted dialogue that Morgan brought into class the next day. The scripted dialogue was particularly helpful for students who had difficulty producing their own work but wished to participate actively in the discussion. It also provided students with the opportunity to read English dialogue, which in turn allowed Morgan to explore the politics of intonation. As students debated the multiple meanings of "Oh," in diverse intonation contexts, they drew on a range of experiences that might otherwise have remained unspoken.

Dialogue

This is a very important element of critical pedagogy practice and theory, but the term is broader than its normal use:

> Only dialogue, which requires critical thinking, is also capable of generating critical thinking. Without dialogue there is no communication, and without communication there can be no true education. Education which is able to resolve the contradiction between teacher and student takes place in a situation in which both address their act of cognition to the object by which they are mediated. Thus, the dialogical character of education as the practice of freedom does not begin when the teacher-student meets with the students-teachers in a pedagogical situation, but rather when the former first asks herself or himself *what* she or he will dialogue with the latter *about*. And preoccupation with the content of dialogue is really preoccupation with the program content of education.
>
> (Freire, 2000, pp. 92–93)

At the same time, there are many obstacles to it, placed in our way by inexperience, poor working conditions, and institutional pressures:

To develop dialogic talent, a teacher needs institutional support and student cooperation to run a seminarlike discussion rather than a traditional lecture class. Many school districts and academic departments mandate certain texts to be read and material to be covered in sequence. At this level of outside management of the classroom, the teacher cannot easily close the door and ignore the authorities. Lecturing machine-gun style then becomes a political compulsion restricting dialogue. Under these limits, the teacher is compelled to become a verbal delivery system covering the official syllabus in nonstop teacher-talk. Other obstacles to dialogue include the teacher's professional status, gender, and race, because new teachers and adjuncts, women, and teachers of color bring less authority to the classroom than do veteran, white, male, full-time instructors. As I argued earlier, authority is gendered, racialized, and age-based. With differential authority attaching to skin color, sex, age, and faculty status, teachers have unequal positions from which to attempt dialogue.

(Shor, 1996, p. 89)

It should be clear from this that, as Wallerstein (1983a, p. 15) says, "a Freire approach to dialogue assumes students equally determine classroom interaction." The term, then, goes beyond a narrow meaning of a two-person oral interaction, and covers students "bringing their concerns and personal agendas to class" (ibid.). It includes reference to and implies use of pair and small-group work.

Auerbach and Wallerstein make clear dialogue's roots in critical thinking, in turn reflecting a critical theory of society. It would be on the basis of their developing, perhaps different theories of society that students might challenge each other in dialogue, or indeed a teacher might ask a student to develop and clarify their position.

The goal of dialogue is critical thinking (or conscientization from the Portuguese) and action. Critical thinking starts from perceiving the root causes of one's place in society—the socioeconomic, political, cultural, and historical context of our personal lives.

(Auerbach & Wallerstein, 1987b, p. 1)

But Shor suggests that dialogue also prevents misuse of power:

Dialogue transforms the teacher's unilateral authority by putting limits on his or her dominating voice and calling on students to codevelop a joint learning process. The teacher opens the process to greater student participation, less student resistance, and more fertile contact with student thought and experience.

(Shor, 1992, p. 90)

Perhaps it needs to be said, since I am writing about language classrooms, that by dialogue I do *not* mean a text, or genre, of the kind that often appears at the beginning of a language textbook, and is a representation of a supposed interaction between two speakers of the target language. Instead, I am using the term to cover relatively informal interactions between pairs of students, among groups, and of course between teacher and student(s). Although Freire takes up the term and uses it both concretely and as a very deeply theorized central concept in his philosophical writings, most practitioners of critical pedagogy, when talking about their classroom practice, use it alongside "discussion."[11]

If a teacher were planning to move a conventional classroom practice in directions hospitable to critical practice, perhaps dialogue would be a single point to be identified to work upon—if, that is, the class were one in which students were socialized into not questioning the teacher during the body of class time, and if it were one in which teachers lecturing on grammar and vocabulary points were the norm. It seems to me that the genre would need to be identified as an instructional item that was going to be introduced (by the teacher) and practiced, during small segments of class time over some days or weeks, as a speech event to be learned and/or a new classroom activity. In the majority of classrooms, EFL as well as ESL, considering the whole world, I think that this degree of care might not be necessary overall. But in some classroom cultures it might be.

An appropriate question at this point is, What's the difference between dialogue and discussion? In empirical work on a critical language classroom, Shin (Shin & Crookes, 2005b) has distinguished between general dialogical and group interaction and critical dialogue. The former is broadly equivalent to discussion, valuable in itself, motivating, and important for L2 classroom practice. The latter refers to interactions, both between teacher and student and among students, in which one person's language, whether statement or question, encourages or presses another to consider the basis for their thinking. This is what Freire has in mind as dialogue. Putting this back in Freirean terms: through critical dialogue, students come to name the world in a way that could lead to the world being changed.

A range of mainstream sources could be used to provide sample phrases for handling discussion (and Lam and Wong's 2000 report of fostering discussion strategies in the EFL classroom shows that it is not necessarily easy). A partial account of growth and practice in this area comes from one critical whole language classroom (Edelsky & Johnson, 2004, pp. 131–32).

> Early in the year [Johnson] began modeling ways for the class to negotiate and disagree. .... At first, she gave students opportunities to negotiate innocuous decisions where stating and defending opinions would be less risky (e.g., what time to have recess and who should decide about

seating arrangements). When a real issue presented itself ... students were ready for a serious discussion. ... Johnson praised students who directly acknowledged another's comment or who respectfully disagreed. ... Johnson ... talk[ed] about the value of listening closely, building a discussion on each other's comments rather than just saying something new each time someone else spoke. ... In critical whole language classrooms the topics are often about racial, gender, class, and other inequities. Safety implies that students will be able to voice genuine (not merely acceptable) interpretations, some of which may, to the teacher's dismay, promote injustice and inequity ... The teacher has to protect all interpretations. ... At the same time, the teacher has to make sure that *any position can be interrogated even as it is protected*.

A critical whole language classroom has to be safe for the teacher too. Teachers should be able to present their opinions—but always as just one more opinion. Bob Peterson (1994, p. 40) maintains that when teachers "pretend to have no opinions on controversial topics", they send a message that it is "OK to be opinion-less and apathetic about important issues."

Certainly, this is another element of language practice that can by no means be taken for granted as within the grasp of L2 students working together, let alone L2 students interacting in front of their peers with their teacher in the target language. Yet, to reiterate, it is classically considered central to critical pedagogy.

Critical content in materials; procedures with materials

Content

The simple point I will begin with here is that a language lesson has to have content, and the content always has a perspective, a cultural orientation, and so on. It is never neutral. Therefore, as teachers (working with students) we have choices to make. That said, this brief section will mostly restate the discussion so far, as I have already discussed the area (a) in terms of content that learners bring in, (b) in terms of content emerging from a critical needs analysis, and also (c) in terms of themes (with three levels of analysis, following Shor). (Further consideration of content will also appear especially in Chapter 6.)

One point to note concerns a tension, perhaps, between what I might call the classical critical pedagogy emphasis on codes as the central way in to content versus other positions that rely more on simply a curriculum shift. In the case of the materials extracts from Janks, with their CLA theoretical inheritance, a more direct, less inductive emphasis specifically on language and language awareness was evident. Similarly, "putting the feminine at the center of the curriculum" is a first step in feminist pedagogy (according to Vandrick, see Chapter 6), a step more likely to be taken by the teacher, initially, than students.

A key area of content that has not been emphasized much so far, though central to Shor's practice, is popular culture. This point is developed by Van Duinen (2005, p. 146), as follows:

> Another aspect of dialogic education is in creating a sense of community among students themselves. A socially and culturally diverse classroom is a place where this sense of community is especially important as difference between and among students is usually more prevalent and pronounced. Though there are many ways to address this issue, one in particular is through using popular culture in classroom curricula, discourse, and culture. Using popular culture ... [is] a way to make connections to students' historicity in the world, but there are other benefits to this approach as well. Jabari Mahiri (1998) ... argues that using popular culture in the classroom can act as a unifying and equalizing force in culturally diverse classrooms. Students find commonalities and shared interests with each other and with teachers when their consumption and production of popular culture texts are recognized, validated and then used to shed light on academic texts and literacy practices.

It could be argued that popular culture is so colonialized by mainstream concepts that relying on it alone might be a dangerous strategy. There's always the problem that the teacher is usually a few years (if not decades) behind whatever younger students think that popular culture is. And this may be a particular stretch for non-indigenous teachers in EFL settings (though it was used most effectively by one indigenous critical EFL teacher, Shin, discussed later in Chapter 6).

In many cases content must conform to national curricula. Critical teachers will undoubtedly be alert to ways in which ambiguity in specifications can be exploited. Cowhey teaches a unit on activism, claiming that it comes under civics and government, using as a guide for her students in this material the phrase "laws and rules keep us safe."

Procedures

The term "participatory" is so central to Auerbach's understanding of critical pedagogy that she uses participatory curriculum development as more or less synonymous with critical pedagogy. So it might seem that participatory procedures are a sine qua non for critical pedagogy. However, they do not appear so visibly in the sample materials themselves. Participatory procedures can be a challenge to manage, at least to start with. Certainly bringing students into the decision-making concerning content is more time-consuming than making that decision unilaterally, outside of the course, by the teacher or by higher authorities. Also it may involve roles and procedures that are unfamiliar to students. Thus it should not be taken lightly, and a teacher could certainly choose to experiment directly with this, even without making use of any other elements in my list.

To repeat, this can mean use of pre-written sample materials, preferably as a way to get things going, and preferably supplemented or overridden rapidly by content brought in by students, suggested by them, and in this day and age, in well-resourced classrooms, found by them on the internet.

Influenced by Cowhey, I want to add that participatory procedures seems likely to be aided first, by the accumulation of materials, but also second supplemented, under favorable conditions, by the development of a list of community resources that can constitute or supply materials. These can actually be volunteers or supporters of the classroom, as well as public resources and officials.

Democratic, participatory, and critical assessment

The older literature on critical pedagogy had little to say about testing or other procedures for assessing the learning of students: "Critical pedagogues have made little, if any, mention of this topic" (Van Duisberg, 2005, p. 142). In early critical FL, Crawford-Lange (1981, p. 267) preferred to see it in terms of participatory course evaluation as did Auerbach and Wallerstein (1987b, p. 7):

> Evaluation of students' progress with a problem-posing curriculum demands an approach different from other teaching methods. Because the curriculum constantly evolves from student issues teachers can't measure fulfillment of predetermined objectives or test outcomes. Problem-posing evaluation concerns a broad spectrum of students' abilities to articulate their issues in English, generate their own learning materials, redefine their views of the world, and take the risks to act in their daily lives. Because students' abilities change over time, problem-posing requires a process evaluation of both the expected and unexpected changes. In concert with the entire approach, evaluation can be an empowering tool. Students can learn to evaluate their own learning and to reflect as a group about the actions they have taken. The first three units of the Student Book introduce the concepts of self-evaluation and group evaluation with specific questions for students to evaluate the curriculum and their actions. To start the evaluation process, look at the effects of codes on student learning and on promoting discussion and action. Did the code tap a generative familiar theme? ... Did it foster student understanding of root causes of the problem, and was action taken? ... What was the result

of the action and how would they do it differently next time? Finally, what new problems did it uncover to pursue in the curriculum? Evaluation about actions reinforces the purpose of education as personal and social change so that students can become actors in their own worlds.

Similarly, in one of the few critical treatment of the topic, Keesing-Styles approaches the matter by initially working through core extracts from the theoretical literature critical pedagogy, remarking (p. 14) that "few, if any, of the theorists offer pragmatic suggestions for an alternative pedagogy of assessment." She eventually arrives at some general principles, as follows (2003, p. 11):

> To achieve a critical approach to assessment, it must be centered on dialogic interactions so that the roles of teacher and learner are shared and all voices are validated. It must foster an integrated approach to theory and practice, or what Freire would preferably term as praxis—theory in action. It must value and validate the experience students bring to the classroom and importantly, situate this experience at the centre of the classroom content and process in ways that problematize it and make overt links with oppression and dominant discourses. It must reinterpret the complex ecology of relationships in the classroom to avoid oppressive power relations and create a negotiated curriculum, including assessment, equally owned by teachers and students.

She then draws on Shor (1992, p. 144), and quotes him as follows:

> the instruments used to test and measure students should be based in a student-centred, cooperative curriculum. This means emphasizing narrative grading, portfolio assessments, group projects and performances, individual exhibitions, and essay examinations that promote critical thinking instead of standardized or short-answer tests.

These suggestions, perhaps slightly more manageable than those of Auerbach and Wallerstein's, probably reflect Shor's own more institutional location as a teacher. Kessing-Styles is dealing with student teachers. She reports being able to work with student-generated assessment criteria, as initially applied to the evaluation of practice teaching sessions, but then extended to "essays, projects ... reports and the construction of resources" (2003, p. 16). She also reports briefly the use of student-generated assessment tasks. She mentions being explicit about the themes of a course, and then students can self-assess with reference to those themes that are of most relevance to them. She notes that a gradual approach is necessary to introduce and guide students in self-assessment; a process that develops over several years with these student teachers.

Critical language pedagogy specialists can turn to the recent upsurge of critically oriented work in language assessment that has developed because language testing specialists have come to see how essential a critical perspective is in the highly power-charged area of testing. Much important work, mostly taking the form of critique and argument, has been done within the language testing community (Shohamy, 2001a; McNamara, 1998; McNamara & Roever, 2006, *inter alia*). Within this literature also can be found descriptions and analysis of alternative classroom practices, as well as a perspective to be presented to our students as they face the much less pleasant "real world" of high-stakes imperialist English (and other) language testing (though the focus is more on the standardized test and its ethical implications than teacher classroom practices). In this literature, Shohamy (2001a) is helpful though she approaches the matter with a focus on the testing establishment and testing experts, rather than on the critical language teacher who is trying to figure out how to do testing and assessment in their own classroom that is consistent with a critical language pedagogy.

An important feature of democratic forms of testing is their use of multiple sources of evidence.

> [T]ests are limited in what they can assess and that there is therefore a need for procedures [i.e., other forms of assessment] to assess areas that cannot be tapped by tests. The application of collaborative and shared models is of special importance in the classroom as it provides students with the experience of democratic assessment behaviour from an early age as they become aware of the need to guard and protect their rights from the assessment machinery of centralized bodies.
>
> (Shohamy, 2001a, p. 380)

Because so many of the problems of testing also come from levels above that of the individual teacher, Shohamy's warnings and suggestions about moving towards participatory and dialogic testing should also be considered (Shohamy, 2001a). She starts from some brief remarks of Freire about evaluation, that emphasize the need for a dialogic perspective here too, and then extends that to encompass testing and assessment procedures that are based within institutions and communities, in which negotiated procedures and practices can be located.

> [N]ew models of assessment follow principles of shared power, collaboration and representation, and can therefore be viewed as more democratic. ... Such approaches change the balance of power between tester and test-taker and assumes that the tester is no longer the 'know it all' who owns all knowledge ... Adopting democratic principles along such lines implies that the act of testing is a mutual effort between

testers and test-takers; other sources of knowledge are also important, e.g., construct-assessment knowledge via dialogical and cooperative means as well as groups of people such as parents, teachers and peers. ... In some approaches, local groups—test-takers, students, teachers and schools—share power by collecting their own assessments, using multiple assessment procedures (portfolios, self-assessment, projects, observations and tests). ... The professional tester serves mostly as a facilitator who assists in the strategies of collecting the information and in its interpretation. In other models power is transferred from central bodies to local ones, such as when external examinations are abolished in favour of local and internal assessment. ... [T]he preferred model, in the classroom as well, is not a transfer of power, but the sharing of power with local bodies. ... This approach can then be applied on the national, district or classroom context. It suggests therefore that assessment of students' achievement ought to be seen as an art, rather than a science, in that it is interpretive, idiosyncratic, interpersonal and relative.

(Shohamy, 2001a, pp. 378–79)

Obviously it would be nice to have more detailed case-based accounts. Shohamy's own experiences within the language testing community in Israel allow her to report on some such cases, not always positively (Shohamy, 2001b). Also at the national rather than classroom-based level, a partial example from the past is the existence of 13 local examining boards administering "national" exams in the UK, between 1965 and 1986.[12] During their time, local schools had input into the curriculum to be examined, and both conventional exams and student reports on long-term projects, overseen and validated by school teachers, were submitted and jointly evaluated. (Students did not have a say in the proceedings!)[13] The local, somewhat negotiated operations ceased more or less at the time a National Curriculum was introduced, itself the opening salvo in the "standards movement" and the shift to central government control of education in the UK, the US, and elsewhere. This appears to be consistent with the description by Moss (1996, cited in Shohamy, 2001b) of "contextualization and shared authority with regard to certification" (Shohamy, 2001a, p. 380). But it seems that more local reports and case studies of procedures and practices in testing and assessment of critical language teaching are badly needed.

Action orientation

An action orientation is conceptually important for critical pedagogies. Close, in one sense, to our area, are existing courses which by definition have an action orientation, namely service-learning courses. These may address a range of matters in the community that seemed to call for action, usually plugging

---

TASK: SEARCH AND CORRESPOND

Despite the importance of this topic, critical assessment appears to be an element of critical pedagogy that is less well-developed (even) than any others. Search for accounts, whether published or oral and informal, of any aspects of testing practices that have a democratic or participatory element. If necessary, write to specialists and ask for their help and advice.

---

students into existing socially supportive institutions. A key question is, are those actions based on a critical analysis of society? Students volunteering with a soup kitchen will not be "critical action" if there is not a consideration, preferably with appropriate materials and dialogical structure, of what this issue really means to the students and to society from a critical point of view. On the other hand, if courses of this kind already exist, they could be useful to critical pedagogues, and for that matter, proposing a service learning option or course could be a first institutional step in the direction of a critical pedagogy.

Critical pedagogy intends to facilitate students being inserted into the creation of their own histories, as Freire puts it. A starting point here, prior to action itself, is activism itself as a theme or curriculum content. In Edelsky and Johnson's (2004) critical whole language program,

> a critical curriculum informs students about activists of all ages. After all, activists and equity movements are also part of a cultural heritage, even though that information is rarely foregrounded in school curricula. Critical teachers seek out resources (interviews with activists, songs written about resistance, literature about activists, movies, and videos about rarely taught events) to show what ordinary people have done, usually banding together with others, to change things on behalf of the less powerful …
>
> (p. 135)

Students in this program interviewed family members who had tried to carry out some form of social improvement. They also learned about activists. They then were encouraged to articulate any role or possibility they imagined, in which they could themselves have an active role in improving society.

Auerbach and Wallerstein's materials often present a step involving action research to find out what people think or what problems they are facing in a particular area, usually at work. On the basis of such investigations, students have further content to bring to the class. In addition, on the basis of this material and further discussion or exploitation of it, the general critical pedagogy literature seems to intend that students will be individually or collectively prepared to act in their places of employment, families, schools, and so on, to deal with problematic situations or even people they may encounter. Or collectively, students will take some sort of action, in engaging with representatives of the state, of the bureaucracy, or other relevant entities. The school itself is also often a target for such actions.

One may ask, if a teacher intends to manifest a critical pedagogy but his/her course doesn't result in action, does it then in a sense "fail" to be critical pedagogy? My answer is no, for a couple of reasons. First, this element is one of the most challenging parts of a critical pedagogy and I would not wish to discourage beginners. Second, all teachers know that the day their course concludes is not the end of the course's effects on students. Seeds are sown that may not in fact grow for years, combining with a multitude of other effects, the development of the student, and the eventual arriving of fruitful conditions. A critical pedagogy class may clearly raise awareness of an issue, and that may not ripen into action until much later, and/or until conditions are favorable or the issue becomes a crisis. I think that a teacher beginning to explore critical pedagogy should not feel that a lesson or module had to result in action. Wallace (1999, p. 103) comments:

> However, classrooms need not be some kind of dress rehearsal for supposed real life beyond them, if we believe that education has inherent rather than utilitarian value. In the case of the Critical Reading class there was a concern to link the classroom world with social institutions beyond it. And action was certainly an option for individual students to follow up, as they wished. … Nonetheless, the course was not centrally committed to furthering specific or immediate forms of action.

But now, let us ask, what are some of the actions that the literature reports or suggests. I'll provide a few examples categorized by student type and age. The younger the students the less challenging these actions should be, of course. One of the most inspirational works on critical pedagogy with elementary students (not language-related: Cowhey, 2006) has as its first major action the preparation and delivery of Thanksgiving food (pumpkin pies) to homeless people. (This requires considerable resources, including a principal willing to open a school on a snow day, parents with cars available with no notice, a Mayor and a homeless organizer willing (by appointment) to meet with elementary students, boxes donated, and eventually the actual distribution around the homeless shelter by the students.) Another, perhaps typical, action that Cowhey documents is her class of elementary students (mostly not second language learners) jointly writing a letter to "the Mayor." One does not know, usually, if the students even receive an answer. Edelsky and Johnson (2004) commented, "The classic 'letter to the president' is not effective activism—especially under the current administration" (p. 135). In other cases it seems that students do succeed in persuading university administrators, or even legislators (Ferguson, 1998) to do things differently.

Although classic Auerbachian work, because of its adult ESL immigrant orientation, suggests that the action involved be directed towards the larger society, the internal institutional conditions of education are clearly also a legitimate target, and the outcomes don't have to be revolutionary to still suggest the possibility of making change. This is the position of Flowerdew (2005, p. 145), whose critical component of an EAP course in Hong Kong resulted, over several years, in a variety of internal projects:

> Carrying out these projects very often gives students a sense of empowerment as they feel they can facilitate change in academic matters. Such projects also raise the issue of power relations existing between undergraduate students and professors who have the status to activate change. Although it may seem rather surprising that undergraduate students could be empowered to effect changes to the academic curriculum, this, in fact, has happened in a small way. For example, a group of biology majors investigating the mismatch between the undergraduate biology curriculum and future career prospects of biology students recommended that more compulsory Mandarin courses be included to give biology students a competitive edge when applying for business-related posts. The students reported that in their interview with the professor concerned, he agreed in principle with their recommendation and said he would raise this issue at a higher level.

The EAP critical literature sees the regular courses that students may take after service English courses (or concurrent with them) as "a site of struggle" (Benesch, 1999, p. 315) and a situation which itself could be improved by the action of the (ESL) students. Similarly, Benesch's ESL students, faced with a lecture class in psychology but concurrent with experiencing a critical pedagogy of EAP, exercised their "right" to be heard, their right to ask questions, their right to give the professor feedback (about his lecturing, his not writing key terms on the board, not citing the section of the textbook under discussion, not providing a proper syllabus, and other issues).

TASK: REFLECT

The last subtopic, action, is the one that seems particularly in need of research. Outline the steps needed for a piece of teacher-research, participatory in nature, that would enable you to get a handle on the connections between an element of critical pedagogy, and action outcomes.

In closing

I would like to remind the reader that I am taking some liberties in this chapter, for expository purposes. Probably more elements of critical language pedagogy could be identified; and anyway, surely a holistic perspective is more appropriate to the spirit of critical pedagogy (rather than one that cuts things up into little separate pieces). On the other hand, I take comfort from the remark I quoted at the beginning of the chapter, from Auerbach, that the exploring teacher may work on first one, then another aspect of this practice, and in a cyclical and reflective manner develop an overall practice in this area. If this is to succeed, then those partially separable elements must be identified, before being rejoined in advanced or more developed work—as I was trying to do here.

Questions for discussion

1   Which of the various options or elements presented in this chapter do you think you could move forward on first, easiest, fastest? Why? Which are more challenging, and again, why?

2   Think of some issues you and your fellow teachers or students face in your own daily life. Imagine you were leading a discussion intended to surface them as problems to be addressed. What would be some good "codes" to use?

3   As Flowerdew's case indicates, actions don't have to be "big". What are some actions (if any) that students could be involved in, in your context?

Notes

1   For another fairly concise set of key critical pedagogy "tenets"—historicity, problem-posing, dialogic, emancipatory, and praxis— see Morrell (2003, p. 8).

2   Freire (1982, p. 28) refers to praxis as "reflection and action on the world in order to transform it."

3   The scare quotes are deliberate. What is mainstream itself varies from context to context. Some progressive elements are in some parts of the mainstream (consider "inquiry-based approaches"). Nevertheless, I use this term for want of a better.

4   For general L1-related review, see Brookfield (1999).

5   Although perhaps this is too conventional a position. Anecdotal reports suggest that unruly urban classes might work better when given a chance to discuss and investigate life issues more relevant to them than the prescribed neutral textbook or curricular material.

6   This vital area of classroom practice is ignored by language teaching specialists. The vast literature of classroom management ranges from the authoritarian to the critical, and all language teachers need at least some orientation to it. Critical, communicative, and/or task-based language classrooms with their emphasis on group work and activity imply considerable management demands. Besides the occasional chapter in a pedagogy text (e.g., Crookes 2003) only a handful of titles are available (e.g., Wright, 2005; Farrell, 2008; cf. Sakui, 2007).

7   Needs analysis to derive curricular objectives was a standard part of curriculum theory at that point (e.g., Tyler, 1949); yet language specialists operated on the position that students needed to learn "the language," i.e., the complete set of grammar rules and vocabulary. That is, they took an English for General Purposes position, which didn't fit well with students who had immediate instrumental needs and only a short time to learn; a group whose increasing prominence was influential in the development of needs analysis as a central concept in L2 syllabus design procedures.

8   "The 1990s and beyond have seen a move to an overarching articulated curriculum with syllabuses planned at a local level within learner 'pathways'. ... This change came through providers' responses to student demands for greater clarity in their learning programmes and from teachers who were finding the individualised system time-consuming and difficult to implement" (Cooke & Simpson, 2008, p. 156).

9   He also references Elsasser & Irvine (1992) using "the Freirean 'generative theme' method to negotiate the syllabus with students" (Shor, 1996, p. 59) and a number of other sources discussing "shared authority" at this point.

10 Interestingly, they refer to humanistic education as a source, and specifically the philosopher Bertrand Russell, here. Russell's work on education (e.g., 1926) is long-forgotten, though he was another who had a hand in an early free school (Gorham, 2005).

11 Besides Freire, one prominent theorist involved in matters of language, Bakhtin, also made extensive use of the term 'dialogic'; in Bakhtin's case he was identifying an internal quality of language, even of individual words and phrases. This is a sense of the word that is not being addressed here; however it is occasionally (confusingly?) used in discussions that lead into or are closely linked to critical pedagogy (e.g., Wong, 2006).

12 http://en.wikipedia.org/wiki/Examination_boards_in_the_United_Kingdom

13 I draw here on personal experience.

4

RADICAL OR CRITICAL PEDAGOGY

Beginnings and elements

Where to start?

Knowing where things come from is important; in fact, asking about where ideas, concepts, practices and proposals are coming from is a crucial aspect of critical thinking. We must "historicize"—put things into historical context as social developments; and we must also ask "Who benefits?" at the same time.[1] In this chapter, I will describe early developments that fed into the traditions that later became known as critical pedagogy, and so for this chapter I am using a more general, less time-bound term, "radical pedagogy." Allocating space to relevant historical traditions of teaching here supports the relevance and practicality of the kind of teaching and language programs I'm advocating. It does so by heading off responses that such work is impossible, since that's not what the historical record shows.

In some cases, the things that people say "can't be done here" have *already* been done, in one form or another, but were discontinued for some reason. Alternatively, they may have to some extent been taken up and become part of the scenery. (An example of a proposal that was quite radical in its day, but is now the default, is co-education.) Historical analyses can also focus attention on what enabling factors were necessary for early radical pedagogy, and then we can see if some of them are still present, or perhaps are no longer present and have to be reinstituted or replaced. In addition, a review of the history will give us a better or more comprehensive sense of the ideas we inherit, or the full range of ideas and practices we can draw upon, which are more diverse than is generally realized.[2] After we informally accumulate a sense of the range of practice and ideas, I will summarize them as a short list of elements or components that can be found in the historical record. Many of them also appear in present day critical pedagogy.

Let me start once again with a general definition: critical pedagogy is teaching for social justice, in ways that support the development of active, engaged citizens who will, as circumstances permit, critically inquire into why the lives of so many human beings, including their own, are so materially (and spiritually) inadequate, be prepared to seek out solutions to the problems they define and encounter, and take action accordingly. And then, within that whole area of education, as second language teachers we focus on language and culture, which to a large extent make us who we are. Thus we can talk about "critical language pedagogy," as some specialists and practitioners have been doing off and on for some thirty years now.

One view of where to start investigating the history of this topic, a view of where the trail starts, is that articulated by one of the most prominent writers in this area, Henry Giroux. In a recorded conversation,[3] he talked about precursors to Freire and critical pedagogy but then stated the conventional viewpoint, which is (as he puts it) "the archive really should begin there [with Paulo Freire]." And there's no question that the work of Brazilian educator Paulo Freire is extremely important. But Freire, like everyone, didn't start from scratch. For quite some time he didn't even use the term "critical pedagogy"— in the recording Giroux recalls proposing it to him as a less challenging term than "radical pedagogy," which was also in use at that time and is a longstanding broad cover term for this same area. The first use of the term in print was Giroux (1983, p. 40), as Giroux was engaged in developing additional theoretical bases for critical pedagogy through exploring a stronger connection to the Frankfurt School of "critical theory," which Freire had made only a little use of in his own work.[4]

We could work backwards further into the past from Freire (as did Taylor, 1993), but as a place to start and look forward I'd like to select a moment which is widely regarded as a point of "rupture" in history, the French Revolution. That will enable us to pick up some threads of educational thought that I think should be worked back, explicitly, into the fabric of radical pedagogy.

Historical background to radical education

In 1789, as social conditions deteriorated in France (because of starvation, the effects of financial crises, and an authoritarian but incompetent government) political events moved towards a rapid and violent transformation of society. At first national elections produced a representation of grievances to the king which was still in support of the monarchical system. But events were quickly taken over by those with firmer (and more radical) views about how society should be run. By 1792, a republic had been established.

For a few years, quite remarkably modern practices were initiated in the Central Schools, public sector schools promoted by the state, spanning high school and lower college level education. These included

> virtually no admission requirements, no graded classes, and no set term of years of study … Instruction was by "courses" rather than "classes," that is, each teacher taught only his own subject; and lecturing, supplemented by questions and discussion, was favored over drill and recitation. All courses were electives for the students, and examinations were optional for the professors. There was no religious instruction. … The planners meant to favor science and mathematics and a modern approach to other subjects, so that the student of grammar, for example, was not to learn arbitrary rules but to understand the reasons underlying them. … The faculty of each school was self-governing; there was no principal or head. … They were "comprehensive" in stressing both cultural and vocational aims, and in teaching the sons of both professional elites and artisan and shopkeeping families … The schools were likewise open to the community in that each had a library open to the public and adults were welcomed in the classrooms to hear lectures or observe scientific demonstrations, so that instruction of the young was blended with continuing education. … We can infer with some certainty that in 1799 there were about 10,000 students in the Central Schools.
>
> (Palmer, 1985, pp. 243–44, p. 249)

Not surprisingly, because of poor political and economic conditions, this system was not well administered. From 1799 on, Napoleon increasingly took over the reins of government and strengthened central control of education. The Central Schools were revised in 1802 and steadily moved towards a highly centralized national curriculum before the return of the monarchy in 1814 (cf. Bailey, 1998).

The legacy of the French Revolution, across Europe and beyond, in the minds of many people from rich to poor was substantial, however. Ideas about democracy, social change, and for that matter about freer forms of education appropriate to the children (not to mention university students) of a free society had been awakened and would never again be put to sleep. After decades of war associated with Napoleon's imperial ambitions, the first half of the nineteenth century moved to a close with revolutions in many European countries.[5] These had been revolutions mainly driven by the middle class associated with a broad movement of "liberalism." However, the working class and the rural peasantry were increasingly radicalized. This was the height of the industrial revolution in Europe; the new industrial proletariat were experiencing bitterly cruel working conditions, the rural populations were starving, and trades unions were on the rise; various political movements often with interests in education struggled and organized. States were weak by twenty-first century standards and did not have a monopoly on education. Some states were not even interested in controlling or developing it. So it was not too difficult for small, informal, local schools to be started up by individuals with a particular, possibly radical, vision of school or society, or for an organization, such as a trades union, to set up classes, both for children or for adults (cf. Gardner, 1984; Humphries, 1981). A range of trends opposed to the mainstream developed, reflecting the impetus provided by the French initiatives just sketched, early "liberal" ideas, and the Romantic movement. Some flowed into the progressive tradition in education (Röhrs & Lenhart, 1995); others were more radical.

The most distinctively radical of the trends in question was termed "integral education." This referred to the education of both mind and body (as distinct from the overly academic education generally found in schools at that time). Also, it was explicitly designed for working people, with vocational features but emphasizing the desirability of non-industrialized forms of work. It was anti-individualist, de-centralized, and cooperative; and involved adult as well as child education, and was promoted by left political theorists, among them Proudhon, because it also drew on radical critiques of society and a view of an alternative society that could be attained. It occurred first in a small set of schools (initially in France: Robin, 1869–1872; Beach, 2008) from where it spread, under the influence of a teacher-administrator called Francisco Ferrer, to Spain, at the beginning of the 1900s (Avrich, 1980). Ferrer developed a small organization and disseminated these ideas further through publications. Ferrer schools were started in Europe, South America, China, and Japan. Ferrer's ideas for his "Modern School" (e.g., 1913) pulled together many ideas that were radical at their time but are commonplace nowadays: coeducation, active learning, a scientific investigative approach applied throughout the curriculum, emphasis on the practical as well as the theoretical, and the use of the physical environment as a learning context and source (Smith, 1983). These schools continued to exist as a distinct tradition outside of the state sector until the 1950s in the US.

Another intriguing precursor in radical education was the influential French educator, Freinet, whose work on international relations between schools, using school-to-school communication across national borders, has been long-lasting and was reintroduced to language teaching by Cummins and Sayers (1990, 1995). In Freinet's system, students wrote and printed their own materials, negotiated their own work schedules with the teacher, left the classroom to do investigative work in the community, and in various other ways manifested a range of ideas from the alternative pedagogies in play since the French Revolution. In his later years, after World War II, Freinet developed a large network of schools whose classrooms exchanged their work and letters and by implication were engaged in L2 learning; L2 specialists Cummins and Sayers (1990, 1995) identify this as a precursor to modern internet-based school exchanges and "learning networks." Freinet was associated with both anarcho-syndicalist and communist teachers' unions, and his own publications were a sustained critique of mainstream education.[6] Cummins and Sayers focus their attention on the way that Freinet took control of the content (and process) of education by focusing on materials development, making it central to his approach and under the control of the students and the network of schools he established, something which is even easier these days with schools networked via internet and with continuing advances in the tools of media creation. They comment:

> computers and other forms of technology can support and enhance a project of possibility that actively challenges the hegemony of the dominant group. This is accomplished by withdrawing "learning" from the pre-scripted texts controlled by the dominant group in society and by recreating the generation of knowledge and the development of critical understanding as a shared enterprise that is jointly elaborated by participants in a learning network. Within this type of network or "construction zone," the generation of meaning is directly and actively under the control of the learners; and all participants, both teachers and students are, by definition, learners.
>
> (1990, p. 26)

In the US, other influential educational developments had no connection to the working class or to radical politics, but drew their inspiration directly from the work of Pestalozzi (1781/1910, 1801/1898; see Bowers & Gehring, 2004) and the romantic ideas of Rousseau. The Parker School is a central example because its founder visited European progressive schools (between 1872 and 1875) and wrote extensively on the philosophy of his school (e.g., Parker, 1937, originally published 1891); Campbell, 1967; Shannon, 1990). It was taken over and closely associated with the University of Chicago, which is where the highly influential philosopher of education and progressive theorist John Dewey also ran a school and became well known.

For language specialists, Dewey is important because he put an activities-based curriculum in the mainstream (cf. Task-Based Language Teaching (TBLT): Samuda & Bygate, 2008). For criticalists, he is important because he advocated for schools a central role in the improvement of society, and because the Progressive Movement, which he was associated with, for a time featured in the mainstream of American education. He also called for, though may not have implemented, participatory curriculum development (Nicholls & Hazzard, 1995; Dewey, 1938). We should note that in practice Dewey obtained much from pre-existing models, the "schools of to-morrow" he and his daughter analyzed in Dewey and Dewey (1915; cf. Stone, 1999). He also spent two years in China, and the uptake of his ideas by Chinese educators in the late 1920s, including their critique from the left by Tao Xingzhi (Wang & Zhang, 2007) also suggests that any idea that activity or task-based approaches with a social justice orientation are somehow purely "Western" or cannot be used in non-Western countries, is questionable.[7]

There was a smaller group within the progressive movement who came to be called the social reconstructionists (often identified as precursors to critical pedagogy: Giroux, 1981; Stanley, 1992). Their main representative was Counts (e.g., 1932). Reconstructionist ideas for social change were also to be found in a widely published and used series of social studies textbooks (e.g., Rugg, 1931; cf. Evans, 2006). Given the central concerns of the present book it is particularly interesting that reconstructionist influence came about particularly through this textbook series. The prominence of Rugg's views, and perhaps the extensiveness of the use of his books, led to his becoming a lightning-rod for opposition to both progressive and social reconstructionist views (Riley & Stern, 2002) and under the patriotic pressure of the run-up to World War II, many of these developments faded away.

A tradition that is not usually drawn upon in discussions of radical education is the free school tradition. Free schools are typically characterized by their emphasis on direct democracy, absence of coercion, and personal growth. Stereotypically, attendance at classes is optional (though students are required to be on the school grounds or in other spaces within the school). The most famous is the small, private, residential school in the UK known as Summerhill. Instituted by its charismatic founder, A. S. Neill, it has consistently offered an extreme challenge to the mainstream in its attachment to an extreme conception of freedom, direct democracy, and absence of coercion, mainly on psychoanalytic or therapeutic principles (Appleton, 2000). The historical inheritances of Neill go back to Danish "folk high schools" and German schools of this kind. The latter were described by an American observer (Washburne & Stearns, 1926, p. 110) as follows:

> Schools with no program, no course of study, no grades, no examinations, no rules, no punishments—with their whole work centered on the development of each child's soul from within—these are the [four] public experimental schools of Hamburg.

These state-supported initiatives lasted from 1919 to 1925 and vanished as the political winds changed in Europe at that time (Wallace, 1995), though they resurfaced later elsewhere. After World War II such developments of alternative educational ideas long-standing in the European traditions of *Aktivitetspedagogik* (Köhler, 1936) and *l'education nouvelle* were re-established (cf. Holt, 1976, on Denmark). Various options in alternative education, including free schools, were initiated with state funds in the US during the 1970s and some of them have managed to maintain themselves since then. The tradition continues to exist and is international in scope (Nagata, 2007). While these schools, then as now, collect together many of the options in alternative pedagogy, they tend not to be based on a socio-political critique, as opposed to an individualist and psychological critique. They have even been criticized by some on the left (e.g., Wright, 1989, p. 114; for example, for their laissez faire character: Freire, in Shor & Freire, 1987). Another criticism of Summerhill and by implication other free schools is that being private and often residential they charge fees that inevitably make them middle-class institutions. This position is resisted by Mercogliano's (1998) account of an independent free school located in a poor neighborhood of New York which draws its students from the local (diverse, poor) communities.

The social movements of the 1960s brought about simultaneous and extreme changes in many aspects of society, including education, around the world. Some of the rapidly spreading developments in education generally, outside of authoritarian polities (of both left and right), during the period 1960–1980 included moves to co-education, abolition of school uniforms, establishment of school councils or other forms of representative democracy in regular state high schools, introduction of sex education, learning contracts, some forms of participatory syllabuses (including at state level), some forms of local control of otherwise national curricula, grade inflation (especially in US universities), far greater overall access to higher education (often at low or zero cost), increased unionization of teacher workforces (including at tertiary level), occasional unionization or organization of "school students" at national levels, and intermittent radicalization of university students, who then played a sometimes violent and at least confrontational role in national political change in countries as diverse as Korea, Japan, France, Germany, Greece, Colombia, the US, and so on.

Adult education and literacy movements were prominent in the less developed countries, in some cases associated with radical political change or the coming to power of revolutionary governments. One of the central figures of contemporary critical pedagogy, Freire was heavily involved in this part of the changes, being exiled from Brazil for literacy work in the 1960s, advising revolutionary governments in ex-Portuguese colonies in Africa in the 1970s and influencing radical educators widely in the 1980s. That is to say, when the historical narrative arrives at this point, it has caught up with the so-called beginnings of critical pedagogy.

As a coda, let me try to bring the story up to the present time. The 1980s (very roughly) were a time during which, in many parts of the developed world, the pace of progressive social change slowed, and was replaced in some cases by a shake-up in state education systems. On the one hand, there were dramatic alterations in the political and educational landscapes in the ex-Soviet Union and also the Peoples Republic of China (e.g., Deng, 1997), towards much greater freedom. At the same time, under UK and subsequently US governments (of Thatcher and Reagan), the audit culture and accountability regimes in education were started, which have been emulated in many other countries and have severely reduced the autonomy of teachers (and the quality of education for many students, particularly those in poorer areas; Ravitch, 2010). At the same time, in applied linguistics, there were important conceptual developments in many areas. Of the greatest importance for the topic of the present book, social and political conceptions of language, of English as an international language, of the ELT publishing industry, of curriculum, and of second language learning processes, all became much more visible than before. Much of this can be rolled up under the heading of critical applied linguistics, of which critical language pedagogy is a component; one that arguably pre-dates the establishment of critical applied linguistics but which fits with it just fine.

Elements of these historical critical pedagogies

A questioning response to this historical account might ask "Are any of these old stories particularly important?" as we prepare to engage with the present and the future. One might also ask "What in these schools and programs was truly radical?" (or critical, recognizing that that term had not been developed in those times).

Well, clearly the teachers who proposed and carried out the initiatives mentioned themselves held views of the individual, of the child in particular, and of society, which were a challenge to dominant views. Many clearly had a naturalistic view of learning and development. Many held views of society which were based on an analysis of it which was negative and "radical," both in a political sense and in a psychological sense. Where countries were monarchical, we could expect our early alternative teachers to be anti-monarchical. Where cultures were dominantly Christian and where the Church played a major role in society (which was true for all the European countries), we could expect them to be anti-clerical. By the late nineteenth century, they would have had a political stance in favor of the peasantry or the working class, and some (for example, Ferrer, Proudhon, Tolstoy, and possibly Freinet) were explicitly associated with anarchosyndicalist positions. The twentieth century progressives might have had socialist outlooks. Insofar as these educators were also feminists, they favored and implemented co-education. Psychological radicals in the free school movement were opposed to the psychologically and sexually crippling oppressiveness of dominant society; and we have seen in the term "integral education" an orientation to learning through action and a unified view of mind and body.

What about classroom practices? We can see some evidence in their prescriptive and descriptive writings in favor of dialogue and a caring perspective or interaction with children at least. The free school tradition is clearly associated with direct democracy in school or program governance.

As for syllabuses and materials, the progressive tradition has primarily an activity-based curriculum, but this was pretty much preset by the teachers and administrators. Freinet is of particular interest and a radical pedagogy precursor because of his student-made, printed, and internationally disseminated materials.

Within the historical record as I have sketched it at present there is also what we might call a critical language awareness approach, or critical discourse analysis. Rugg's reconstructionist textbooks (e.g., 1931) printed samples of newspaper reports and encourage analyses that are alert to differences in writer's viewpoint and to obfuscation; CDA *avant la lettre*. This becomes more visible with Freire and his emphasis on literacy. He also has an action orientation that is more explicit than that of the precursors. On the other hand, it is not clear what the historical precursors to critical pedagogy thought about testing and assessment, although the free school tradition would probably have thought the whole idea unnecessary.

In closing

My concluding point is this. It is intellectually and possibly emotionally important for critical language teachers to see themselves as part of a confluence of long-standing traditions, within what could broadly be called radical education. Giroux's assertion that the archive starts with Freire is partially true, particularly when we focus on language, but Freire himself consciously drew from preexisting nonmainstream ideas in education (philosophy, religion, and so on). And indeed, there were undoubtedly elements of the radical tradition that he was not familiar with. The availability of information in the early twenty-first century makes it much easier to look back; and it should thus make it easier to see oneself, as a critical language teacher, as part of a strong, indeed everlasting, tradition.

Questions for discussion

1 What sort of history of education, or of language teaching have you been exposed to? To what extent have you been provided with a unitary story of progress?
2 Let me put this another way. What conceptual differences exist between the procedures of schools during the French revolution and schools today? Is this progress, regress, or just a difference in values?
3 What aspects of critical language teaching are close to or identical to the historical record presented in this chapter, and which are different? What is the significance of the differences, if any?

4　Do you think it is easier, in any sense, to learn a second or foreign language in an educational institution now, than it was a hundred years ago? Is the average language school (course, program) more "efficient"? If so, why? From a critical point of view, does it make sense to answer this question as it applies to all learners? If not, how would you modify an unhedged answer to the first question?

Notes

1　These questions have been identified as crucial elements of a critical perspective in many places. For an early example in TESOL, see Bartlett (1990). Or Smyth (1987, p. 20):

- Where did the ideas I embody in my teaching come from historically?
- How did I come to appropriate them?
- Why do I continue to endorse them now in my work?
- Whose interests do they serve?
- What power relationships are involved?
- How do these ideas influence my relationships with my students?
- In the light of what I have discovered, how might I work differently?

2　I am not the first person to advocate this strategy for critical education. Apple (1988, p. 178, cited in Cummins & Sayers, 1995) noted: "[B]y seeing how teachers have *helped make their own history* (contradictory though it maybe), by once again restoring their (and our) collective memory of the range and success of particular political and cultural struggles, we take a large step toward making such struggles legitimate once again."

3　http://www.youtube.com/watch?v=UvCs6XkT3-o. "On the origin of the term, Roger Simon had talked about it, but I think it began with discussions with Paulo. ... We [with Donaldo Macedo] had rejected the term radical pedagogy. ...It would not allow most educators to take the leap of identifying with it. ... So we used the term critical pedagogy."

4　One other important early figure in North American critical pedagogy, Roger Simon, suggests that the term was in use in the OISE Critical Pedagogy and Cultural Studies Forum shortly after 1979 (Simon, 1992).

5　As well as anti-colonial revolutions and wars of independence in South America that brought an end to Portugese/Spanish colonialism there by about 1822.

6　Again, not springing out of nothing but to some extent a continuation of progressive European educational ideas associated with *l'education nouvelle*.

7　He traveled extensively outside the USA; his ideas were widely and sometimes loosely interpreted in many countries, but often made common cause with indigenous versions of modernization and progress in circulation internationally (Popkewitz, 2005).

5

RELEVANT UNDERSTANDINGS OF LANGUAGE AND LEARNING

A common position in studies of language learning and teaching is that language teaching practices should be founded on theory, often theories of language learning. Accordingly, in this chapter I will try to say something about two areas of relevant theory, specifically theories of language and theories of learning, as they might relate to learning and teaching in critical language pedagogy. I will address them mainly as resources for deepening our understandings. There are many different conceptions of theory, of course, though the dominant conception emphasizes its generality and universality. On the other hand, critical pedagogy comes from a diversity of traditions, some of which take account of historicity and specificity rather than generality, and which also look for an integration of theory and practice. Given that the historical extent of critical pedagogy itself is clearly a span of fifty years, not to mention its precursor radical trends going back several hundred years, what we have in the field of critical pedagogy is continual cycles of theory, conceptual change, and practice, all interacting, within continually changing socio-political and cultural environments. At an individual level, we often find cases in which active and forward-thinking teachers try out and develop practice under the immediate pressure of classroom need and personal values, and then academics follow along trying to put labels on things, with the intention of examining, promoting, or dismissing them, and certainly with the intention of informing others about them.[1] Many of the prominent authorities in the traditions canvassed so far in this book were both teachers and theorists. Therefore, perhaps it would be better to say that teacher-researchers in this area (as in others) theorize their practice, as well as turning to the parallel developments of theory outside language teaching itself, that may constitute resources for further developments of what is often called *praxis*—theoretically grounded practice. And this itself contributes to further cycles of interacting theory and practice.

That said, the understandings of language and of learning that were associated with early conceptualizations of critical pedagogy were, at least, concerned with adults developing L1 literacy under conditions of oppression; they were not primarily concerned with second language learning. Also, they had only tenuous connections with established learning theories or theories of language. The literature of critical language pedagogy does not engage strongly with mainstream theories of language and engages only weakly with theories of second language learning (though it implicitly theorizes these areas itself). Despite this there are developing literatures in second language learning and in analyses of language that are at least partially relevant to the practices of critical language pedagogy, and it is important to briefly review what theoretical resources have accumulated in these areas which may assist our practice and our critical philosophies of language teaching.

Theories of language

Many students of a second language around the world are taking courses that focus on the structures of language. But many of those who study a second language want to communicate, that is, do things with words (cf. Austin, 1962). The idea, clearly, is that words are for active purposes; we humans use them to perform particular functions (rather than consider the structures on which those functions are hung); among other things, we use them to act on the world (and act with each other). In this functional conception of language, language connects with social structures and patterns of interaction to get things done.[2]

In both the structural and functional conceptions I have just identified, language is generally seen as neutral and under our command for everyday matters. This understanding is helped by the idea that language is often understood as an inert or transparent entity. If instead, however, it is seen as something with a social history, or even more, something not necessarily entirely under one's control, it may be clearer that language can be seen as doing things (directly or indirectly) to society in general, and to learners (and their identities) in particular. They may see language as a tool, or indeed a weapon, sometimes used for social change, and sometimes used against the weak. The integration of language with social matters is sometimes referred to as discourse processes, or sometimes just "discourse" (cf. Fairclough, 1992; Foucault, 1971; Mills, 1997).

Once radical pedagogy developed an interest in language, as it did most notably with the early work of Freire, it adopted a perspective in which language helps or hinders a person from understanding (and acting on) the world. According to Taylor (1993, pp. 35–36), Freire's conceptions of language were probably influenced by Febvre, the French scholar of history and of *mentalités*.[3]

Taylor also views Freire's practice of decoding as "a specific application of" discourse analysis. However, Freire did not provide any systematic theory of language, writing about it mainly in philosophical terms. At more or less the same time, the field of applied linguistics was seeing a flourishing of functional theories of language that could be used in L2 teaching, particularly in the work of Halliday.

Halliday was initially a linguist and teacher of Chinese, who subsequently worked with English language teachers while developing a wide-ranging theory of language. He begins with a radical understanding of society. In an autobiographical note (Halliday, 2002, p. 118), he writes:

> My time in China had been more or less evenly divided between two regimes, nationalist and Communist. I had been impressed by the achievements of the Chinese Communist Party, and I had studied a certain amount of Marxist theory. It seemed important to apply Marxist principles to the investigation of language. ...

Halliday says that he developed his theory of language, Systemic Functional Linguistics (1961, 1973[4]) partly in response to questions emerging from the work of Bernstein (e.g., 1961, cf. 1971–1975) on "how the social order was reproduced, and potentially transformed, through language" (Halliday, 2002, p. 124–25). This is a concern almost identical to that of Freire.[5] The theory concerns itself with the many ways that the functions performed by language, both at the level of the sentence or utterance, and above that level, in discourse, show themselves, can be achieved, and are organized. Theorizing language above the sentence also allowed for other developments in language analysis to be used in L2 teaching. During the 1970s and beyond, the idea of genres, or text structures, became part of many second language teachers' everyday conceptions of language. It is important that L2 users of a language be able to use genres effectively if they are to succeed in society or achieve the goals implicit in the tasks of communication; and as genres come with often unspoken rules concerning their structure, these must be analyzed and taught if non-mainstream learners are not to be disadvantaged.[6] So this perspective facilitated theory and analysis of the role of power in discourse. Academic developments with a critical perspective developed out of this in an early "critical linguistics" in the late 1970s. This was developed by Fowler and others at the University of East Anglia in the late 70s, and was later subsumed by Critical Discourse Analysis (Hart & Lukes, 2007). The idea of a critical linguistics doesn't mean that a purely structural analysis of language is somehow wrong:

> The prevailing orthodoxy of linguistics is that it is a *descriptive* discipline which has no business passing comments on materials which it analyses;

neither *prescribing* usage nor negatively evaluating the substance of its enquiries. But I see no reason why there should not be branches of linguistics with different goals and procedures, and since values are so thoroughly implicated in linguistic usage, it seems justifiable to practise a kind of linguistics directed towards understanding such values, and this is the branch which has become known as critical linguistics. … Now, the word "critical" could be intended, or taken to be intended, to denote negative evaluation, but this negativity is not necessarily the aim of critical linguistics. As far as I am concerned, critical linguistics simply means an enquiry into the relations between signs, meanings and the social and historical conditions which govern the semiotic structure of discourse, using a particular kind of linguistic analysis. This activity requires a very specific model of linguistics. The model has not only to identify, and to label reliably, certain key linguistic constructions; it has to relate them to context in a specific way. … Halliday's systemic-functional linguistics … is specifically geared to relating structure to communicative function, and this model provides most of my descriptive apparatus. …

(Fowler, 1991, p. 5)

This perspective was taken up, and indeed taken over, by those who emphasized its application particularly to discourse, within the school of thought known as Critical Discourse Analysis (CDA).[7] Its analytic methods were taken over by CDA, particularly by Fairclough (e.g., 1995). Fairclough explains the antecedents of his work and its educational orientation or intention, as follows (1990, p. 8):

The theme of "language and power" (and related themes such as "language and ideology", "language and social control") is I believe being forced upon us by the increasingly prominent role language is playing in establishing, reproducing and changing, power relations as these social and cultural changes proceed: This is not a new role but an intensification of a role which has been extensively documented in contemporary thought—in Marxist work on ideology (Althusser, 1971; Gramsci, 1971) and its extension to discourse (Pecheux, 1982), in Foucault's (1977) studies of discourse and power and Habermas's (1984) work on strategic versus communicative uses of language, and in more empirical work on media discourse, language and gender, etc. … Such an approach is also educationally motivated: the functioning of discourse in the management of change and in the constitution of a changing social order makes critical language awareness, as part of a language education programme, an essential prerequisite for effective democratic citizenship.

In terms of a conception or theory of language, it is the "D" of CDA that is the core. Increasingly, language as discourse (which is to say, as a social practice) is the understanding that is drawn on by critical applied linguists. Many key aspects and sources are summarized by Rogers (2004, p. 5), who draws on Gee (1996) to emphasize the roles of discourse.

> Gee (1996) made a distinction between little "d" and "D" discourse. Little "d" refers to language bits or the grammar of what is said. "D"iscourse refers to the ways of representing, believing, valuing, and participating with the language bits. Big Discourse includes language bits, but it also includes the identities and meanings that go along with such ways of speaking. This distinction helps us see that the form of language cannot exist independent of the function of language and the intention of speakers. Further, Gee [2004] asserts that Discourse is not merely a pattern of social interactions, but is connected to identity and the distribution of social goods. Gee (1996) set forth a number of theoretical propositions about Discourses.
>
> 1. Discourses are inherently ideological … They crucially involve a set of values and viewpoints about the relationships between people and the distribution of social goods, at the very least, about who is an insider and who is not, often who is "normal" and who is not, and often, too, many other things as well.
> 2. Discourses are resistant to internal criticism and self-scrutiny because uttering viewpoints that seriously undermine them defines one as being outside of them. The Discourse defines what counts as acceptable criticism.
> 3. Discourse-defined positions from which to speak and behave are not, however, just defined internally to a Discourse, but also as standpoints taken up by the Discourse in its relation to other, ultimately opposing, Discourses.
> 4. Any Discourse concerns itself with certain objects and puts forward certain concepts, viewpoints, and values at the expense of others. In doing so, it marginalizes viewpoints and values central to other Discourses. In fact, a Discourse can call for one to accept values in conflict with other Discourses of which one is also a member.
> 5. Discourses are intimately related to the distribution of social power and hierarchical structure in society, which is why they are always and everywhere ideological. Control over certain Discourses can lead to the acquisition of social goods (money, power, status) in a society. These Discourses empower those groups that have the least conflicts with their other Discourses when they use them. Let us call Discourses that lead to social goods in a society *dominant Discourses*, and let us refer to those groups that have the fewest conflicts when using them as *dominant groups*.

TASK: EXEMPLIFY

It will be easier to digest these ideas if we test out some examples. What are some examples of ways language can be used to conceal or neutralize events that might be thought of as unethical if viewed from a critical standpoint? (If you can come up with these, you are presumably engaging in critical language analysis. Would you agree that second language students should be able to do this, too?)

Given Gee's definitions, can you come up with some examples of possible Discourses? Try them out on friends, colleagues, and other readers of this work; see if they agree with your selections as good examples of Discourses.

Applying critical theories of language in the critical language pedagogy classroom?

As a preliminary point, note that a critical linguistics doesn't mean we throw away the analysis of sentence structure provided by mainstream linguistics, or particularly the pedagogical grammar that arises out of it (cf. Morgan, 2004). As Shor (1992, p. 35) says,

> [It is not the case that] students have nothing to learn from biology of mathematics or engineering as they now exist. Neither does it mean that students reinvent subject matter each time they study it or that the academic expertise of the teacher has no role in the classroom. Formal bodies of knowledge, standard usage, and the teacher's academic background all belong in critical classrooms. As long as existing knowledge is not presented as facts and doctrines to be absorbed without question, as long as existing bodies of knowledge are critiqued and balanced from a multicultural perspective, and as long as the students' own themes and idioms are valued along with standard usage, existing canons are part of critical education (p. 33).

Yet there will presumably be plenty of things we want to do (as teachers) or want our students to learn that will not be aided by merely having available a conventional structural or functional theory of language, and which will, we may suppose, be aided by a critical theory of language. So *can* we assume, then, that the practical aspects of critical language pedagogy are adequately supported by this critical theory of language? Canagarajah (2005, p. 933) comments questioningly as follows:

> Though we have a well-established critical tradition on orientating to sentence-level rules from the time of critical linguistics (see Fowler &

Kress, 1979) and stretching up to more recent forms of critical discourse analysis (see Fairclough, 2000; Gee, 2000), there are very few research projects using this approach in classroom learning. Although exemplary articles on how critical linguistics can help classroom language learning are available (see Fairclough, 2000), they haven't inspired active research.

At first blush this assessment seems a little too negative.[8] The work of Wallace (2003, pp. 33–43) may provide a start.

Wallace's (2003) book has at its core an account of her classroom practices and some specification of materials used, in a voluntary critical reading course offered to advanced EFL students at a post-secondary university college in London in the late 1990s. In the course, she made use of Hallidayan SFL concepts as she and her class read and analyzed a range of carefully selected texts. The linguistic theory used for pedagogical purposes was SFL. This was applied in the course of doing critical discourse analysis of the text. She hoped to foster students' awareness and helping them use such analytic strategies, thereby raising their ability to respond appropriately to power-laden and obfuscatory uses of language and use language as a tool of power themselves.

Here are some quotes in which she explains a bit more about how her approach to critical language awareness and critical reading makes use of SFL:

> [SFL] takes a wide view of context to move beyond the immediate textual environment in order to take account of the cultural landscape. Because functionally grounded, it sees all human language as "shaped by the social functions it serves" (Chouliaraki and Fairclough 1999: 140). Halliday's is essentially a social grammar. This makes it compatible with a conceptualisation of reading as social practice and texts as social artefacts (Wallace, 2003, p. 31)
>
> [It uses] a simple conceptual framework of three contextual features …: field, tenor and mode which serve to interpret the social context of a text. The grammar thus offers the possibility of looking at whole texts in their social context: the ideational, interpersonal and textual functions of language, linked respectively to field, tenor and mode and exemplified by features of grammar such as transitivity, mood, modality and cohesion, are linked to features of the social situation in which the text arises, namely its content, the relationship between producer and receiver and the overall function or rhetorical mode of the text, whether descriptive, narrative or expository.
>
> At the same time, Halliday (1990, pp. 24–25) allows for depth … propos[ing] four levels of language use, the first most salient kind relating to the use of obvious logical anomalies such as "eventually we will run out of food. We must learn to live with this"; the second to lexical effects,

as observed, for example in ritualised collocations such as … "delivering the curriculum"; the third relates to what Halliday calls the "outer layer" of grammar, as evidenced in function words such as pronouns, while the fourth is at the most concealed level … the hidden grammar.

(Ibid.)

Although Wallace's was a course she called critical reading, the more widely used term for work of this sort is "critical literacy." To some extent critical literacy is the pedagogical application of basic concepts in or from CDA. Many critical literacy case studies certainly reference CDA.[9] Wallace, after the exposition of Hallidayan linguistics excerpted above, goes on to provide "an account of a framework or pedagogic procedure which illustrates how critical language study informs teaching and learning … [this is a] mapping out of the territory of critical literacy pedagogy" (ibid., p. 33).

> One kind of framework which makes strong reference to criticality, although it is ostensibly concerned with what it calls the design of social futures more widely, is that offered by the NLG [New London Group] (Cope & Kalantzis 2000) [also focused on by Canagarajah, 2005, earlier]. … This model moves from situated practice, to overt instruction, to critical framing concluding with transformed practice. … By situated practice the NLG mean immersion in a community of learners engaged in authentic everyday literacy experiences. Kalantzis et al. have however argued elsewhere (e.g., 1990) the limitations of education which favours experiential modes of learning: mere immersion in practice, however authentic, will not always in itself promote learning. Situatedness or contextualisation needs to be supported by explicitness so that understandings can be raised to consciousness. This principle motivates the stage of overt instruction when aspects of texts and reading are made explicit and key terms introduced.

Thus Wallace uses the basic terminology of SFL as a pedagogic tool, a critical pedagogic grammar. In the third and fourth parts of this approach, there is "critical framing," in which students step back from texts which they have previously analyzed. Finally there is transformed practice in which the learner makes use of their new understanding of language in an active way. This work supports a related but simpler more pedagogical model of Lankshear (1994) which is specific to written texts only, which Wallace uses to "guide [her] account of the key phases of a critical literacy pedagogy (ibid., p. 35).

> 1. knowing literacy (or literacies) critically, that is having a critical perspective on literacy/literacies generally;

2. having a critical/evaluative perspective on particular texts;
3. having a critical perspective on—being able to make critical readings of—wider social practices, arrangements, relations, allocations, procedures and so on. which are mediated by, made possible and partially sustained through the reading of texts.

(Ibid., p. 34)

In partial and preliminary summary, then, critical-functional theories of language are required by critical L2 pedagogy, indeed, are implicitly drawn on to explain how it is that reading the word (in a particular way) enables one to read the world. Furthermore, pedagogic grammars of a critical kind can be used and (according to Wallace) are useful in assisting the learning of a second language for critical purposes. Put another way, it could be suggested that we regularly need a critical language awareness strand, involving explicit instruction along with the established, task-oriented, experiential modes of critical L2 pedagogy.[10]

TASK: REFLECT

How has your awareness of language changed during your time as a student and a teacher of languages? What sort of understanding of learning were you presented with when you started teaching? How did it change, and why?

Theories of learning

The academic part of the field of language teaching and learning assumes that teaching practices should be supported by theories of learning. At the same time it has been recognized that the separation of theory and practice implied by the use of two distinct terms is a problem (e.g., Crookes, 1997a, 1998; Pennycook, 2001, p. 3). A useful response is to replace the two terms with one: "praxis"— forms of practice that are based on theory and which are used to develop theory. Nevertheless, it is still useful to ask about the concepts and forms of our theorization of practice, their sources and influences, and the directions in which they might move. As critical language teachers we could ask, "Is our practice adequately stimulated or encouraged by theories of learning, or by an understanding of conceptions of learning associated with a critical perspective on second language development?"[11] Equally well, from a critical point of view, one could view the area skeptically: "Is it not the case that mainstream theories of SLA (precisely because they are mainstream) will involve conceptions of language and of learning that are hostile to the critical social science conceptions underlying critical pedagogy?" Let me put the matter another way: shouldn't a critical pedagogy have associated with it an appropriate (presumably critical) theory of learning? And does one, or even more than one, exist? In this section I will review sources for critical theories of learning (and critical theories of language learning). These are distinguished to some extent concerning their disciplinary locations. First is critical psychology, next is socio-historical activity theory, then identity theory, and finally social theories of learning.

A couple of preliminary points first. Theories of learning can be located in the disciplines of psychology (behavioral, cognitive, not to mention neuropsychology), social psychology, educational psychology, sociology, sociology of education, and anthropology; and perhaps even in linguistics. Dominant conceptions in these disciplines are insensitive to class, race, gender, and so on (or have been until recently). Older theories in second language learning, emerging from the 1970s, show the strong influence of individualist cognitive psychological conceptions of learning theory. This limitation no longer holds; a range of conceptions of language learning contend or coexist (cf. Mitchell & Myles, 2004; Seedhouse et al., 2010). In addition, I should mention that very different understandings of theory, or of the role of theory, co-exist. Dominant conceptions see theory as providing general and causal explanations; alternative perspectives see theory as being locally valid interpretations of key aspects of the phenomenon under consideration, and/or overarching interpretive perspectives which direct our attention to important aspects of the phenomena we are concerned with.

Finally, in exploring theories of learning some time should be spent *within* the field of critical pedagogy with the work of Freire. His writings are broadly in the area of curriculum theory, or philosophy of curriculum,[12] rather than in disciplines more commonly hospitable to the development of theories of learning. For critical language teachers, his conception of what is ideally to be learned is, of course, more than just "language." In his terms, this would be "critical consciousness." In the final part of this section I will attempt to characterize it and speculate on how it is acquired, that is, sketch one more relevant learning theory.

TASK: REFLECT

Can you give some examples of the way other social sciences feed in to applied linguistics? Think of another discipline you know something about … Probably its dominant manifestation is non-critical; can you come up with an example of this? What is needed for a social science to have a critical version?

Critical psychology

Critical psychology was developed in Germany beginning about 1968 (Tolman, 1994), under the direction of a central figure, Holzkamp, who died in 1995.[13] Work in this tradition in English was promoted by Sullivan[14] (1984, 1990) and continues (e.g., Prilleltensky & Nelson, 2002; Fox et al., 2009; Prilleltensky & Prilleltensky, 2006) though it is still marginal.[15] For second language learning and teaching specialists a limitation is that it orients to the practice of clinical psychology and to the psychotherapeutic end of psychology, as opposed to orienting to learning, at the educational end of psychology.[16] Part of its content is critique of mainstream psychology. Critical psychology's understanding of learning denies that we learn alone, somehow isolated from society, or think alone, without others to think and act with. And it is also dismissive of the conception of the person that psychology operates with (de-sexed, de-classed, un-located, and so on). Schraube (2000, p. 49), in summarizing some of Holzkamp's central concepts, uses language that will be quite familiar to readers of Freire:

> In his historical analysis of the human psyche, Holzkamp pointed out that on account of the societal form of human life, we, in comparison with other creatures, can always create a *changing relationship* to the world which we inhabit. Humans do not live *immediately* within a natural environment, where *meanings* dictate the activities of living beings, but rather in a *mediated* social world, where meanings *reflect possibilities of action* and allow for a *consciousness* of the world. It is this unique relationship that creates our awareness of *being a subject*. Regardless of how determined given conditions in life may be, the individual subject always deals with them in a *relationship of possibilities*. We humans are subjects who can always act.

That is, in Freirean terms, as a result of conscientization (see later), people are inserted into history as individuals who collectively act on the world to change it. Holzkamp is taking up a conception of the person, of the psyche, of the psychological, which is not that given by mainstream society.

This or related work also appears under the heading of liberation psychology, and more generally within "community psychology." Also, it ties up rapidly with identity theory, because we can ask: "What has been learned when a critical understanding of an L2 is acquired?", and the answer would be, an ability to function with critical understanding and anti-oppressive action in another culture; which would be a form of radical acculturation and thus of identity shift (see Watts et al., 1999; Watts et al., 2003).

TASK: COMPARE

Find a typical introductory textbook of psychology. How is it organized? How much of it concerns learning? What are the other main topics? What assumptions are made about how we can best understand learning, in this kind of approach? Is this the dominant understanding in society? If so, why?

Critical socio-cognitive theories of learning

Are there more well known or more well developed learning theories that may be of use to us? Yes. An important line of work in this area began with the search among psychologists in Soviet Russia for psychological theories which could be located within understandings of human learning that would be consistent with the social theory of Marx, popular in that time and place. With hindsight, one might say this would have referred to the learning of humans as typically located in a class society, subject to oppression through societal structures, and having the potential to act on their worlds, through work, so as to improve them and develop as persons. It would direct our attention to the means by which they engage with society in the process of learning, as well as the effect of that development on who they are and become. And the object of learning in general would be the development of consciousness. However, the story is not so simple.

The individual who began this work, Lev Vygotsky, lived in Russia at the beginning of the twentieth century. He died at the age of thirty-six, having produced a substantial and diverse oeuvre and stimulated the development of many lines of investigation (e.g., 1926/1997). A crucial element of his work for critical perspectives is his introduction of the concept of mediation into theoretical understandings of learning. This focuses our attention on the cultural elements which stand between the learner and what is to be learned, and facilitate or hinder that learning. Vygotsky presents a view of learning as inherently social, as occurring particularly between individuals with greater and lesser amounts of knowledge, and taking place through dialogue.

Shortly after his death, political opinion turned against Vygotsky's primarily cognitive perspective, moving back to favor Pavlovian behavioral psychology (that Vygotsky had previously successfully opposed).[17] During the next twenty years, research in Vygotsky's line was actively discouraged by Soviet authorities; his publications were suppressed in Russia and were also not available in the outside world. From 1956, with a change in the political climate, this line of work gradually revived partly because of the efforts of his colleagues Le'ontiev (e.g., 1959) and Luria and their many collaborators and students. Le'ontiev provided a constructive critique of Vygotsky's work, and developed its social and contextual content. Comparatively small amounts of this kind of work were then published and through translation became influential in the English-using parts of the world from the late 1970s on.[18] They influenced the development of social theories of informal learning[19] and separately have been taken up by Engeström into what is now called activity theory (e.g., Engeström et al., 1999).[20] Both these lines of development are of interest because of their social orientation; but there is also questioning and criticism concerning a lack of "criticality" in these lines.[21]

Core elements of Vygotsky's work are increasingly present in studies of SL learning (see e.g., Lantolf & Thorne, 2006). This is normally referred to as socio-cultural theory. But modern (non-SL) research in this area of this kind, as well as Vygotsky's original work (Morss, 1996) has been criticized for its lack of attention to inequities associated with class and race, not to mention gender and other sites of oppression (Panofsky, 2003). There certainly have been numerous studies of class (and other sites of oppression) in relation to formal contexts of learning, i.e., school, early work in the sociology of education (Bernstein, 1961; Bowles & Gintis, 1976), and subsequently ethnographies of education (e.g., Heath, 1983; Willis, 1977). This work, over many years, has empirically identified ways in which lower-class students (women, minorities) lose out in the classroom. Critics would say, however, that these socio-cultural studies do not theorize over their contexts and combine the results in terms of a theory of learning which is both general and at the same time sensitive to the culturally and historically located nature of the learner. One attempt of this kind is that of Panofsky. Panofsky lists five categories of cultural elements which mediate learning (usually positively) and are themselves part of culture. Being part of culture, they are likely to be present under favorable circumstances, and absent or distorted under unfavorable circumstances. They thus provide the possibility of explaining, in a systematic way, the diversity of learning associated with oppressive and discriminatory circumstances versus favorable and resource-rich circumstances.

(a) *Cultural activities* such as producing goods, raising and educating children, making and enforcing policies and laws, providing medical care. It is through these activities that humans survive and develop themselves. They are basic to the ways in which individuals interact with objects, people, and even oneself.

(b) *Cultural values, schemas, meanings, concepts.* People collectively endow things with meaning. Youth, old age, man, woman, bodily features, wealth, nature, and time mean different things in different societies.

(c) *Physical artifacts* such as tools, books, paper, pottery, eating utensils, clocks, clothing, buildings, furniture, toys, games, weapons and technology which are collectively constructed.

(d) *Psychological phenomena* such as emotions, perception, motivation, logical reasoning, intelligence, memory, mental illness, imagination, language, and personality are collectively constructed and distributed.

(e) *Agency*. Humans actively construct and reconstruct cultural phenomena. This "agency" is directed at constructing cultural phenomena and it is also influenced by existing cultural activities, values, artifacts, and psychology.

(Ratner, 2000, p. 4, quoted in Panofsky, 2003)

Panofsky reviews a large number of studies of learning and social class; ranging them against the above system of categories, she finds that social class results, within schools, in differential treatment of students' attempts at learning (teacher response to errors, in-class productions, actual selection of curricular materials, ways of handling misbehavior, articulated expectations, etc.) to such an extent that it is plausible to talk in terms of a different *consciousness* being produced through lower-class students' experience of the relational features of school. The cultural activity of school, as experienced by these students, involves a different set of physical artifacts, differential evocation of psychological phenomena, and differential development of agency, coming out of the fact that school itself presents cultural values different to those of oppressed groups. In developed countries, school students themselves have experienced an extensive period of "symbolic violence," says Panovsky. The children in the countries studied in this line of work share many of the experiences that the illiterate peasants that Freire worked with, in many aspects of their experience of formal schooling and in particular in the effect on their consciousness it has had (and it hardly needs to be added that this line of argument and research extends to other sites of oppression, such as race and gender).

The implications of this empirically grounded development of the mediational aspects of culture explain many cases of failure to learn in mainstream schools; they also suggest that teachers working with what Freire would call oppressed groups have to consider a range of supplementary strategies, as he did. In various places Freire refers, for example, to ways in which he helped peasants who had short and unsuccessful experiences with formal education realize that they *did* have knowledge and agency; and he placed this kind of activity or discussion near the beginning of a course. That said, this developing critical theory of learning has yet to be systematically exploited in pedagogical terms.[22]

A prominent form of social learning theory was developed by Jean Lave (e.g., Rogoff & Lave, 1984), a social anthropologist who originally worked on informal learning in everyday (non-school) settings. Her approach was extended by Wenger in more middle-class and business-oriented contexts, taking up the interest in apprenticeship that Lave had begun (Wenger, 1998). The perspective has become popular partly, I suspect, because of the uptake of Wenger's work in business management contexts (cf. Contu & Willmott, 2003). It centrally focuses on how "communities of practice" develop and how a learner apprentices, socially learning to participate and learning in general through social means. It has been criticized for its insensitivity to power; it may however develop in this respect.

> From the point of view of critical theory, being socialized into the practices of a community includes learning one's place in the sociopolitical organization of those practices. Researchers who incorporate critical theory into their exploration of second language learning argue that one must account for relations of power in order to gain a fuller understanding of the practices and interactions in which learners participate—and thus of their learning processes. But what is more important, these researchers contend that this understanding should then lead to social and educational change such that more equitable social relations can be effected, particularly in the interests of disenfranchised groups and individuals. It is interesting that, in contrast to the theory of legitimate peripheral participation (Lave & Wenger, 1991) in which learners are viewed as learning their marginalized participation, critical theorists tend to view marginalized members of a community as having their access to learning blocked because they may be prevented from participating meaningfully in target-language social practices.
>
> (Zuengler & Miller, 2006, pp. 42–43)

Bucholtz (1999) provides a detailed account of how interpersonal power differentials actually prevent legitimate peripheral participation (see also Pavlenko, 2000). On the positive side, however, it is interesting to see Lave and Wenger's concepts being used by critical pedagogists to explain some of the underlying features of learning that they document as having taken place. For example, consider Duncan-Andrade and Morrell's (2008, pp. 11–12) account of projects they undertook with urban youth to foster learning, operating very explicitly out of a critical view of society (with an explicit focus on race) and a participatory curriculum which makes active use of the concept of a community of practice. This approach raises the possibility of a counter-culture community of practice.

> We advocate for an urban education model that utilizes critical counter-cultural communities of practice (4Cs), developing a critical and engaged citizenry with a democratic sensibility that critiques and acts against all forms of inequality. In short, communities of practice can be defined as follows:
> - Who: "groups of people who share a common concern or a passion for something they do and who interact regularly to learn how to do it better"
> - What is it about: it's *a joint enterprise* as understood and continually renegotiated by its members

- How does it function: *mutual engagement* that binds members together into a social entity
- What capability does it produce: the *shared repertoire* of communal resources (routines, sensibilities, artifacts, vocabulary, styles, etc.) that members have developed over time (Wenger, 1998).

A counter-cultural community of practice recognizes the existence of a dominant set of institutional norms and practices and intentionally sets itself up to counter those norms and practices. In urban classrooms, a countercultural community of practice responds directly to structural and material inequalities in the school and the larger community. The developing counter-cultural community of practice intentionally targets alienation, intellectual disenfranchisement, despair, and academic failure to be replaced with large quantities of community, critical consciousness, hope, and academic achievement.

To develop these critical counter-cultural communities of practice in our own work with urban youth, we attempted to employ the five steps of the cycle of critical praxis [a classic action research formulation]: identify a problem, research the problem, develop a collective plan of action to address the problem, implement the collective plan of action, evaluate the action, assess its efficacy, and re-examine the state of the problem.

Developing a full-blown alternative community, or at least a group of people in a school who think and act differently, seems a highly desirable base for critical forms of learning.[23]

TASK: REFLECT

The isolation of critically minded persons, adrift in a materialistic, individualistic media-dominated culture of passive consumption, is a problem. To what extent, if at all, do you have access to a constructive counter-culture?

Activity theory is a development of Vygotsky's position that a human learns by way of tools and artifacts that mediate interaction with the environment. This insight allows for culture, not to mention class, to enter into the theoretical context of learning. Activity theory proper came about (explains Thorne, 2005, p. 395) through

> Leont'ev's ([1959]/1981) formulation that emphasized the genesis and mediation of mind through *sensuous human activity* … Activity in this sense

refers to social relations and rules of conduct that are governed by cultural, political, and economic institutions ... Leont'ev and subsequent activity theorists elaborated this shift by more formally operationalizing the roles of communities, the rules that structure them, and "the continuously negotiated distribution of tasks, powers, and responsibilities among the participants of an activity system."

(Cole & Engeström, 1993, p. 7)

Swedish psychologist Engeström (e.g., 1987, 1991) built out the mediation concept to explicitly specify and include rules, division of labor, and community as theoretically crucial components.[24] In addition, he specified a transformative orientation or tendency. In that (I suppose) he accepts the idea that we learn in order to act, often to act so as to improve matters. As his major exponent for our field, Thorne (2004, p. 63), writes: "The goal of activity theory is to define and analyze a given activity system to diagnose possible problems, and to provide a framework for implementing innovations."[25]

Research using the framework of activity theory was not initially explicit about a critical orientation (Thorne, 2005, p. 396, cf. Blunden, 2010).

A central challenge ... is the assumption by [researchers in this tradition] ... that scientific concepts and formal schooling have a positive valence for all populations ... This idealized perspective is in direct contradiction to the research of reproduction theorists and critical pedagogues ....

(p. 396)

But he adds that this is under correction:

Practitioners of ... activity theory are attempting to address these issues, however, by focusing greater attention on power and agency[26] in their analyses, particularly by including concerns voiced in the critical sociology of knowledge literature (see Jocuns, 2005).

In that case, the future-oriented, innovation-oriented nature of activity theory can be pressed into service:

But equally important is for outcomes of a local action to enhance an individual's capacity to perform relevant and competent identities. This is one aspiration that activity theory shares with critical pedagogy—not only to cultivate developing expertise at the level of communicative performance, but also to support one's continued development as a person. As Lantolf and Pavlenko (2001, p. 145) suggested from an activity theoretical perspective, SLA is "about much more than the acquisition of forms: it is about developing, or failing to develop, new ways of mediating ourselves and our relationships."

(Thorne, 2005, p. 401)

These developments are particularly visible in a recent collection (Sawchuk, Duarte, and El Hammoumi, 2006). The concluding chapter in that volume (Sawchuk, 2006) draws on the author's empirical work, particularly interviews with Canadian working-class laborers, to discuss the implications of class-consciousness for learning. His focal students are trades union members engaged in informal learning (and quite dismissive of formal learning). Using concepts of activity theory, Sawchuk formalizes his findings in terms of activity systems that relate to aspects of working-class life and identity and support social forms of learning more appropriate and supportive of working-class culture than those of formal (middle-class) school.

Recent developments of activity theory may bridge the gap between learner and social and cultural context in a way that is necessary if the implications of the word critical are to have an impact on learning theory.[27] Also, as a *situated* learning theory it draws our attention to the institutional context for learning, and indeed reminds us of the limitations of school as we know it. Once again I am reminded that Freire primarily worked in non-formal, adult education settings outside of the conventional school. For critical second language teachers, school is often part of the problem, rarely part of the solution, which is why considerations of the wide range of institutional options must be part of the agenda of critical language pedagogy. This point will be taken up in Chapter 7.

What, anyway, is to be learnt? It is not simply language, even as a set of practices but must include conscientization: a different way of thinking about (and acting on) the world, mediated by language.

Critical (post-structural) theories of identity and second language learning

During the period in which applied linguistics began to be established as a field (say, the 1960s), the dominant conception of the person (and of identity) in the social sciences was one that derived, ultimately, from liberal political theory. All people were considered equal, politically, and were supposed to have equal rights; intelligence and ability to learn were considered to be basically equal and certainly *not* linked to concepts such as race or gender. (This position was itself an ethically grounded response to earlier dominant conceptions which had denied the intelligence of women, blacks, and various other groups.) During this period, in applied linguistics and second language studies, then, identity was seen as relatively fixed, a feature of a person in relation to his/her class, ethnic group, etc. (cf. Tajfel, 1982). A simple willingness to acculturate was considered as potentially motivating some instances of SL learning, in situations where immigration was possible (e.g., Schumann, 1978). However, from the standpoint of the present day, fifty years later, this conception of identity can be seen as relatively simplistic. In an important review of this area, Ricento comments on the early investigations: "[T]here was little emphasis on the interaction of an individual's multiple memberships based on gender, class, race, linguistic repertoire, or on how these memberships were understood and played out in different learning contexts" (2005, p. 898). In hindsight one could say it was "under-theorized," in that it was a change in theoretical perspectives rather than empirical concerns that moved this work forward. By the mid-1990s our field began to seriously pick up on changes in the conception of personal identity that had been developing elsewhere in the social sciences, so that it became seen as not fixed, nor merely associated with membership in socially determined, structural feature of society such as class, or race, or gender. This more fluid and multiple understanding of identity is often referred to as "post-structuralist."

The idea of "multiple memberships," the idea that identities can shift, and the idea that learning an additional language might be intimately involved with identity, have been very stimulating of research. Numerous observers of our field (see Block, 2007, for an authoritative overview) identify this development with the work of Norton (e.g., 1995) in particular; she in turn references the well-known work of Foucault, and Bourdieu, and the less familiar work of Heller (1982, 1987, 1995), and draws from them major concepts that informed her influential studies of L2 learner identity in Canada. In this work, the shifting identities of these learners are theorized as playing a major role in what Norton terms their "investment" in English. Zuengler and Miller (2006, p. 43) comment:

> [L]anguage and identity ... has gained footing in the field and become a research area in its own right. It has been addressed in a special issue of TESOL Quarterly (Norton, 1997a) as well as in numerous other publications. From a sociocultural perspective, our identities are shaped by and through our language use (Norton, 1995, 1997b, 2000; Pavlenko & Blackledge, 2004). ... [S]ociocultural approaches to learning ... often explore and critique the ways in which the patterning of power relationships can legitimate some identities and forms of participation but devalue others. ... [L]anguage learners have much more at stake than merely developing competence in an additional linguistic code. As [critical pedagogy specialist] Morgan (1998) notes, "language 'conditions' our expectations and desires and communicates what might be possible in terms of ourselves—our identity—and the 'realities' we might develop" (p. 12).
>
> (Zuengler & Miller, 2006, p. 43)

In his survey, Ricento (2005, pp. 895 and 899) summarizes some of the key features of this area, which he too notes has been the subject of much publishing and research in recent years.

> Within sociocultural approaches … identity is not viewed as a fixed, invariant attribute in the "mind" of the individual learner. Rather, identity is theorized as a contingent process involving dialectic relations between learners and the various worlds and experiences they inhabit and which act on them. The implications of this approach for SLA research can be summarized. First, the assumption that SLA researchers and educators should operate with is that "speech, speakers, and social relationships are inseparable" (Norton, 1997b, p. 410). …
>
> [And on the other hand,] theories and research in SLA that do not take into full account the social aspect of language learning and use cannot be taken seriously. … An individual's identity in L2 contexts is mediated by the reactions of others to that individual's social and cultural position, which, in turn, can influence that individual's motivation to learn.
>
> (p. 899)

This last sentence in particular should evoke echoes of the work of Panofsky summarized earlier. Those in oppressed positions in society who are trying to learn an L2 can clearly be seen as likely to be negatively impacted by all sorts of vicious cycles of interaction, motivation, and identity, in their language learning efforts.

Going back to the historical orientation of the beginning of this section: insofar as identity was considered at all in SL studies, most work done before the mid-1990s would have seen it as singular and primarily concerned with national or cultural identity. Class, race, and gender as aspects not only of identity but also as sites of oppression, were not considered. Thus there was no role for critical conceptions of the person to play in understanding second language learning in general. Or (to be fair), the matter was not entirely ignored in the *talk* of second language specialists. During that period I often heard colleagues acknowledge that "SES predicts school success." But I also observed the mainstream perspective taken, namely that language teachers generally had no options to address this within their role as teachers, and there was little or no intention to work against this conception of their role. Social change was certainly to be advocated and if possible to be engaged in, as a matter of personal choice outside of the teaching role, but the study of second language learning (let alone teaching) did not have a role to play in this, a view which was (and remains) the dominant position in our field.

Where are we, then, in terms of a theory of the person appropriate to critical SL learning? It seems that we must have a conception of the person which may be close to that arising from a pragmatist, community-oriented, and possibly performance-oriented theory of society; the individual is in society, and the individual and society have a mutually constituting relationship (involving discourse processes), *and* society is characterized by difference, diversity, and conflict. Communities socialize individuals, but the individual only exists (and performs his/her many roles) in relation to the many communities s/he is simultaneously a member of. The person is not only located, or positioned, in these multiple webs of power, but also acts within them, on them, and is acted upon by them, with varying degrees of agency not only to result in benefit for her/himself and associates but also on occasion to alter the way these structures themselves are constituted.

TASK: REFLECT

Explore this conception of the person by interpreting it as it might apply to you. To what extent would you accept that you have been constituted by discourses? To what extent do you see society as conflictual rather than unitary? To what extent do you have agency regarding social structures? To what extent is your identity shifting rather than fixed? (etc.)

What (else) is to be learned? Acquiring critical consciousness

In his earliest writings, Freire regularly used a Portuguese word, *conscientizaçao*, to refer to one of the main goals of his work, and of critical pedagogies. If this goal is to be attained through critical pedagogy, we presumably need to extend our theories of learning to accommodate this. The term is related to "consciousness," and in English translations of Freire's work is often called "critical consciousness" (though it may also be translated as "consciousness-raising" and simply transliterated as "conscientization"). To understand it, let's consider first the term "consciousness," as explained by a critical psychologist, Martín-Baró (1994, p. 38, p. 41):

> Consciousness is not simply the private, subjective knowledge and feelings of individuals. More than anything, it represents the confines within which each person encounters the reflexive impact of his or her being and actions in society, where people take on and work out a knowledge about the self and about reality that permits them to be a somebody, to have a personal and social identity. (p. 38) … [This] supposes that persons change in the process of changing their relations with the surrounding environment and, above all, with other people.

Clearly a theory of the development of consciousness is closely related to a theory of identity development, which was the subject of the previous sub-section. Now consider how Martín-Baró defines learning—as

> not only a matter of elaborating and reinforcing a sequence of stimuli and responses; more significantly, it structures the way a person relates to his or her environment, shaping a world where the individual occupies a place and social interest take on concrete forms.
>
> (Ibid., p. 39)

This can be put directly in terms of the desired outcomes of critical pedagogy, as Torres does (1994, p. 83):

> Literacy training, nonformal education, and public popular schooling developed by liberation pedagogues have an explicit conscientization goal, and particularly the development of class consciousness and historical consciousness.

It also justifies course content concerning critical theories of society within critical pedagogy, because

> [t]hrough critically understanding their social system, people grasp the constraints on their psychology and behavior. This awareness opens up the horizon to new possibilities for social action and for new forms of identity and other psychological processes.
>
> (Ratner, 2000, p. 427)

Going on now to critical consciousness or *conscientizaçao*—the term pre-dated Freire and was popularized by Camara, the influential, socially active bishop of Recife (Freire's home town). He refers (Camara, 1969, p. 74) to it as "the term we have coined to express this work of ... stimulating consciousness" (cf. Mackie, 1981b). He was an early influence on Freire (Roberts, 1996). In Freire's characterization of social change, modernization in Brazil was associated with a change in individuals' consciousness.[28] Freire claimed that as people developed an understanding of social and political processes, they were more willing to engage in thoughtful and empirically-exploring ways of improving matters, rather than dwelling on the past, engaging in polemics and merely emotional responses to problems. He suggested that this development was a response to involvement in democratic political contexts, which increasingly existed in Brazil during the post-World War II period (until the military coup that resulted in Freire's exile).

In Freire's early work, different levels of consciousness can co-exist in an individual. But attempts to more narrowly define and systematize his remarks on the subject into a formal stage theory (W. Smith, 1976) also laid it open to criticism. Understood as consciousness-raising, the term was the focus of criticisms of Freirean pedagogy, because it was identified as the imposition of culturally alien ideas on traditional groups, or as implying an elitist position in which the teacher has a higher level of consciousness than his/her students. Subsequently, Freire avoided the English term "consciousness raising" (Roberts, 1996, p. 186).

Roberts (1996, p. 188) draws together the concept of conscientization with that of praxis:

> Praxis is the *synthesis* of reflection and action. Freire speaks of conscientisation as "the process by which human beings participate critically in a transforming act" (Freire, 1985, p. 106), and stresses: "there is no conscientisation outside of praxis, outside the theory-practice, reflection-action unity" (p.160). Conscientisation, Freire notes elsewhere, "can only be manifested in the concrete praxis (which can never be limited to the mere activity of the consciousness)" (Freire, 1976, p. 147). I propose, therefore, that rather than separating the two concepts out, as many people attempting to apply Freirean ideas do, conscientisation and praxis ought to be seen as *necessarily* intertwined. Conscientisation, I submit, is the reflective component of praxis. Hence, when one engages in praxis, one is of necessity being conscientised. Conscientisation occurs in the transforming moment where critical reflection is synthesised with action.

He also places it in its social context, since it arises out of Freire's continual insistence on the importance of critical dialogue among individuals, between learners, and with the involvement of a teacher who also is a student or learner (cf. Freire, 1976, pp. 146–47, quoted by Roberts, 1996). This is emphasized by Freire's earliest use of the term to refer to a change in collective consciousness in a specific country and time, and of his specification of "thinking, acting and knowing as *social* events" (Freire, 1976, pp. 134–35, quoted in Roberts, 1996, p. 192). It is also suggested here that becoming aware of the socially constituted nature of consciousness is also an aspect of conscientization.

> Conscientisation is concerned with expanding the range of discourses within which people might actively (and reflectively) participate. This is not merely a shift in "sign systems", but a change in the concrete practices of everyday life. There is thus a material as well as "intellectual" basis to conscientisation. Being critically conscious implies a continuous process of transformation. People who undergo conscientisation are constantly being re-constituted, as they critically reflect upon reality, act, change both themselves and the world around them, reflect again on the new reality which results from transformation, carry out further actions as necessary, and so on.
>
> (Roberts, 1996, p. 193)

This image of the individual in social context being an individual "on the move" and to some extent capable of experiencing differing forms of consciousness at different times and across different discourses shows, Roberts argues, the ability of the Freirean conception of conscientization to coexist with recent theories of identity (such as those briefly discussed in the preceding subsection).

The term is very definitely still in play. For example, critical consciousness is identified as a target in the recent critical (race) pedagogy of Duncan-Andrade and Morrell (2008), who report a range of pedagogical initiatives that worked against the norms and possibly self-images of black students in an inner city US school. Among them, work on extra-curricular activities, such as basketball, turned out to be particularly effective in promoting a collective rather than individual form of consciousness and a context for mutual aid:

> We worked hard to develop a counter-culture in the program, one that normalized excellence and collective achievement. We did this, in part, by raising students' awareness of the critical "double-consciousness" demanded of them if they were to become successful in school and the larger society. Du Bois (1903/1996) explained the idea of double-consciousness as the effect black people in America experience by having to struggle with two "warring ideals." Many urban youth of color experience this effect. On the one hand, they are "American" but never fully accepted as a group in a society that often portrays them as purveyors of social pathology and non-intellectual. They are also aware that they are connected to distinctive cultures (pan-African, pan-Latino, pan-Asian) but that living in the United States means they might never fully realize this identity. A critical double-consciousness is realized when a person faced with this internal battle is able to develop a critically conscious response to these conditions.
>
> (pp. 84–85)

The authors explain that personal, one-on-one conversations with students about the realities of life in a somewhat hostile educational environment were very important in this process, though they also then encouraged their students to extend and share that perspective and lessons learned with peers. They encouraged peer mentoring and shared study sessions, both informally and through summer camps.

The theoretical positions here return conscientization to its origins in early forms of critical race theory and also emphasizes the importance of the anti-individualist position in theories of learning and practice that are of use to critical pedagogy. A theory of the development of conscientization is a necessary part of the learning theory apparatus of critical language pedagogy.

In closing

This chapter has covered a rather broad area, or set of areas. None of these theoretical areas have been developed with particularly tight connections to critical language pedagogy (though Wallace's use of SFL in critical reading is probably the closest). I have canvassed a wide range of traditions, including more obscure ones (like critical psychology); I hope it is clear that I did so to alert readers to how much is out there and how significant intellectual traditions can be found to underpin critical language pedagogy, along with those also originally plumbed by Freire and his predecessors. While mainstream disciplines of social science are and should be critiqued by critical perspectives (because otherwise they are themselves tools and sources of oppression) so, ideally, the relationship between critical language pedagogy and its theoretical domains is interactive and cyclical. Critical L2 learning theory should benefit from and be developed by critical L2 practice, and vice versa. In the end, we must remember that the target is praxis.

Questions for discussion

1   What sort of linguistics, or pedagogical grammar, have you used or experienced, in second language teaching or learning? Under what circumstances do these theories, or sources of formal information about language, need to be supplemented by something more critical? Can you think of some instances of teaching a second language where the need for this might be particularly acute?
2   Can mainstream theories of learning that talk in terms of a decontextualized system of structures in the mind co-exist with critical theories of learning that talk in terms of people learning together in sociopolitical environments?
3   Could conscientization be seen as a legitimate instructional goal if the broader context was teaching for enhanced citizenship? In your experience, what learning experiences have resulted in a personal change in values or an altered disposition to act on social justice values?

Notes

1   "By having a learning theory I do not mean being able to précis Piaget, Skinner and Bruner. I mean being able to state one's own best-educated understanding as to how people come to internalize new information or to perform new operations. ... Certainly Year I children can very easily be encouraged to talk about how they learnt to talk. Teachers can likewise examine the learning theory implicit in their classroom practice" (Boomer, 1982, p. 5).
2   Going back to the Prague school of linguistics, to Bühler, and Malinowski, near the beginning of the twentieth century.
3   That is, ways of thinking, forms of consciousness, or worldviews characteristic of a particular time and place (cf. Febvre, 1962). Febvre was a precursor of Foucault; whose ideas in turn inform Gee, considered shortly.

4 Martin & Rose (2007) is a recent exposition; Thorne & Lantolf (2006).
5 During the 1960s he worked closely on linguistics materials for English language teachers, calling the products "a monument to linguistics as a democratic force, a theoretically informed activity being put to community service" (ibid, p. 124).
6 However, just because a woman or a person of color *can* "correctly" carry off a written or spoken genre, such as an employment application, that doesn't mean they will get a job in a racist society.
7 CDA continues to develop particularly as a result of sympathetic critique such as that of O'Halloran (2003).
8 Though a recent search of the main index for our field (*Linguistics and Language Behavior Abstracts*) gives only about six hits for "critical literacy" in the title, twenty-nine as keyword, and many of those were not related to second languages.
9 E.g., Kramer-Dahl, 2001, writing about efforts to foster critical literacy in Singaporean classrooms, refers directly to the work of Comber, Fairclough, Clark and Ivanic & Simpson.
10 A long-established theme, but still timely, as the recent June 2008 conference on the topic in Hong Kong indicated.
11 Indeed, it could be said that the teacher's feeling that theory is irrelevant, which has prompted so many academic pieces of writing by worried academics (including me), comes from an incompletely articulated feeling that the classroom is so different, and so much worse, than the contexts that early SLA seemed to imply. And indeed, early SLA hoped indirectly to improve, if not radicalize classroom teaching. It emerged from an era that was very skeptical about the value of classroom teaching at all, and from a time when conventional classrooms were pretty much thought of as a waste of time. Unfortunately the cultural critique associated with it got lost as it aspired to scientific status and became enmeshed with a very un-social conception of the person, or (cognitive) system, that was doing the learning.
12 The disciplinary structures are different by time and language. His work is *pedagogia*, but this is not well translated by the word "pedagogy." It is more like "curriculum theory."
13 http://en.wikipedia.org/wiki/Critical_psychology
14 Also at OISE, like Simon and L2 specialists in the area.
15 Though Grötluschen (2005) points to some interaction between prominent learning theorist Lave and a central figure of critical psychology, Holzkamp; and Billig (2006) analyzes the apparently rapid growth of critical psychology in the UK.
16 With the exception of the work of Sullivan (as O'Sullivan, 1999). And indeed, perhaps we have to think in therapeutic terms if the victims of oppression are to be successful in learning.
17 In particular, work on child development was singled out for political proscription; and this was an area that Vygotsky was particularly associated with. See Yasnitsky (2009).
18 "The "Vygotsky boom" ... dates back to 1978 when the book entitled Mind in Society was published under Vygotsky's name" (Yasnitsky, p. 1); though his *Thought and Language* had been published, in English by the prestigious MIT Press, much earlier, in 1962. Why was there no Vygotsky boom at that time? Perhaps because of the nature of the writing itself. Yasnitsky (2009, p. 95), refers to "highly idiosyncratic discursive practices of [Soviet scientists] motivated by censorship requirements for publication ... [Leonte'ev] was asked ... "why do you write in such a complicated, convoluted manner?" He replied: "Long ago life taught me to write so that nobody could deliberately take a quote of mine out of its original context and, use it as evidence against me to send me to jail" ... (Yasnitsky, 2009, p. 104). "[L]ater publications ... typically avoided any references other than those to the classics

of Marxism-Leninism ... [and did not reference other empirical or theoretical work, nor] the authors' close and direct collaborators, for instance to the studies of graduate students or research assistants" (ibid., p. 106).

19 Especially those of Cole and of Wertsch (e.g., Wertsch et al., 1995) and of Lave (e.g., Lave & Wenger, 1991).

20 Theories direct our attention, and conceptualize the object of investigation, as well as simply providing causal explanations or interpretive understanding of what is to be investigated. "Activity theory is a powerful and clarifying descriptive tool rather than a strongly predictive theory. The object of activity theory is to understand the unity of consciousness and activity." (Nardi, 1996, p. 7). Nardi (1996, pp. 10–11) also advocates for activity theory as a general guide or meta-theoretical perspective on learning: "One would like to be able to develop a comparative framework, perhaps a taxonomy ... that would help us as we pursue design and evaluation activities. It would be desirable to be able to go back to previous work and find a structured set of problems and solutions. Activity theory will help us to achieve this goal."

21 "SCT [sociocultural theory] is not inherently critical, activist, or political, or morally assertive ... [but] The future of SCT, as I see it, includes an activist, revolutionary ethic." (van Lier, 2004, p. 17)

22 Perhaps some indication of pedagogical implications of this kind of perspective on non-mainstream learners is provided by Feuerstein's work, though it is not necessarily informed by a critical theory of society (Kozulin & Rand, 2000).

23 See also Hodson (1999) for a similar perspective to foster the entry of minority students into scientific pursuits and practices, when otherwise science is seen as white, male, and mainstream.

24 Nardi (1996, p. 5): "Zinchenko (1995) discusses the differences between cultural-historical psychology and activity theory, calling them 'two strands of research.' He notes that cultural-historical psychology has been more concerned with the problem of meaning, while activity theory has contributed a focus on object-relatedness. The cultural-historical school emphasized mediation by language, while activity theory has concentrated on mediation by tools (explaining its attractiveness to those of us concerned with technology). However, there is nothing incompatible in the two 'strands'; rather, they reinforce one another, and I concur with Zinchenko (1995) that we should 'look at [the strands] as mutually amplifying one another ... [each] enriching the other.'"

25 Theories direct our attention, and conceptualize the object of investigation, as well as simply providing causal explanations or interpretive understanding of what is to be investigated. "Activity theory is a powerful and clarifying descriptive tool rather than a strongly predictive theory. The object of activity theory is to understand the unity of consciousness and activity." (Nardi, 1996, p. 7) Since we are in the area of social theories of learning, including (anthropological) studies of informal learning (Lave's original home), one might ask why not simply draw on them, in all their situated diversity. The response of Nardi (pp. 10–11) is "every account is an ad hoc description cast in situationally specific terms. Abstraction, generalization and comparison become problematic. An ethnographic description, although it may contain much information of direct value for design and evaluation, remains a narrative account structured according to the author's own personal vocabulary, largely unconstrained and arbitrary. Ethnography—literally, "writing culture"—assumes no a priori framework that orders the data, that contributes to the coherence and generalizability of the descriptive account. This leads to a disappointing lack of cumulative research results. One would like to be able to develop a comparative framework, perhaps a taxonomy ... that would help us as we pursue design and evaluation activities. It would be desirable to be able to go back to previous work

and find a structured set of problems and solutions. Activity theory will help us to achieve this goal."

26 "Agency as it is construed in activity theory is "never a 'property' of a particular individual; rather, it is a relationship that is constantly co-constructed and renegotiated with those around the individual and with the society at large" (Lantolf & Pavlenko, 2001, p. 148). ... [O]ne way to view the relational construction of agency is provided by the more recent formulations of activity theory ... where an individual is mediated not only by material and symbolic tools, but also always by social formations such as immediate communities of practice ... as well as distant or even imagined communities (e.g., Anderson, 1991 ...)" (Thorne, 2005, p. 400).

27 "It is important to note that SCT has its roots in a common intellectual and activist lineage that also informs critical pedagogy and structurationist sociology. Hence, part of what I see as an important development in SCT is to continue to strengthen these ties and collaboratively to develop an increasingly critical research and activist apparatus for use in developmentally focused research. From this perspective, SCT and post-structuralist approaches are not in competition. Rather, they share aspirations for political engagement, while also offering distinctive contributions to the project of critical scholarship. A distinct difference between SCT and most other research frameworks is that it does not separate understanding (research) from transformation (concrete action). Modern activity theory in particular, though also used descriptively and analytically as a diagnostic framework, is fundamentally an applied methodology. That is, it encourages engaged critical inquiry through which an investigation would lead to the development of material and symbolic-conceptual tools necessary to enact positive interventions. Y. Engeström (1999) expressed this potential through the idea of *radical localism*, the notion that the capacity for change is alive in the details of everyday practices that, en masse, make up society." (Thorne, 2005, p. 403).

28 This reflects the influence of the concept of *mentalités*, from Febvre, mentioned earlier.

6

DEVELOPING DOMAINS
OF RADICAL LANGUAGE
PEDAGOGY

At the present time, there are several distinguishably different strands of thought and practice that can be grouped under the label critical pedagogy. Historically these strands to some extent began as distinguishable entities, and can be discussed separately. On the other hand, since they all have emancipatory intent and to some extent learn from and inform each other, it is also valuable to group them together. The label "radical pedagogy" is one term that is sometimes used to do so (Gore, 1993). It is very important to recognize that though I present them separately in this chapter, reflecting how they were initially conceived, these days they are indeed seen as interacting and overlapping.

Within a short space of time after critical pedagogical ideas became prominent in the 1960s, radical curricular and practice strands also struck out on their own beyond the concept of class that was central to the Freirean conception. Some of these lines drew on Freire but also drew on other traditions. Or, to put it in a more nuanced way: a range of not particularly prominent alternative emphases, mainly curricular, pre-existed Freire in education. Following the attention gained by critical pedagogy, these lines assimilated Freirean emphases into their own tendencies, while developing independently. The most prominent of these are educational initiatives related to gender and race. In the initial phases of development that I am referring to, these concepts were seen in "essentialist" terms: women (all women) were different from men in specific respects and at the same time any woman was essentially the same as any other woman. (Second wave feminism ignored race, class, and sexual orientation.) Perhaps these sorts of perceptions provided helpful dynamism to social movements. Here is how educational philosopher Peters (1995, p. 51) summarizes the matter:

Within the old identity politics of the 1960s, social movements introduced some theoretical refinements, splitting and questioning the priority of class as the leading collective subject whose goal was emancipation. There was greater recognition, in particular, of race and gender as specifying in a non-reductive way lines of oppression. In an important sense these social categories depended, in their early stages, on essentialist readings: it marked them out in contrast to the other dominant modernist readings of political identity—those of class, and of nation. Where the notion of class permanently broke apart the idea of a homogeneous collective unity of nation, those of race and gender led to a greater understanding of an internal social differentiation. Yet these social movements still subscribed to the old logic of identity as stable and homogeneous categories. ....

Gradually but with increasing strength from the 1980s on, it became clear that the essentialist conception of these alternative sites of oppression was quite inadequate. In due course, a sense of the multiplicity of identity became signaled by the use of the term "post-structural."[1] I turn to Peters again (1995, p. 52) for a concise summary of what the term means in this context:

> The poststructuralist critique of the subject and of reason was instrumental in unsettling the modernist discourse of identity, in taking the process several stages further. It problematized the category of the individual as the last vestige of a rationalistic liberalism that has privileged the Cogito— the self-identical and fully transparent thinking subject, the origin and ground of action—as *the* universal subject against which all irrational others are defined. It carried out this critique in a way that problematized not only the unity of the subject but also that of any group, which, on the basis of an alleged shared experience, may have been thought of as a unity or singular actor.

Clearly, if critical pedagogy shows sensitivity to diversity, to the different tropes of oppression, this is likely to make radical pedagogical initiatives of all kinds more practical and more relevant to a variety of groups. In organizing the material below under a range of single subtopics, I am at risk of appearing to suggest that a person can be defined by just one of them, which is more or less the opposite of what a post-structural position would require. So this is primarily for purposes of exposition (though closely related to "strategic essentialism": Spivak, 1987, p. 205). At any rate, we are now in an area in which identity, diversity (and the subject) are central concerns, and beyond a position in which class is the single site of oppression.[2]

Yet at the same time, perhaps there is less of this material in existence than one might think, when it comes both to analyses of how race, gender, etc., play out in language learning and language teaching and in particular (as usual) actual detailed examples of materials are rare. And more reports of practice are needed.

Feminist

Feminist pedagogy is probably the first and clearest example of a perspective separate from but related to critical or radical pedagogy. It can be seen as arising generally after Freirean critical pedagogy had established itself not only as a practice but also as a concept and line of research and publishing in academia. Specialists began using the term "feminist pedagogy," both drawing on Freirean ideas but also critiquing them and to some extent separating themselves from them.

Where and when did feminist pedagogy manifest itself? It's possible that women's consciousness-raising groups were one initial location (cf. Bailey, 1977). Foley (1999) drawing on Alvarez (1990) points to the range of learning that took place (by women) in the Brazilian women's movement (from 1968 till the restoration of democracy). But specifically pedagogical analyses come mainly from the US higher education literature initially. In these discussions, a jumping-off point was simply that gender had been completely ignored in the critical pedagogy literature of the 1970s. Kenway and Modra (1992) surveyed the situation and find these complaints beginning in 1980.[3] How to deal with the ignoring of feminist principles or gender as a site of oppression in the practices of critical pedagogy? One possibility was the simple matter of selecting curriculum material that puts the woman at the center of the material: "[C]urriculum developers have designed new courses (e.g., Women's Studies, Family and Work Studies), attached new units to current courses, and totally redesigned existing courses" (Kenway & Modra, 1992, p. 142). This initial move had its own problems: making curriculum more woman-friendly was done with essentialist conceptions of women in mind, and "this sort of essentialism is being challenged from a number of different directions, as matters of class, ethnicity and race become the concern of feminist teachers and researchers who increasingly recognize that students' identities cannot be reduced to one particular structural factor" (ibid., p. 145).

Another substantial option appeared to be the possibility of having different processes in the classroom that distinguish it from one which is competitive and in that sense, patriarchal. Among various writers taking this line (cf. Maher, 1985), Schniedewind's explorations and depictions (e.g., 1975a, b, 1978/1987, 1993) of "feminist process" have been reprinted more than once and constitute an important core element of feminist pedagogy. In her 1978 paper Schniedewind puts forward her ideas in terms of five "process goals":

1   mutual respect and trust;
2   shared leadership;
3   cooperative structures;
4   integration of cognition and affect; and
5   action.

This perspective is advocated for use in women's studies classes, i.e., in higher education contexts where a focus is already on curricular material and educational goals relevant to women (from a feminist perspective).[4] In an analysis of feminist pedagogies, Kenway and Modra (1992, p. 159) review Schniedewind's work and note its indebtedness to Freire.[5] They also note limitations in its applicability, pointing out that the feminist pedagogy in question is based on the writer's experience in "single-sex classes in tertiary institutions," whereas, "most feminist school teachers teach the dominant curricula and seek ways of making these 'gender inclusive.'" Sattler (1997, p. 154) comments:

> It is important to highlight the fact that feminist theories and feminist practices about education are not always cognizant of the realities of schools. It is important that these theories be informed by the material conditions of schools and schooling so that theory rises from practice and possibility rather than theory dictating practice.

In her accounts of the practices of feminist high school teachers,[6] she states (1997, p. 174) that "In practical terms this results in a great deal of resistance to curriculum that is externally imposed." Teachers she encountered "resist[ed] not only the state-standardized curriculum but also ... academic feminists" who ran teacher-education workshops which, they felt, put them under pressure to use literature or teaching materials that went beyond what their students or their teaching circumstances could handle. In terms of practices, the basic pattern Sattler is drawing on is of language arts teachers who have enough freedom (the chapter is subtitled "behind closed doors") to choose and use course readings (fiction and non-fiction) that articulate a feminist perspective, and use them as the basis for classroom discussion. Some feminist teachers emphasize retaining conventional teacherly authority (e.g., Duncan & Stasio, 2001) because of the resistance from students that will otherwise make teaching difficult, or put differently, feminist teachers must "develop a classroom based on the 'authority' radical feminism has granted to women in the process of subverting and transforming patriarchal culture" (Friedman, 1985, p. 207).

Turning to the L2 literature, an initial point of departure, perhaps conceptually prior to drawing on women-friendly material, are analyses of existing materials which demonstrate their gender bias. In an extended review of identity in L2 learning, Ricento (2005, p. 901) notes that:

TASK: REFLECT

Pause for a moment … It could be the case that in many developed societies some elements of feminism have become part of mainstream culture. If so, you may feel inclined to say "I am not a feminist" and then when pressed articulate many values consistent with feminist views of society. So, are you a feminist, or not?

Content analyses of ESL textbooks published in the 1970s and 1980s revealed stereotyped male and female roles and promoted the use of masculine generics such as "he", "man", or "mankind" … Other more recent studies have found stereotypical portrayals of gender roles in EFL textbooks published in Japan … and Russian textbooks published in the United States …

He (ibid.) also points to

research … concern[ing] "Gendered agency in second language learning and use' [which] explores the intrinsic relationship between gender and agency in the process of L2 learning and use. … Of particular interest to ESL/EFL educators are studies that show that women around the world are learning English as a means of liberating themselves from the confines of patriarchy (Kobayashi, [2002]; Matsui, 1995).

Vandrick has been the most prominent exponent of feminist pedagogy in ESL contexts (1994, 1995, 1999, 2000, 2005a, b). Her central recommendation is a straightforward suggestion to move towards feminist pedagogy through developing and using woman-friendly curriculum: "[U]se writings by and about women as often as possible—not necessarily with any fanfare" (2005b, p. 5). She has in mind particularly college-level ESL, in which original readings or other materials brought in by the teacher are staple fare (1995, p. 5):

The students can honestly be told that these topics and discussions are an important part of current U.S. and worldwide culture and politics. Readings on women's issues can be integrated into various units and activities related to academic reading. A newspaper article on a women's issue can be part of a unit on reading magazines and newspapers and how this differs from reading an academic text or other types of books. The class can discuss the differences between reporting, editorials, and feature writing, and ways in which women's news has been marginalized in women's or style sections. The image of women in advertising can be examined. Another point that can be addressed in this discussion is the influence of advertising on the editorial content of periodicals. … This kind of analysis raises awareness and promotes caution about regarding the written word with too much reverence or assuming that writing is neutral. Articles about women who have been successful in various fields, or have been political, religious, or moral leaders and thinkers, provide role models for students. Fiction and poetry can also be used to illustrate points about women's lives and concerns. Again, this is an opportunity for students to learn all the customary elements of literature: plot, setting, character, theme, and so on. …

At an interactional level, the feminist ESL classroom teacher cites women as authorities whenever possible, uses women as examples, uses women's names and female pronouns in sample sentences or grammar point teaching, and certainly calls on women in the class as often as men. Vandrick is consistent with many other feminist pedagogues in advocating cooperative rather than competitive learning, and on the matter of power and authority in the classroom (mentioned earlier) says these must be "dealt with explicitly." That is to say that at least if gender-related oppressive patterns of interaction occur in the second language classroom, they must be named and taught against (cf. Crookes, 2003a, pp. 35–36).

Now turning to actual altered practices, lesson plans, and materials if we can find them, as usual the earliest treatment of this theme concerns ESL (not EFL or other L2) classes. For example, Petrie (1985) summarizes women-friendly aspects of a course for returning non-traditional adult ESL students in Canada. Her class used a range of pre-existing L1 materials:

> [V]ideo-tapes such as *Women Want* and audio-tapes, such as *Women in Power,* assigned for homework, provide listening practice and elicit considerable comment for class discussion. Individual students have prepared short oral presentations on such topics as *Working Mothers and Guilt Feelings, Rape, Men's Liberation* … Readings may be chapters from *Women Unite!, An Anthology of the Canadian Women's Movements* [Discussion Collective no. 6, 1974], *Women in the Canadian Mosaic* [Matheson, 1976] … Role play is widely used; e.g., acting out the role of employer and applicant, male supervisor and female employee, husband and wife (the latter, of course, having female students play the male role and males the female role).
>
> (Petrie, 1985, pp. 62 and 64)

Continuing with suggestions for materials; more recently, Schenke (1996) is a short account of an "advanced-level [ESL] writing class in Canadian culture consisting mostly of women students" (p. 156). Noting the students' shared interest in soap operas, Schenke selected a range of moderately challenging authentic feminist analyses of popular literature and media (where too difficult, they were paraphrased and rewritten by her). After this,

> the question arose as to what a feminist soap opera might look like and what would be required more generally for the production of (in their words) "antisexist" media. To help us think about this, we watched an excerpt from a soap opera produced by the Inuit Broadcasting Corporation in resistance to the cultural and racial imperialism of Canadian television in English.
>
> (Ibid., p. 157)[7]

The product was "a written paper linking personal histories and viewings with the analyses offered by the readings." So this was work intended for advanced learners. But drawing on this initiative, one can imagine that for much lower level students, still, some carefully selected extracts of soap operas, supplemented by well-prepared discussion of concepts with which to analyze them (needing pre-taught vocabulary, perhaps) seems possible under favorable circumstances. Soap operas might very well be a topic in almost any conventional "English conversation" course or textbook; missing, I am almost sure, would be the conceptual tools for a feminist analysis. It is noteworthy that in one of the few studies in this area involving L2 learning of a language other than English, Ohara et al. (2001) used popular culture of the target language, in the form of TV commercials, as the content to be critiqued from a position that recognized the oppression of women in mainstream Japanese society. In this case, students analyzed gender roles in these short, vivid, and easily accessible elements of culture, and then rewrote and acted out new versions in which gender roles were reversed or creatively manipulated, taking up suggestions of reversal similar to those mentioned by Petrie (earlier).

An interesting opportunity arises for feminists (and other critical language teachers) working in EAP because they may have classes that coordinate closely with regular content classes. Suggestions for how to exploit this have been provided in the important work of Benesch (e.g., 1999)—her treatment of a curricular topic with feminist import helps us explore what the practical classroom manifestations of a feminist pedagogy look like. At that time she noted initially that: "Just as feminist issues have been absent from many ESL classes, feminist theory has not yet had a significant impact on second language (L2) theory and practice" (p. 101). She drew on Maher and Tetreault's (1994) analysis of feminist classrooms in the US to identify four main areas of difference: "authority, mastery, voice, and positionality." Student experience is accepted as a source of authority and expertise; mastery becomes a matter of students interpreting information on the basis of feminist perspectives; voice (the ability to speak and be heard) should apply to all and positionality means the multiple positions of students and teachers are acknowledged as the basis for understanding. These four principles constitute concise guidelines for practice here.

A recent collection in this area (Norton & Pavlenko 2004a; summarized in Norton & Pavlenko, 2004b) is significant for several reasons. First, it is published by TESOL itself; thus showing support from the leading professional organization for the topic. Second, a major section of the book is devoted to EFL contributions, including several from Japan. Third, it strongly espouses (and explains) a post-structural perspective. On this last point (which I brought up a few pages earlier), this time starting from gender as the primary focus, Norton and Pavlenko (2004b, p. 504) say they view it from a post-structural point of view

> as a complex system of social relations and discursive practices, differentially constructed in local contexts. This approach, situated within a post-structuralist framework, foregrounds sociohistoric, cross-cultural, and cross-linguistic differences in constructing gender. We do not assume, for example, that all women—or all men—have much in common with each other just because of their biological makeup or their elusive social roles, nor do we assume that gender is always relevant to understanding language learning outcomes. Instead, we recognize that gender, as one of many important facets of social identity, interacts with race, ethnicity, class, sexuality, (dis)ability, age, and social status in framing students' language learning experiences, trajectories, and outcomes.

Feminist pedagogy, in these accounts, proceeds particularly by way of curricular content (as has already been indicated by many of the previous quotes and references). For example, Simon-Maeda describes her gender and language issues course (in a Japanese post-secondary institution) as a "feminist course." It contains material on

> gender inequality from a linguistic perspective, including sexual harassment in the school and workplace, domestic violence, sexism in textbooks and the media, and sexuality. In addition to the lecture format, students complete worksheets and engage in journal writing.
>
> (Norton & Pavlenko, 2004a, p. 9)

In terms of interaction and process, Simon-Maeda (2004, p. 128) describes the course as "lecture type."

> During the first 60 minutes, I introduce a certain topic related to the linguistics aspects of gender inequality. … Students then get into groups

of four or five people for about 15 minutes and complete a worksheet ... that contains questions or points for discussion ... The remaining 15 minutes of class time are reserved for journal writing. I regularly collect the journals and make a few comments (in English) ...

(Ibid., p. 130)

Cohen's chapter in same book (2004) describes a university course whose full title is "Academic Preparation and Linguistics Theories and Advanced Reading/Listening Comprehension." Class size was about twenty-five, three-quarters female; the course met six hours per week for a year. Again, the most obvious feminist pedagogy strategy is making the curriculum content much more inclusive and indeed sensitive to a feminist perspective on the content, which in this case is the English language itself, along with EAP strategies. In the course, she used L1 academic "textbooks shaped by a feminist problematic of gender" (p. 157) such as Skutnabb-Kangas (2000) and by comparison a textbook (Barber, 1997) "which assumes a patriarchal ... frame of reference" (ibid.) along with video reports on cultural matters from Japanese TV, and worksheet tasks she designed, all of which focused students' attention on aspects of gender and language. Through "an explicit critical feminist pedagogy" (p. 155) Cohen fostered "interpretive skills: the skills required to negotiate the intersecting cultural narratives of class, gender, sexuality, ethnicity, and national identity." Her recommendations for "developing critical feminist engagement in the classroom" are the following maxims: "Encourage Dialogic Engagement With Text ... Ask and Elicit Many Types of Questions ... Raise Awareness of Pseudogenerics ... Have Students Question Prescriptive Grammar Rules ... Explore Markedness" (p. 161). Pedagogically, there is heavy emphasis on discussion, group work and student-led presentations, as well as use of teacher-student email in preparation of student work and presentations.

It would appear that the emphasis in these reports of feminist pedagogy in EFL/ESL is on skillful, indeed highly informed and creative selection of content, along with use of consciousness-raising discussion and activities, and crucial attention to the development of voice and the allowing or fostering of agency in the classroom. The details of the cases reported (which space limits prevent me from more than alluding to) are persuasive and would prove helpful to teachers beginning to explore feminist perspectives, though in general it seems these are exceptionally confident and well-prepared teachers, in some cases with quite a few years of experimenting and exploring critical alternatives, often working with advanced students and under favorable conditions. No pre-prepared model materials have emerged in published form from these initiatives, though possibly direct correspondence with some of the authors could be productive for the inquiring or beginning teacher.

TASK: SEARCH AND CORRESPOND

My teacher students have found it surprising that I believe that academics have a moral responsibility to respond to inquiries in their field, and that specialists will actually write back to them. I think that this is in fact highly likely in the small world of critical second language studies. So if you find yourself in a position to begin feminist pedagogy, why not attempt to open email correspondence with feminist pedagogues and ask them about materials they've used?

Anti-racist

Race is a quite belated topic to gain attention in the second language teaching scene. A *TESOL Quarterly* special issue on the topic (Kubota & Lin, 2006a) can be taken as a turning point perhaps, though Curtis and Romney (2006) is based on a TESOL convention panel of 2001, so that date is perhaps a better marker for increasing attention in our field to this topic. In the introduction to the *TESOL Quarterly* special issue (Kubota & Lin, 2006b), the authors identify critical pedagogy and critical multicultural education (cf. Kubota, 2004; May, 1999; Weil, 1998) as the two main perspectives informing second language teaching that is intended to work against race as a site of oppression. To introduce the topic I will sketch its historical development through the tensions between critical and non-critical multicultural education, and between the latter and anti-racist education.

Multicultural education was a curricular development of the late 1970s and provided some space for education intended to work against racism. It did so primarily by developing content for use in the mainstream of curriculum, particularly in high school courses such as civics or social studies and perhaps history, that promoted knowledge about different groups ("ethnicities," whether immigrant or indigenous, but essentialized and homogenized as non-white), mostly positioning them as outsiders to a dominant culture. This is a tendency that goes back to the introduction of active governmental concern with race relations and the education curriculum across the main English-speaking countries from the early 1970s on, with broadly similar features (led by Canadian national policy developments in 1971; Moodley, 1999, p. 148). Not long after the introduction of multicultural curricula, emanating from mainstream, dominant (white) cultural perspectives, they began to come under criticism from those who favored a more radical position. The resulting debate was to be found in a number of countries[8] (UK, Canada, Australia, South Africa, and New Zealand). Those on the left questioning multicultural education were associated with the term "anti-racist education" (except in the US, which preferred the term "critical multiculturalism"). The anti-racist position on multiculturalism was that it merely promoted a "typees and tacos" view of diverse cultures. This reduced pernicious racism to a superficial and relativistic form of cultural difference, which while apparently celebrating "diversity," did so in ways that failed to expose the power relationship between dominant white culture and the various oppressed minorities which were instead presented as part of one big happy multicultural family. In the UK at least, this critique was drawn upon both generally and in ESL (but without being clearly integrated into L2 pedagogy; Levine, 1981; Levine & Bleach, 1990; Sarup, 1991).

The turn to the right[9] in the political administrations of many English-dominant countries coincided with increased immigration and diversity in many of them. This resulted in a change in trajectory for state support for multicultural educational and social policies along with increased central control of educational curricula[10] and controversy over language (Cameron, 1995). May and Sleeter (2010, p. 2) refer to multicultural education in the US as being "rebuffed" and "unraveled," with associated policies of affirmative action for minorities as having been "dismantled." In the introduction to a recent collection on "intercultural education" in Europe, Bhatti et al. (2007, p. ix) remark that "in countries such as England and Sweden … the very notion of 'multicultural' education is seen to have had its day … In the Netherlands the idea of a multicultural society has officially come to an end. There citizenship education for integration has been used to replace intercultural education. [Yet] in Greece and Italy inter-cultural stands for valuable communication and a sincere attempt to understand diversity …." These authors also draw on the practical realities in which more people identify with more than one ethnic or racial term, or just identify as of "mixed" backgrounds; a similar line is taken from a theoretical perspective by those who fuse multicultural analyses with postmodern perspectives on homogeneity versus hybridity. Our understanding of race-oriented critical language teaching initiatives needs to be set in these wider international political and policy contexts. At the same time, we can note limitations of the educational discussions of anti-racism and critical multiculturalism, which (according to May and Sleeter, 2010) have not made much contact with non-English-dominant countries, with the exception of Banks (2009). In fact, the ethnic diversity of many nation-states (for example, Malaysia or India) has in some cases been reflected in government educational policy for many decades without use of an explicitly multicultural terminology. At the same time, although few if any cases of national policy align with critical multiculturalism, there is greater willingness among elites, and greater pressure from minority groups, for at least some degree of multicultural orientation in curriculum worldwide; it is important to set the sometimes limited discussions of this topic in the wider international and comparative education context (Banks, 2009).

TASK: REFLECT

This is quite a difficult area. Well, perhaps they all are. But before you press on into the detailed review that follows, why not pause for a moment and reflect, or share, how you describe yourself in race-related terms. And consider (and explain to others, as appropriate) what you understand by the term "race" and how it is used, and/or fits or doesn't fit, into your language teaching context.

In a recent review, Kubota (2004) comments that second language teachers are sometimes believed to be "naturally sensitive to cultural and linguistic diversity" (p. 3) and as a result are "usually regarded as liberal advocates for multiculturalism" (ibid.), by which she means views and actions which "promote tolerance, acceptance, and respect toward different cultures … supporting equality among them" (ibid.). This position tends, however, to accept meritocratic and individualist conceptions of nation-states and the role of citizens within them, which she says, "in the school context … is played out as universal, neutral and difference-blind institutionalism" (p. 32). Moving on to expound critical multiculturalism (which she sees as basically the same as anti-racist education[11]) for the ELT/ TESOL field, Kubota (2004) identifies several key features or principles.

1 *Explicit focus on racism and other kinds of injustice at the collective level.* In the first case, this means that in curriculum content, racism is not presented as manifesting merely in individual interactions, nor capable of being overcome by the isolated efforts of individuals. At a more analytic level, it "focuses on how certain groups of students are disadvantaged in educational decisions such as tracking, testing, funding, curriculum, pedagogical approaches, and language of instruction" (ibid., pp. 37–38).

2 *Nonessentialist understanding of culture—Problematization of difference.* By this Kubota means that anti-racist or critical multicultural educational theory and practice recognizes non-homogeneity and change within cultures.

3 *Culture as a discursive construct.* Kubota has previously (1999) analyzed the "construction" of images or descriptions of essentialized groups of Japanese learners of English, constructions put together by TESOL specialists. Here (2004, p. 40) she makes this point more generally:

> As culture is a discursive site of struggle, multicultural education is a field where certain ways of thinking (color blindness, power evasion, etc.), educational practices (equal treatment of all students, celebration

of ethnic festivals, etc.), and various texts (visual images, descriptions of different cultures, etc.) are constructed and contested. Multiculturalism as a discourse also reflects and produces certain power relations. There is an implicit assumption in liberal multiculturalism that whiteness is the norm against which all other racial groups are defined and is thus superior. Critical multicultural education deconstructs not only our knowledge of culture, but also the meanings of multiculturalism.

4   *Critical multiculturalism is for all students and is pervasive throughout the curriculum.* Thus we can see that this perspective again is likely to manifest as a primarily curricular initiative. One hopes that it would be implemented by teachers using dialogue, orienting to inquiry, and emphasizing the agency and perspectives of their students. Focusing on language teaching in this context, Kubota (1999, p. 29) advises that

> the teaching of the dominant code needs to be grounded in a critical understanding that no particular culture or language (or variety of a language) is superior to others, that learning the dominant cultural and linguistic codes does not have to mean sacrificing one's cultural and linguistic heritage, and that the learner can appropriate the dominant linguistic and cultural codes in order to advocate cultural and linguistic equality in the wider society.

Applied linguistics has been strongest in the research behind critical multicultural initiatives through documenting the mismatches in discourse practices and conventions between minority students and their teachers in mainstream classrooms (e.g., Heath, 1983; Scollon & Scollon, 1981). This implies that an essential feature of all classrooms should be culturally appropriate pedagogical practices. These two characteristics in the pedagogy of critical multiculturalism are indeed suggested by most expositions (e.g., Weil, 1998; Nieto, 1999), but these are of course oriented to the L1 context. The question for us, however, is how does this manifest when working with second language learners, whether in domestic (e.g., ESL) settings or internationally (most obviously, EFL cases). In fact, critical pedagogy itself has been criticized for ignoring race (Haymes, 2002; Leonardo, 2005), so perhaps it is not surprising that the small literature in our area, basically accumulating only in the last ten years, mostly consists of personal narratives by second language teachers and occasionally students which relate events relevant to their status as teachers and people identified or identifying as of a particular racial status. Even outside of the L2 context, critical multicultural education lacks reports of practical classroom interventions. I proceed to briefly summarize the two primarily pedagogical reports that Kubota and Lin presented in their special issue.

To get a sense of what the practicalities of anti-racist education might look like in a classroom that focuses on language consider a famous early path-breaking teaching initiative in this area, "Discrimination Day" (originally taking place in 1968). In this simulation, a US teacher (Jane Elliot) separated her class into two groups (based on eye color) and then carried out a range of regular classroom activities with them in the course of which she actively discriminated against one group and in favor of the others. She was trying to make students feel what it is like to be treated differentially on the basis of "minor" external features. She documented her innovative simulation and conducted anti-racist teacher education workshops based on it. This work (Elliott, 1973) is famous; besides written accounts there were early video or film reports of it and video versions are easily accessible.[12] It has taken forty years, but TESOL has now caught up with this. In the recent *TESOL Quarterly* special issue just mentioned, Hammond (2006) reports adapting Elliot's simulation for Japanese EFL students. She ran classroom activities closely matching Elliot's, over two semesters and accumulated student reflections along with her own observations of this. Analyzing her data two ways, she initially reports that participating in the experience heightened Japanese EFL students' understanding of racism. But a second pass through her data, using concepts from critical pedagogy, led her, she says, to a different and slightly less positive finding. Student reports included ways of avoiding the topic, ascribing racism only to active emotional commitment on the part of the dominant group, and so on.

From a practical point of view, this study is of particular interest because it made use of a simulation, and reminds us of the potential strengths of simulations, an established activity type in second language teaching, to encompass more complex material. Simulations have a long history and have been used in language teaching at least since the beginnings of CLT (cf. Fletcher & Birt, 1979), but do indeed (as Hammond's report reminds) require a great deal of planning from the teacher, sometimes extra resources, and usually longer blocks of time and a complete departure from regular (textbook-driven) course material. On the other hand, even non-critical simulations, moving on beyond communicative materials, offer substantial potential for in-depth use of language and treatment of topics, as is clear from Hammond's account.

The other main practical example that Kubota summarizes is that of Taylor (2006).[13] This reports on one of a number of annual three-day "camps" for high school ESL students in Canada; the specific event is also described as a residential "leadership retreat." It took place outside of regular school classes (which reminds us how important extra-curricula initiatives can be for critical pedagogy) and was funded and supported by Canadian provincial education and teacher education authorities. The "Year 2000 ESL Equity Leadership Camp" participants were drawn from the very diverse Toronto schools and represented fifteen ethnolinguistic groups.

Central to the camp curriculum are students' personal experiences as the basis of shared insights, analysis, embodied knowledge construction, positive identity building, and leadership development. Understanding leadership as the capacity to analyze and collectively act on the architectures of power shaping the social and material conditions of learners' immediate worlds, activities aim to build active alliances around shared values and visions. In the 3-day program, mixed-school Family Groups engaged in:

1. Ice-breakers and team building activities; pair interviews.
2. Viewing a video dramatizing the ways linguicism, racism, and xenophobia can marginalize, isolate, and disadvantage ESL students; debriefing personal responses and experiences.
3. Learning to analyze racism and other forms of discrimination at the individual and institutional levels based on examples from personal or immediate experience.
4. Analyzing in school groups how antidiscriminatory and welcoming their own school is; developing and presenting an action plan (a timeline of specific collective steps to improve different aspects of their school with the support of attending teachers).
5. Making confidential written commitments to individual action plans or resolutions.
6. A reunion of all participants a month after camp to present progress reports, problem-solve, reconnect and renew momentum.

(Taylor, 2006, p. 525)

TESOL standards are another place to look to get a sense of the current state of play in the field concerning this topic. The standards for teacher education promoted by the US-based TESOL organization state that "candidates are aware that racism and discrimination have effects on teaching and learning." They also say that "candidates consistently use an anti-bias curriculum and materials … [and] deliver instruction that includes anti-bias materials and develop a classroom climate that purposefully addresses bias, stereotyping, and oppression." The precise term "anti-racist" is not used, but racism is explicitly mentioned and, by implication, teachers and teacher education programs are enjoined to foster teachers' capabilities to use an "anti-bias curriculum." Given the absence of materials and research emanating from TESOL, this might be a challenge. Reviewing standards for TESOL teachers from elsewhere, I found that the Australian equivalents were more explicit.[14] In answer to the question "What makes an accomplished TESOL teacher in Australia?", The Australian Council of TESOL Associations states as its very first disposition, that "TESOL teachers espouse the values of cultural inclusivity, multilingualism, reconciliation and anti-racism." The last two terms signal, I believe, a stronger position than that of TESOL in this area, with "reconciliation" relating to the

Truth and Reconciliation Commissions used by countries which are making a serious effort to come to terms with violent racist actions in their past. On the other hand, US national standards outside of TESOL are severely criticized by Vavrus (2002) for avoiding language that would in any way promote critical multicultural or anti-racist teacher education.

To take the exposition a little further I am dividing the orientations L2 practice might have in this area into four domains: mainstream, ESL, EAP, and EFL.

The heading "mainstream" can refer to the situation in which the teacher is operating as part of a general teaching force within a school which has a multicultural orientation. Quite possibly the teacher is white, or at least not from the ethnic groups of the student body. This requires the teacher to make a sustained effort to get to know more about "their students' wider cultural networks and identities" (for which enhanced teacher education is also needed: Lea, 2010, p. 41). It implies teaching critical literacy within a multicultural curricular context (Locke, 2010, referring to New Zealand schools). It can include efforts to simply include the students' L1 in the classroom ... not necessarily an easy thing to do in the existing and increasingly constraining audit culture classrooms, with their scripted lesson plans mandated. In a relevant recent case study, Bartolomé's student teachers (2010, p. 57)

> discussed and designed various practical interventions that range from consciously creating a plan for first language inclusion in their [English-only] classrooms, by "pushing the boundaries" of what is allowed by the state ... Students recognize that, as state employees, they are limited in terms of how far they can "push the envelope" at their place of employment. Nevertheless, they are equally conscious that they can overcome these restrictions by engaging in parent and community organizing efforts *outside* their own school districts.

"ESL" in this context implies teaching a second language to immigrant groups and within that having a focus not only on racism, but also teaching the language needed to interact in racist or racially charged situations. This would be by direct analogy to critical pedagogy in which the problematic aspects of students' lives form the content of class. The critical literacy or critical language awareness equivalents of this imply working with texts and media that contain implicit or explicit racist meanings. At a first level of analysis, I conceptualize teachers working with ESL students on their behalf. But if I recognize that the dominant cultures of most developed countries are themselves shot through with racism, then an anti-racist perspective involves sharing and developing a cultural analysis that goes beyond the conditions of the immigrant students and includes an analysis of indigenous groups (Hawaiians in Hawai'i, Maori in New Zealand, Aborigines in Australia, First Nations in Canada, and so on).

EAP: first of all, EAP does not just address the language of academia; it includes providing an understanding of the university as a culture and a place of study. In critical EAP this of course is a critical understanding, and includes the possibility of aiding L2 students at universities to take action to improve their access to learning. Adding in a race focus implies recognizing and presenting an analysis of the extent to which a university too, or academia in general, can manifest racist positions and practices. And again, this can include action to work against such positions.

Finally, EFL: in EFL contexts, anti-racist teaching is teaching about the culture of the target language from a critical point of view and may also include addressing racism within the host culture as well, as Hammond (2006) illustrated. In addition, Kubota (2004, p. 46) reminds us about the common EFL situations in which students and teachers are non-white. She points out that

> whiteness and white supremacy are relevant not only to white people or societies inhabited by them, but also to other people and societies. … Whiteness is indeed worldly in that it imposes the white norm and worldviews onto the ways that non-white people around the world think and communicate. Thus, it is necessary for teachers and students, white or non-white, to critically examine how their ways of thinking and communicating are regulated by Eurocentric norms in an imperialistic paradigm.

This leads us (drawing again on Kubota, 2004, p. 46) a little further into several central concepts that also must be the focus of reflection, discussion, and critique. First, the native speaker construct, which is very much associated with being white. And second, L2 teachers' own consciousness. Kubota (2004, pp. 44–45) cites Harklau (2000; see also Nozaki, 2000) as noting that

> some high school teachers often viewed immigrant students as belonging to a fixed imaginary cultural group with hardworking, attentive, and diligent qualities, although others viewed the students as lacking cognitive abilities. These identities are reinforced by instructional practices in which students are encouraged to disclose their immigrant experiences through writing personal stories or they are rewarded for being hardworking and well-behaved. In contrast, in a community college ESL class. where these same learners were positioned vis-a-vis newly arrived immigrant students, they were viewed as difficult students for their rudeness and lack of cooperation and academic skills. This study demonstrates that identity is neither neutral nor inherent but constructed by teachers' perceptions of the Other.

Third and finally, the language itself needs to be both scrutinized and appropriated. Kubota (2004, p. 46) draws on two prominent critical applied linguists, Pennycook (1994) and Canagarajah (1999). The former suggests that within critical pedagogy, we should teach the standard language, but do so in a critical way, noting its involvement with "domination and subordination," rather than taking it as truly normative. We should not avoid standard English, as this can lead to "marginalization or ghettoization' (says Canagarajan, 1999, p. 176) but critically negotiate its use.

Anti-racist education is intended for all groups in a society, to foster understanding, and to encourage accepting attitudes and behaviors. Clearly this is a very broad area of increasing importance, in which much work remains to be done; indeed, for language teachers an area whose surface as only just been scratched.

TASK: EXPLORE

Baby steps are needed here. Consistent with a central concern of this book, what could materials look like in this area? Find and share any piece of authentic realia, or non-language related teaching material, of relevance to your locality, that could be a starting point for an L2-related class in this area.

Sexual identity, oppression and pedagogy

Oppression related to sexual identity[15] is a fact. Increasingly, it is an issue addressed in education systems, though it is a newcomer in these areas and initiatives are likely to experience even more resistance than those related to class or race. Investigations into second language curricula and pedagogical practice in this area are fewer than those related to other sites of oppression considered in this chapter. Taking a fully international perspective, as second language specialists must, it is necessary to recognize that the sympathetic perspectives to be found in some cultures (including some non-Western cultures) are matched by entirely unsympathetic official stances in many countries and educational systems. Discrimination is sometimes mild, but all too often is extreme, with state-sanctioned and state-condoned violence, as of the moment of writing, occurring on a daily basis all around the world.[16] Even countries where "hate-crimes" are punishable by law, experience such crimes quite often, again up to and including murder. Thus it hardly needs to be said that sexual identity is a focus of oppression; so stigmatized and extreme is oppression in this regard that it is only in the most recent years, and in quite a small way, that options to oppose it through education, either in mainstream education and or in language teaching, have become visible. Language learning and movement between cultures becomes particularly important as the difference between cultures, for individuals facing sexual identity oppression, is potentially one of life or death, and thus language teachers can expect to encounter quite a few students engaging in "sexual migration" (Nelson, 2010, p. 446; Carrillo, 2004).

Nelson's (1999) article "Sexual identities in ESL" is an indication of a change in the wind for L2-related publication on this topic.[17] There had been almost no treatment of the topic in TESOL writing prior to this, though a small amount of potential curriculum material with positive treatment of lesbian and gay identities existed (e.g., Bösche & Hansen, 1983).

Increasingly, modifying curriculum options, along the lines suggested by Vandrick for feminist pedagogy and feminist L2 curriculum (see above), are possible given the GLBT-positive literature that has begun to be available in this area. Some of this material is referenced in Vandrick's later discussion of the matter (Vandrick, 2009, p. 105). However, Nelson says that simply obtaining and using inclusive materials can be problematic. First, teachers may not have relevant knowledge; second, "[I]f these representations come only from the target culture, are they sufficiently inclusive?"; and third and more strongly, "[A]iming for tolerance presupposes intolerance [so] only two possible positions are created—to be either tolerant or intolerant" (1999, pp. 376–77). Nelson points out that theoretical work in this area has gone beyond conceptualizing and defending lesbian or gay identity, and has moved forward to draw on "the linguistic concept of *performativity* ... in arguing that sexual identity is performed rather than expressed" (p. 375). This facilitates the development of "queer theory," in which all sexual identities are called into question, and all are seen in non-essentialist ways, as performed rather than stable and inherent. Bringing the matter back to practice, this suggests an inquiry approach to sexual identity (with this theoretical base), rather than merely an inclusive curriculum.

In her study which explores this perspective, Nelson interviewed and observed three post-secondary ESL teachers who were "interested in sexual identities in ESL and had previously worked with the topic of lesbian and gay identities in the classroom" (1999, p. 379). In the part of the study that Nelson reports in her 1999 paper, it is first of all of interest that the (US community college) ESL class observed was in a gay neighborhood "in a city where discrimination based on sexual identity is illegal" (p. 380). This makes the topic one which immigrant and refugee students would naturally encounter in their lives in the vicinity of their educational institution, as Nelson explicitly reports (p. 387)[18]. However, the course in question was a grammar-based one, not a thematic one. In the short piece of the lesson Nelson analyzed, the students were studying a unit on modal verbs, which included a worksheet written by the teacher. The worksheet contained sentences that depicted "scenarios" concerning which speculation (using a modal) was required. In this case, the sentence was "those two women are walking arm in arm" and student produced follow-on utterances or written sentences with the modal "could." One student produces a possible sentence: "They could be lesbians" (p. 381). This is then taken up in more thematic discussion, with questions such as "'Is this true in your country?' and 'Do you remember when you discovered in the United States it was different?'" (p. 381), and the holding-hands scenario is extended to men. This allowed an extended discussion among the students, men and women from a range of countries including from Asia, Central and South America, and Africa, in which personal experience and opinion are articulated and drawn upon. There is some similarity to the Freirean concept of a code here.

> This task was developed in a way that makes it accessible and potentially relevant to any student, as anybody whether straight, queer, or none of the above—could see same-sex affection and speculate about what it might mean. ... Furthermore, the task calls for not just one but three or four interpretations of each scenario, which accomplishes several things. Asking for multiple interpretations serves to underscore the uncertainty often associated with reading sexual identities. This uncertainty demonstrates why verbs sometimes need to be modalised, and it also allows students to raise the possibility that the two women are lovers but does not require that they do so, as there is no right answer. Because the teacher had the students discuss their written answers in small groups, the students were exposed to even more speculations (and the teacher had the chance to circulate and find out how students were responding to the task before deciding whether further work was needed).
>
> (Ibid., p. 387)

In other work in this area, a combination of an inquiry perspective and a thematic curriculum that facilitates engaging with this topic is found in Nguyen and Kellogg's (2005) study. Here too, ESL post-secondary students (at a community college) were placed in a position of discussing and exploring the topic of sexual identity. One difference is that the course was something approximating a sheltered content ESL course, whose primary content or topic was "civil rights." This obviously legitimated a range of social justice topics. The other notable difference is that discussion was by way of Computer-Mediated Communication (CMC), in this case an online discussion board. Finally, note should be made of O'Mochain (2006) which shows that the area can be developed in EFL contexts as well.

TASK: RESOURCES

Attitudes and practices in this area are changing fairly fast in some parts of the world, yet tragedies are also reported on a very regular basis in the world press. What is the situation in your cultural context? What institutional support resources, if any, exist? Are you aware of any pedagogical initiatives on this topic in your vicinity? If working with a group, share details.

Peace and environmental education

Another curricular strand I would like to identify and at the same time encourage more of, is peace and environmental education. From the perspective of a broadly defined critical pedagogy, environmental, peace, and global education can be seen as perspectives that share values with critical pedagogy though to varying degrees predate it. Accounts and examples of practice in these areas make it clear that these are curricular perspectives that typically provide direct instructional content of factual and values-clarification nature, and develop language and communication skills in regard to these topics, with discussion to absorb the concepts. In many cases they encourage forms of action, either in terms of changed lifestyle or active citizenship. There is not a lot of L2 related material in these areas, however, but some exploration and exposition is warranted because of the degree of overlap between the area and critical pedagogy.

Peace education

Unlike the "post-structural" group of race, gender, and sexual identity as strands within critical (or radical) pedagogy, peace education clearly predates the social movements of the 1960s. Stomfay-Stitz (1993) claims an ancestry back at least to Horace Mann, founder of the common school movement in the US, in the first half of the nineteenth century. This is supported by Harris (1988, 2004), who refers to the growth of peace movements in the nineteenth century in response to the Napoleonic wars. These were strengthened by "working men's associations and socialist political groupings. … As the nineteenth century drew to a close, groups of teachers, students, and university professors formed peace societies to educate the general public about the dangers of war" (Harris, 1988, pp. 16–17). These initiatives continued after World War I. Jane Addams was one figure with educational associations who was very active in this movement; another was Montessori. After the catastrophe of World War I, many developed countries experienced opposition to war that manifested in the strong pacifist movements of the time and associated educational initiatives. After World War II, "the first academic peace studies program at the college level was established in 1948 at Manchester College" (Harris, 1988, p. 18). A prominent alternative education figure, later in her life Montessori was active in peace education during this post-World War II period (e.g., Montessori, 1972). But pacifism and opposition to war was seen as pro-communist, and it was not until the beginning of the 1960s and the anti-nuclear movement that peace education and pacifism regained force (Stomfay-Stitz, 1993). During this period and increasingly, the United Nations organization itself is identified as a force in peace education[19] (cf. Boulding, 2000). Its education wing (UNESCO—United Nations Educational, Scientific and Cultural Organization) continues to be an important site for resources, both financial and instructional, in this area. Within many countries, some institutionalization has developed; for example, in the US, Reardon (e.g., 1988) established the Peace Education Center, Teachers College Columbia in 1967.

Harris and Morrison (2003) provide some useful general suggestions in their chapter "Getting started: First steps in educating for peace," as follows. They divide the domain into education in community settings (i.e., adult informal education) and formal school settings. In the latter case, a first step is for the teacher to become informed about peace education and resources for it. They note that prominent teachers' organizations have provided support:

> [T]he Association for Supervision and Curriculum Development [has] already published peace and global educational resources for teachers. In the United States the two largest professional teacher unions, the National Educational Association (NEA) and the American Federation of Teachers (AFT), have actively promoted education for world citizenship, and the NEA has produced a curriculum for nuclear-age education called *Choices.*
> (Harris & Morrison, 2003, p. 104)

They then suggest developing a network of like-minded individuals so as to prevent teachers being isolated (a good general strategy for critical language teachers, of course). The next step is to "infuse" peace education concepts into existing courses. This is initially presented as an initiative of the teacher, but Harris and Morrison also say that "some peace educators have asked their students to help plan a peace event for the classroom. Working with the teacher to plan curriculum gives students a sense of ownership to enable them to take steps to create a more peaceful world" (ibid., p. 108). Going on, they also consider the introduction of separate courses and programs. The suggestions of Harris and Morrison assume, once again, highly resourced teachers with high levels of control over curriculum.

An optimistic illustration of some of these basic ideas, notably "infusion," is provided by Cowhey (2006) who reports teaching peace within her overall critical perspective, to elementary students (mixed L1 and L2).[20] Although there were many discussions of peace in her class, when it came to a period of time where there was considerable public opposition in the US to a war, she did not try to set up a school demonstration with her students but did organize a community event, organized by ex-students and sympathetic parents. This was a two-hour march (in winter), which, she reports, affected her students deeply, made them think, and gave them opportunities to talk with sympathetic and interested adults about matters of concern to them (that had been discussed on and off in class over some months prior to the event). The beneficial results of participation would appear to be consistent with the research of Anyon (discussed in Chapter 8), though Cowhey does not cite her or her arguments.

The attentions of UNESCO to this topic appear to have influenced its uptake by TESOL and applied linguists, with more initiatives appearing from the late 1980s on (Gomes de Matos, 1988). Renner (1991) is a concise but comprehensive and practical overview of the area from the viewpoint of an EFL teacher working in Italy. This report specifies the area of practice as peace education, but the themes treated include environmental education, which illustrates the closeness of these areas, perhaps. Renner follows Harris in distinguishing three levels of curriculum modification: First, a "contributions approach" in which the instructor simply adds activities to the existing curriculum. Renner suggests using a holiday or event as the prompt for this (such as tying some activity to Martin Luther King Day). Or, "using the existing curriculum, the instructor prepares an addendum to it on a specific question" related to peace. What Renner calls the "transformative approach" calls for noting where existing course books manifest "racism, sexism, violence or provide opportunities for real-life skill development of conflict resolution" (p. 4) and rewrite the syllabus in these areas; and finally a "social action approach" in which the "syllabus is completely designed by learner-instructor interaction." Renner provides short accounts of lessons in human rights education, environmental education and AIDS education. In the first case, the outcome of the lesson was the ("upper intermediate") class writing a letter in support of a prisoner identified by Amnesty International. Renner comments (p. 8):

> The students' response to this activity was very positive, even if we had to first discuss the usefulness of writing letters and get beyond the students' distrust of the political system … Young people believe their actions will make no difference. Peace education gives them a sense that they can and do effect change.

Renner also has interesting and useful things to say about how he made use of an L1 resource on environmental education (Steger & Bowermaster, 1990). At one level this work is similar to many (e.g., Brooks & Fox, 1995), with readings on relevant subtopics and discussion questions. Notably, Renner points to the "condensed story board which gets across the main ideas in fairly simple, direct language" (1991, p. 9) and comments that he used the material with "high-level beginners (120 hours general English study)." Since the whole matter of how much of this sort of thing can be done with what level of students is unexplored, this comment should be welcomed. He notes that he explained unknown vocabulary and "allowed L1 for discussion."

Of course, not all EFL contexts are the same. Discussing their work in Vietnam, Tyler et al. (2008, p. 349) say

> [A]lmost all current peace education materials are based on teachers exercising choice and selecting which of a range of options is most suitable

for their class. ... This notion is foreign to traditional teacher training in Vietnam. ... Vietnamese teachers are not used to the idea of "cherry picking" from existing materials to incorporate just some exercises of materials into their own teaching. Also, the use of a variable curriculum would place a strong onus of responsibility on, and might even threaten the security of teachers who will be judged in terms of their conformity to political standards.

One of very few extended reports of ESL practice in this area (more or less) is Morgan (1998, pp. 29–38). Morgan reports this initially as part of his general work in critical language pedagogy; however, the theme and topic of a module lesson that Morgan narrates is his Canadian adult ESL class's responses to the Gulf War, and this is primarily from the point of view of opposition to this or any war, so I think it could arguably be included here. Much of the account concerns how he helped his adult Chinese ESL students in Canada prepare to explain their experiences of war to an L1 teacher and her grade 7 students. The vivid narrative is informative in its own right but could also be used to flesh out the limited textbook and theoretical accounts that I have sketched here.

Of the handful of pre-made materials designed for second language students, I will mention two. First, Brooks and Fox (1995) is a textbook is designed for advanced ESL and EFL students (as well as native speakers, claim the authors), and has a fairly conventional structure of a large set of authentic readings, with pre- and post-reading exercises, discussion questions, and writing prompts. The twenty-four readings cover "(1) working for a healthy environment; (2) developing peaceful relations between men and women; (3) educating families and children for a more peaceful world; (4) promoting greater cross-cultural understanding, (5) exploring spiritual values, and (6) working for a better world" (p. viii). Second is Duffy (1995), a teacher-friendly volume of analysis and materials that was an outcome of the TESOL Summer Institute of that year. It covers conflict and conflict resolution, cultural understanding and moves on to more directly peace-

---

TASK: REFLECT

Perhaps peace education is one of the less-provocative ways in to critical pedagogy. It is relatively difficult to be in favor of war, in most places these days. (I hope I am correct in saying that!) On the other hand, probably many language students and their teachers will not have much familiarity with peace studies as a substantial curriculum area. What are some strategies or arguments you could initially come up with to justify introducing this kind of material to classes and courses you are familiar with?

related matters through a study of the life of Mahatma Gandhi. It is immediately useful and practical, though probably calls for at least intermediate level students. It is also a gateway to many online resources in an area that is far more developed outside of TESOL (and critical pedagogy) than inside it.

Environmental education

Environmental education as we know it today traces its inheritances to the Nature Study movement of the late nineteenth–early twentieth century, and in the US to Conservation Education, which was a response to the Depression and the dustbowl environmental disaster in the US Midwest of the 1930s. On the basis of these substantial and long-term developments, the nascent environmental movement of the late 1960s had no difficulty developing initiatives in print (Swan, 1969; Stapp et al., 1969). L2 specialists Jacobs et al. (1998) view the Belgrade Charter of 1975, sponsored by the UN, as a landmark after which substantial development of this area began to take off.

L2 manifestations in our academic literature are fewer than one might perhaps expect (but see Brown, 1994; Cates, 1990; Jacobs et al., 1998; Lopez et al., 1993). Early, Brown (1994) gave a short statement of a variety of publishing initiatives that indicated mainstream and ESL action in this area along with peace and global education (including a 1993 special issue of *EL Forum*). Concerned scholars in our field have raised these matters in the past (Cates, 1990 cites Rivers, 1968; or see Bragaw et al., 1981, for an early world languages position), but it could be argued that as a result of growth in mainstream curriculum in environmental education, resources are greater now than they used to be and also that this is an area where what was radical before has become more mainstream now. That is to say, the green/environmental line is occurring so widely that to use curriculum material that advocates peaceful citizen action to decrease global warming is not going to get you into trouble. And there is a lot of L1 material, including child-friendly social issues picture books.[21]

I have not seen any evidence that material in this area is particularly different in its processes. Most of it seems basically to be a curricular option. Stempleski (1993) is a good paper providing an overview of the area with particular reference to EFL contexts. Perhaps the most substantial current contribution to this area for L2 teachers is Jacobs et al. (1998). They express the idea that "the environment" should be one key theme in language instruction. However, they also emphasize that their approach to "greening the ESL classroom" draws on current trends in language instruction that are also consistent with basic orientations in environmental education, including a learner-centered perspective, the valuing of diversity among students, a holistic, theme or content-based approach to curriculum, learner training with a long-term view, a cooperative orientation, and indeed an action orientation. They then provide a substantial collection of fifteen lesson plans, many covering one to three classes, timed, with some activity sheets and quite specific guides to length and duration, that a teacher beginning in this area could easily use more or less off the peg, with "12- to 19-year-old students of at least high beginner proficiency level … [and] adult language learners" (p. 6).

TASK: REFLECT; EXPLORE

I assert that ecological topics and awareness are almost mainstream these days, so, on the one hand, language teachers may find material on this topic even in mainstream or assigned coursebooks. On the other hand, merely noting the destruction of the environment may not be accompanied by a critical perspective. What steps might be taken to develop such a perspective? Try to obtain an example of how this topic is handled in a regular L2 textbook. Does the material offer any openings to developing a critical perspective here?

Critical English as a foreign language

Critical pedagogy applied in the area of English as a foreign language has some distinctive characteristics that justify a separate discussion. These include questions of cultural appropriacy, sheer feasibility, and the role of outsiders and insiders in educational systems.

The primary point I want to address is the suggestion that certain cultural or geographical areas (e.g., East Asia) are particularly unfavorable locations for this work, for reasons of cultural appropriateness, not for reasons of political oppression. Some domestic and international academics in some countries in this region (e.g., China, Singapore) have denied the utility and applicability of both communicative language teaching and critical approaches in countries with fairly "traditional" school systems and cultural perspectives. Foreign language teachers in these areas have also questioned the applicability or appropriacy of these approaches. It has been suggested that some such assertions are based on a misrepresentation of cultures (Kubota, 1999). Consequently, reports of critical EFL pedagogy from these areas are of interest precisely because there is in some quarters a presumption that such efforts are impossible or inappropriate.

In what follows I provide brief notices of an admittedly small number of reports of critical language pedagogy primarily from Asian contexts (limited to those appearing in English, unfortunately). This is to build a case against the position that critical pedagogy is culturally inappropriate in some areas. That is not to say it is always advisable or practical, for purely pragmatic reasons. After these notices, I make some comments with broader geographical implications.

Korea

Shin and Crookes (2005a, b) report an investigation into critical language pedagogy with a two-part strategy. First, a review of the past of Korean educational culture and patterns in the broader aspects of Korean socio-cultural history suggested that activist positions were possible and indeed had been adopted at various times and locations in Korean education; the recent history of Korean education in particular documents the enormously active and engaged nature of Korean university students in political action. On the basis of this history it was argued, first, that dialogue and critical inquiry were entirely possible in Korean education. Even quite explicitly political positions, including of course anti-colonial positions during the colonization of Korea were natural, though dangerous, for educators. Second, within the admittedly often-constraining state education system, Shin's explorations of critical English language teaching were positive, and further supported our position that critical perspectives in English teaching were possible. Shin's actions were small-scale interventions within existing institutional arrangements: one within an actual high school English class, the other within an after-school English-speaking club, but still with high school students. The study reported examples of classroom discussion showing critical features, and student evaluations of these interventions that showed they were valued by students and consistent with principles of critical language pedagogy. It is what we could call a "proof of concept" initiative.[22]

Hong Kong

Wong et al. (2006) provide a very practical account of efforts to introduce critical literacy into the Hong Kong state high school system. First of all, they report on changes in Hong Kong educational policy which they say clearly encompass a "broad critical agenda across all key learning areas" associated with a new school subject called "Liberal Studies" (p. 131). At the same time, the old public examination system with its emphasis on "decoding texts [and] an instrumental view of literacy" (p. 131) persists. They write that "The notion of the 'critical' is and will remain a contested issue in Asian education systems" but on the basis of their findings they also say that "given the opportunity, Hong Kong students are more than capable of approaching texts from critical perspectives and that classroom pedagogy needs to address what critical means in the context of language education" (p. 132). In introducing their account, they state what should be by now a familiar point:

> [T]he biggest problem [was] for our school's teachers who were used to prescriptive teaching methods supported by commercial available textbooks and have not previously been asked to develop a school-based

curriculum. These were no commercially available resources designed specifically for this program and teachers were asked to use a range of texts from available sources, including newspaper, and develop teaching materials that supported their class. This in turn impacted on their teaching workload.

(Ibid., p. 134)

The two main projects or sequences of tasks they report concern developing a critical understanding of a children's story (Peter Pan, using "a shortened version of a commercially produced reader"; ibid.) and a critical analysis of advertisements in local Chinese newspapers, again drawing on existing materials (in this case, produced by a local university). In both cases, they used the work of Freebody and Luke (1990), their "four resource model," which allows the same material to be engaged with at different levels. First, students worked with the texts as "code-breakers," then as "text-participants" (which requires at least figuring out for whom the text was produced), next as "text-users" (rewriting and acting out a scripted version of Peter Pan, for example), and finally as "text-analysts," clearly the most critical position. Students had to identify the main themes and the intent of the author for the children's story, and in the case of the newspapers, they had to engage in "intensive reading between the lines" concerning the articles, and analyze the purposes of the advertisements. Overall, they observe that the students were from school and from language backgrounds that were not usually expected to achieve well in the higher (critical) levels of the curriculum, but based mainly on self-report data and their own observations, they report that

> students at our school appear capable of demonstrating the skills of text-users and text-analysts through regular engagement in a wide variety of literacy practices … Given the opportunity through a different approach and different materials rather than the normal textbook oriented methods, students will engage with the text from essentially a critical perspective.

(p. 138)

Japan

There have been several periods in the history of the Japanese education system during which the system itself has been progressive, teachers have had radical positions, and students have been extremely active (e.g., Dowsey, 1970; Kato, 2010; Lincicombe, 1995). As with the history of progressive education elsewhere, this is not well-remembered or available to current teachers and students, and the present education system has many limitations that block access to these memories or to the possibility that things could be different (cf. McVeigh, 2002). A related problem has been misperceptions among western TESOL academics about this cultural group important for EFL, leading to Kubota's (1999) correction and rebuttal.

After the period of greatest activism by Japanese students and teachers (the 1970s), responses to the authoritarian nature of state education have led to increasing interest in free and alternative schools, both in Japan and, for those parents who could afford it, abroad (cf. Kuroyanagi, 1982). However, critical pedagogy has not been very much in evidence in the published literature. Takayama (2009) provides an overview of critical education studies in Japan, but provides few empirical accounts outside of the movement for *burakumin* emancipation. Publications in English naturally only provide limited insight into what critical and alternative perspectives are surfacing in Japanese educational contexts. In the language area, one study of critical EFL pedagogy (Konoeda & Watanabe, 2008) has been summarized earlier; McMahill's valuable work is summarized in Chapter 8 (1997, 2001). ELT work also exists originating in Japan with an emphasis on gender and language (e.g., Casanave & Yamashiro, 1996) though the orientation of these authors is not direct to critical or feminist pedagogy.

Singapore

Kramer-Dahl's (2001) report depicts Singaporean education around 1995, when it was being criticized by its own government for stifling creativity:

> a school system where teachers and textbooks function more or less as passers-on of received, finite knowledge and where selection for the 'better' streams and the next level up occurs through a set of rigid, outdated examinations.
>
> (p. 15)

At the same time, she states, at least one Singaporean academic was in print denying the utility or appropriateness of critical literacy on cultural grounds. Kramer-Dahl reports on her offering of a course for undergraduates at a major Singaporean university. The course was entitled Critical Reading and Writing. She notes that the course was marginal in the overall curriculum and thus it was comparatively easy for her to reconfigure it in critical literacy terms. The course was supposed to introduce second-year undergraduates to "writing in the disciplines," but was altered so that in addition they were obliged to reflect on the literacy training they had received and carry out a variety of pieces of writing in which they had to ask themselves "why" a particular structure was to be employed, and also write reflective pieces which documented how they were writing.

Its major goal was to make visible to our students (and teachers) how school and university classrooms and their pedagogical practices work together as cultural technologies in the production of preferred discourses about reading and writing, and preferred positions for students from which to read and write. They could begin to understand that what counts as effective reading and writing in these places of schooling may vary, and be even at odds with each other, but that they are always "normative, political practice[s] ... entailing strategic decisions about who should read [and write], how they should read [and write], where they should read [and write], and to what ends and consequences" (Luke, 1994, p. 369).

Kramer-Dahl concludes that overall the class was successful, but she devotes quite a bit of space to analyses of the resistance of some students, which provides quite insightful understandings of the challenges these students experienced from the course.

It is encouraging to find a report of this kind from Singapore, with its reputation for tight control of its education system and strong centrally planned social engineering; however, Kramer-Dahl does make a point of mentioning the marginal status of the course. Practically speaking, the advanced or indeed bilingual abilities of the students would have certainly facilitated delivery of the conceptual parts of the course.

A more recent paper makes it clear that Kramer-Dahl has not given up nor been fired.[23] Kwek et al. (2007) report on a "pedagogical intervention" that runs contrary to dominant tendencies in Singaporean education:

This paper presents a pedagogical intervention project conducted in secondary English classrooms in Singapore, entitled "Building Communities of Readers among Teachers". The project is positioned against the dominant instrumentalism of Singaporean approaches to creativity and promotes a socio-cultural stance to creativity and criticality in English language education. Currently in progress, the project seeks to foster teachers' rich textual engagements and to connect them with those they provide for their students. Situating the professional development in communities of reading circles, teachers' own, often narrow repertoires of reading are foregrounded, allowing them to experience the struggle of an active engagement with texts, and thus facilitating a reimagining of their reading pedagogies, which at present are highly scripted and authoritative. The ultimate aim is to enable them to re-imagine their reading pedagogies in ways that encourage the creative and critical possibilities that textual openness can bring to classroom practice and learning.

It remains to be seen whether there will be other similar developments.

Iran

Perhaps the perceptions of Iran in its current political formation suggest an even more unlikely venue for critical pedagogy than some of the areas just discussed. However, at least two reports document approaches to critical literacy in classes there. Ghahremani-Ghajar and Mirhosseini (2005) discuss a private high school where critical literacy elements were added to the existing syllabus for an upper level EFL class of thirty sixteen-year-olds. The authors focus on their collection of student dialogue journal entries. In a departure from standard instructional practices, students were encouraged to write freely without concern for formal accuracy; the teacher responded to them supporting this orientation.

> In the cultural context of schools like the one in which we carried out this research, students are traditionally silenced and given no say beyond textbooks and tests. In such a context, being able to break the "culture of silence" (Freire, [1970/]1998) even on paper is a considerable breakthrough towards empowerment. … In the small social context of school and in the smaller context of dialogue journal notebooks, the main realisation of empowerment is students' being able to gain their voice at the minimum level of writing freely.
>
> (ibid., p. 291)

Over the duration of the course, student writing moved from merely descriptive to much more creative forms. Students also wrote evaluations of the course and clearly valued the progressive orientation to student participation, open-ended questions on exams, and made positive suggestions about the style and content of the course.

Izadina and Abednia (2010) report on a critical literacy approach in a state university EFL reading class (in which twenty-two of the twenty-five students were women) conducted during 2008. Even more substantially than Ghahremani-Ghajar and Mirhosseini, they couch their report within the literature of critical pedagogy, though the classroom practices focused on students' development of voice through writing rather than any more active forms. Perhaps this is just good sense. As it is, the authors report that the instructor "is outspoken in his criticism of the status quo and actively tries to encourage critical and creative action on the part of his students" and experiences "disapproval" from his colleagues. They note (p. 55) that "most of the students in the reading class, aware of [the] political structure and religious taste, initially preferred to distance themselves from discussion about political, religious, and other unsafe issues." The syllabus was negotiated; students selected readings based on the relevance of an initial selection to their lives, and this resulted in both neutral topics and at least one more loaded ("deception in mass rallies");

students were gradually introduced into the posing of questions concerning the texts to be read that had a critical literacy orientation. Group discussions and reflective journal writing formed part of the activities used. The authors base most of their analysis of the course on the journals collected, and suggest that participants had the opportunity to develop a range of positive developments likely to be missing from their more mainstream classes, such as increased self-awareness, freer expression of opinions, actual class participation as opposed to silence, and so on. The authors also show an awareness of the necessarily limited nature of the progress they could make (p. 64):

> Despite the great value of these changes in the participants' thinking and reading habits, critical reflection, by itself, is not enough. As implied in the concept of praxis, action inside and beyond the borders of classroom is also of particular significance in critical pedagogy ... In this study, we cannot make claims about how the observed critical reflection of the participants translated into action in society at large simply because the teacher didn't teach any other courses to them and, thus, didn't have regular contact with them at the university let alone outside. However, since the course itself can be considered a context for social interactions with other members of society, the changes observed in the students' styles of interaction with their peers, the teacher, and the texts, can be thought of as samples of critical and creative action that may promote similar behaviors in society.

It may be recalled that students in Iran have been very actively involved in political protest in recent years, as well as experiencing the harshest forms of response from the established authorities, as is all too common everywhere.

Contrasts to the Asian reports

I began by focusing on Asian countries because of assertions that things critical in language teaching can't be done there. Given the role of Freire in the overall topic, one might naïvely assume that, by contrast, there should be a lot of critical pedagogy in non-Asian countries, most obviously in Brazil. However, the real story is mixed. After the renewal of democracy in Brazil, Freire did guide initiatives when in the Ministry of Education of the state of Sao Paulo (O'Cadiz et al., 1998). But these were in many cases not continued under succeeding administrations. Cox and de Assis-Peterson (1999) reported that the outlook for critical ELT pedagogy in Brazil was not positive (cf. Busnardo & Braga, 2001; Rajagopalan, 2004). Jorge (2009) explains that familiarity with and action concerning this concept is split across elite and grassroots sectors in Brazil, including across language teachers. Those in the former group may be quite unfamiliar with it (or hostile); those in the latter quite familiar and making use of it.[24] Critical ELT in Brazil gained some heightened international visibility as a result of the "Critical literacy in ELT" project 2006–2009 which had support from an international group including the British Council Brazil, Brazil TESOL, and the University of Nottingham (see e.g., Hodgson, 2008), but this project has not been continued, apparently.[25]

If South America, with its still-recent history of military dictatorship and later neoliberal regimes has limited and mixed reports of critical (language) pedagogy, surely Europe, with its often progressive political administrations, might be better? Relatively few European education specialists are writing in English on this topic and the topic may appear under quite different headings and educational traditions. Matters critical are probably taken for granted in the alternative educational sectors of the Nordic countries which are still informed by the folk high school (*Folkehøgskole*) tradition. In France the persistence of *l'education nouvelle* is not obvious (Gumbel, 2006; West, 2010) and French education has experienced attacks on its autonomy by central state actors just as in Anglo-Saxon countries. Critical analyses of society to be found in the educational sectors of European countries may not have manifested themselves separately in language teaching in Europe; notable exceptions are Dendrinos (1992), a critique of EFL materials in Greece and more recently Guilherme (2002), a book length treatment of critical culture teaching in an EFL context in Portugal.

Critical and participatory approaches to English in South Africa were vibrant traditions, as illustrated earlier in this book. They continue to contribute (e.g., Janks & Sethole, 2006), and there are occasional reports of use of such ideas elsewhere in Africa (e.g., Schleppegrell & Bowman, 1995).

The reports I have brought together, and the arguments made in some of them, demonstrate that critical EFL is conceptually possible and do-able in all parts of the world: those where it has been wrongly disputed (East Asia), those where it has a long heritage (South America, South Africa), and those where it has a home in other progressive traditions (Europe). Doing it is one thing; should one check once again whether it is really desirable? Some in ELT have argued that plenty of students of English actually have no need whatsoever for it (Rogers, 1982); it is forced upon them, and in that case, critical language pedagogy of English is just as oppressive as regular language pedagogy of English.

I admit that the "need" for *all* students to have English in countries such as, say, Bolivia, Chad, or Indonesia, for example, is not self-evident, even if one accepts that English is the international language of power. It might be true that some members of the workforce in those countries have instrumental needs for English, but whether that means that English should be a compulsory element of elementary and secondary school again could be debated. Part of the problem here is the non-homogeneity of nation-states; the elites and even the educated workforce of capital cities around the world all have a fair amount in common with each other and might have "need" for English. But do rural populations of periphery countries really have any need for English at all? The answer could be "maybe not." *But* rural populations are often oppressed populations. Did the independence movement of Aceh (Sumatra, Indonesia) *need* English? Do the Zapatistas *need* English? Do the Uighurs of China *need* English? Do the occupants of the *favelas* of Rio de Janeiro need English? My answer is a guarded "yes, some." Most of these groups do make use of English (and the Zapatistas are famous for their creative way with words; cf. Marcos, 1999). English gets all these entities resources and publicity and prevents them from being entirely sidelined by dominant media telling their stories from the point of view of the "western media." So having spokespeople who know English probably won't actually hurt them at all..

What "kind" of English do they need, or could they use? The classic instrumental "needs" of Communicative Language Teaching (how to order food in an "English" restaurant, book a room in an international hotel) should make way for real, "critical" needs. Groups and their representatives need English (and other second languages) to talk to the Red Cross, UN peacekeepers, non-governmental organization representatives, international volunteers, diplomats, soldiers or mercenaries from various countries, and the international press and the media. Under the best conditions of international intervention, many representatives of those agencies will be locals and users of the local languages (but often not: Bremer, 2005). So actually, under the worst circumstances, the need for English as the language of international media is likely to be acute.

Finally, note that some governments (e.g., Colombia, S. Korea) have national language policy that aims to make a large proportion of citizens equally competent in the national language and English. In the case of Thailand and Korea, politicians have even proposed making English an official language. In this case, content-based instruction in the L2 is a natural form of curriculum, and all topics relevant to the development of critical and active international citizens are fair game.

In closing

Overall I hope it is made clear here that critical pedagogy has certainly gone far beyond Freire's original conception, and does justice to a greatly extended understanding of oppression and resistance that theorists and practitioners of various radical strands in education have developed. It should also be clear that internationally, critical perspectives on language learning and teaching can happily be entertained and developed which reflect these diverse understandings, although materials and curriculum in these areas have in some cases only just begun to be developed, or must be moved forward from small early initiatives. Finally, can it be done everywhere? Yes, it can.

Questions for discussion

1   Essentializing or not? How do you respond to any of the labels and categories that I have been obliged to use in this chapter? Are you unitary, diverse, or hybrid?

2   Can you make any general remarks about the roles of outsiders and insiders in working in these areas? Or make this a more focused question: supposing you are a male language teacher, and a feminist, would that make you less likely to tackle aspects of women's oppression, but if you did want to address this, how would you do so?

3   Can you think of other curricular areas or sites of oppression which might be emerging at the present time, that might fit into this chapter?

4   What is your opinion about the international dimension of this chapter? Are the prospects for critical EFL worse than for critical ESL? Setting aside generalizations, can this question be addressed for particular regions or types of educational institution?

Notes

1   A term which has very many other more significant meanings, unfortunately.

2   "It must be remembered that despite differences with their predecessors, the French poststructuralists can be interpreted as continuing the enterprise of the critique of the subject through a series of reflections on Hegel. Judith Butler (1987, p. 175), for instance, understands the twentieth-century history of Hegelianism in France in terms of two constitutive moments: "the specification of the subject in terms of finitude, corporeal boundaries, and temporarility" evident in the work of J. P. Sartre and Emanuel Levinas, among others; and "the splitting (Jacques), displacement (Derrida), and eventual death (Foucault, Deleuze) of the Hegelian subject" (Peters, 1995, pp. 51–52).

3   They also noted that "in a recent book written in collaboration with Macedo, Freire has taken a great deal of trouble to respond to the substance, if not the letter, of the criticisms" (p. 157: Freire & Macedo, 1987).

4   She was to continue this exclusive perspective in later work (e.g., 1993).

5   Also attested to by the fact that it appears in a collection entitled *Freire for the classroom* (Shor, 1987).

6   About half her sample of 15 were high school teachers; the others were university teachers.

7   Canada has been and continues to be a location sensitive to this and related topics, and even a source of possible materials. Prominent critical pedagogy expert Morgan refers (1998, p. 15) to "excellent ESL materials ... produced by the Ontario Ministry of Citizenship" which he used in "a lesson about violence against women" (cf. Cumming, 1990).

8   "The details of empirical historical experience may differ from country to country, but, broadly speaking, the fundamental issues that emerge remain the same" (Kalantzis & Cope, 1999, p. 251)

9   UK: Thatcher administration begins 1979; US: Reagan administration begins 1980.

10 UK National Curriculum 1988; New Zealand 1993.

11 "With its explicit focus on racism, critical multicultural education constitutes antiracist education." (Kubota, 2004, p. 38); this is consistent with the positions taken earlier by May (1994) and McLaren (1995).

12 E.g., http://www.youtube.com/watch?v=JCjDxAwfXV0&NR=1

13 In a review of the topic published more recently, Kubota (2010) returns to these and *only* these two studies. This suggests, as May & Sleeter (2010) say in several places, an all-too-familiar disparity between extensive theoretical analyses and few reports of practice.

14 http://www.tesol.org.au/ted/std_t.htm

15 This term avoids implications of perhaps more common alternatives (sexual preference or orientation; Nelson, 1999). The US National Education Association defines and explains the matter as follows:

> Sexual orientation is an identity based on whether someone is attracted to people of a sex different than their own, the same sex, or both sexes (i.e., heterosexual, homosexual, bisexual). Gender identity is a person's internal sense of being male, female, or somewhere else along the gender spectrum. Transgender is an umbrella term for people whose gender identity is different from their biological sex or the sex they were assigned at birth. The acronym GLBT stands for gay, lesbian, bisexual and transgender. While progress has been made since the Stonewall Rebellion in New York City (1969)—widely considered to be a pivotal moment in the GLBT rights movement—GLBT individuals still face discrimination and intolerance based on pervasive stereotypes and myths about GLBT people.

16 Nelson (2010) cites data indicating eighty-six countries in which adult homosexual activity is a criminal offense and ten in which it carries the death penalty.

17 Nelson refers to conference presentations and workshops that paved the way.

18 In a later article (Nelson, 2010) she reports that a nearby private language school in the same vicinity actually had an administrative policy *forbidding* teachers from discussing the topic.

19 http://www.un.org/cyberschoolbus/peace/frame2.htm

20 On resources in this area, Cowhey makes positive mention of Klamath County YMCA Preschool Staff (1993), Morrison & Morrison (1999), Parr (2004), Radunsky (2004), Steig (1984), Seuss (1984), and for the related matter of civil rights education in the US, King & Osborne (1997).

21 E.g., Van Allsburg (1990), Burningham (1994).

22 For other Korea-related cases, see Na & Kim (2003), Kim (2002), Shin (2004), Sung (2001, 2002, 2006, 2007).

23 And is still Associate Professor at the National Institute of Education, as she was when the earlier paper was published.

24 Or making use of it without fully understanding it: Bartlett (2005).

25 See also Farias (2005), writing about critical understandings of EFL in Chile.

7

ADMINISTRATION AND RELATED MATTERS

Inside the system?

In general, language teachers' views can shift over time. To put this in terms related to the present work, we know that language teachers may encounter critical perspectives or politicizing experiences. Language teachers who acquire a broader, more socio-political dimension to their thinking and teaching while they are doing advanced professional studies may experience greater frustration if they merely return to their old position of employment when they complete their course of study. It's possible they may have moved, say, from seeing their primary responsibility as teaching English efficiently, conceived on an individualistic basis, to a position in which their philosophy of language teaching is driven by an ethical analysis; thus merely assisting students to get a high score on the TOEFL, or even helping them to be able to order a meal in a restaurant in English (and suchlike) is no longer professionally satisfying to them. If they come from a mainstream high school EFL context or any context where there is strong central control of curriculum, they may find that they cannot simply return to their school with enhanced "skills" and then carry out "improved" English language teaching. Even in schools which are not so subject to central control, a teacher who is the only one with a critical perspective will find his/her influence to be weak. They thus may find themselves frustrated. Of course, if such teachers have altered their viewpoint while completing advanced studies, they may raise their sights to aim at a new position at a higher institutional level in language education. However, this alone may not result in professional satisfaction. Many of the same sicknesses afflicting lower grade levels of schools are simply reproduced in nominally "higher" education.

In response to this likely sort of professional trajectory, I urge such teachers (and present readers of this work) to first be willing to say "No." Cowhey (2006, p. 222) reports a critically minded teacher (Bill) who, while being interviewed for a position

> asked the principal, "What kind of diversity do you have here?" There was a long pause, and then the principal answered, "We've got a few of them, but they don't give us much trouble." When the principal called to offer ... the job the next day, Bill turned him down. There's no sense in starting to work for an educational leader with whom you have major disagreements from the start.

Besides turning down inappropriate positions, critically minded teachers should be aided to consider the broadest range of possibilities that exist for educational practice involving language. Accordingly, I now present a survey of critical pedagogy orientations from an administrative and institutional viewpoint.

I will begin this administrative review with the question of whether or not, or to what extent, critical perspectives can be pursued within the mainstream parts of state education. After the present introductory section of this chapter I review a range of institutional possibilities, placing more emphasis on those that may offer opportunities for critical pedagogies. A general principle in this examination is that the margins have often been good places for those with a critical orientation. Margins are places where the established order is weak and the writ of law or regulation less effective, so they should be places where experiment and boundary-crossing can flourish. Yet it must be admitted that those are not necessarily the places that will produce secure, long-term employment, or a handsome income and comfortable existence. At the same time, let us bear in mind that critical (language) pedagogy needs critical administrations and administrators.

Countries where central control of education had always been tight have shifted with globalization and other (population and economic) changes over the last twenty-five years. First in the old USSR and Soviet-bloc countries, then in China (Xu, 2000; Zhang & Adamson, 2011), monolithic state education has broken up. Other countries where there is still tight state control are showing signs of change as well (e.g., Japan and perhaps Korea). And once institutional diversity comes in, so do possibilities for at least alternative pedagogical initiatives. Of course, as I tried to make clear in Chapter 4, there have always been educational alternatives, though at some times and places they have been more visible than at others.

Historically, opinion has been divided on the potential and feasibility of any kind of alternative pedagogy in regular state schools. The libertarian or anarchist left in education divides from the authoritarian or statist (Marxist) left, traditionally, on the basis of trust of, or willingness to work within, the state sector.[1] In the run up to the appearance of critical pedagogy (under that name), Bowles and Gintis (1976) had made a strong case that schools merely reproduced the established order and thus it was a waste of time for radical teachers to work in that part of the education system (cf. Althusser, 1971). Freire regarded the adult literacy sector as more likely to be innovative than the mainstream.[2] However, specialists like Shor (1980) and Giroux (1983) disagreed with reproduction theorists, and demonstrated the possibilities to be found from being in the state system. And the work of many individual teachers and organizations in developed countries and elsewhere during the 1970s did indeed show what could be achieved within state education systems. This was during a time of great social change and comparatively lax central control. From the mid-1980s on and the beginnings of accountability regimes for education systems and increased central control of education by the state in countries where there had been some flexibility (UK, US, Australia, etc.), some might again have begun to doubt whether radical themes could be expressed in state institutions.[3] Perhaps the argument is too generalizing; it may be true for the most typical state high or elementary schools, but not true if the state system can be induced to accommodate a range of school types, some more alternative than others (see Chapter 7). So before turning to alternatives within the state sector, let me put down some not entirely positive notes about options and resources for critical teachers in the mainstream.

Content options and resource requirements

It may then still be the case that some well-resourced parts of the public sector in schools and universities with resistant philosophies or teachers can deliver somewhat critical pedagogies. As a case in point, I return to the work of elementary teacher Mary Cowhey to identify her favorable administrative and other resource contexts.[4] She began her career as a labor organizer and activist. She has a supportive principal. Her school is located within striking distance of five institutions of higher education with which it has established relationships, in a small open-minded town in the U.S. northeast. There are school gardens (and a nearby marsh). Rural or at least suburban surroundings allow field trips; indeed, field trips are both allowed and apparently easy to arrange. (In many schools around the world the immediate vicinity of the school is too dangerous or unpleasant to walk the students around.) Writing in 2006, Cowhey claimed to have full control of the curriculum and could change topics easily. There are many parent volunteers, who provide mini-lessons, cover while the teacher is doing administrative work, and assist with field trips. Some parents have cars and are available by phone to assist during the day on some occasions. There is a school library and a range of picture books on diverse topics in the room where she teaches. A parent who is a professional journalist was able to assist the students in making a class newspaper. The local newspaper is willing to publish student work. University students visit the class for durations of some weeks. Cross-age tutoring is possible. After school is over the teacher can "network" with families, meeting parents in person and even going to their homes occasionally. The school has a pen-pal partner school in South Africa.[5] So to turn this around, if critical pedagogy specialists find themselves in administrative posts, they should be attempting to mobilize resources along those lines. Equally, critical teachers need to consider their administrative needs in these broad terms, going beyond the materials and activities used within the classroom.

More democracy within existing institutions?

A term that still appears sometimes, and is intended to indicate a degree of local control and devolved administration is School-Community Based Management (SCBM), also known as School-Based Management (SBM) and even Comprehensive School Reform (CSR). These terms and concepts were outgrowths of the 1980s, in the UK and US where different administrations shared a political viewpoint (Whitty et al., 2000). Central governments combined specification of outcomes from schools at the same time as they granted them an apparently greater degree of local autonomy.

> [S]chool-based management has no 'essential meaning' but needs to be understood within a particular timeframe and a particular politics. Yet a key assumption on which it is based is that consistent and significant delegation is allocated to the school level of authority to make decisions within a broader framework of government guidelines and policies.
>
> (Kimber & Ehrich, 2011, p. 179)

Ogawa (1994), tracking the origin of this movement, dates it to 1986 and the influence of reform-efforts driven by the US National Governors Association. Basically, it was hoped that schools would attempt to reform their administrative structures (and be provided with money and consultant support for doing so) in directions of increased community participation, through parent and teacher participation in committee structures, with principals who would be willing to share authority. On the surface this suggests a greater degree of democracy would be manifested.

I think the simplest conclusion that could be drawn from the many studies of SBM that ensued during the decade following 1986, and a smaller number still appearing, including in countries other than the US (Mexico: Rodall & Martin 2009; Finland: Caldwell, 2008; World Bank, 2007; see also Shatkin & Gershberg, 2007) is that a great deal depends on the kind of community that is induced to participate in school-based management. And in addition, much depends on other central government initiatives. Thus, unfortunately it may be the case that the communities with most to gain from participation, that is, those already marginalized by mainstream education, are exactly those where parents don't have the skills or attitudes to engage with inherently middle-class dominant culture institutions. Perhaps it is the case that we need an organized community *before* this kind of structural initiative can be taken advantage of, at least in the state sector. (See discussion later of community schools.)

In many countries, accountability regimes after the mid-1990s shifted into higher and more oppressive gear. In the US, positive trade-offs between increased devolution and heightened state specification of outcomes were generally lost in the era of No Child Left Behind. Teaching to the test dominated; participatory processes were irrelevant if they did not lead to higher test scores. Indeed, large sections of the pre-existing curriculum were also jettisoned. Not surprisingly the evaluation of such initiatives shows much to be desired (Apple & Beane, 1999; Cook, 2007).

The university/post-secondary sector

Clearly, universities have often been sites of opposition. Despite accountability regimes, the investment that liberals and the left in many countries made in this sector has meant that non-mainstream programs have to some extent been able to resist encroachment or eradication. But the gradual defunding of state universities in developed countries suggests that this cannot be the only option for critical perspectives in education and applied linguistics, and those interested in critical language pedagogy cannot consider this to be their sole location. Indeed, those at work in this sector must be willing to fight a continual struggle. On some occasions specialists must recognize that the contradictions in being funded by political institutions basically hostile to their analyses mean that they may expect to have to leave when the returns to effort diminish, or indeed that they may in fact be pushed out by unsympathetic administrations.

I turn now to the more substantial range of institutional options that go beyond these potentially frustrating locations.

TASK: SHARE EXPERIENCES AND OPINIONS

The do-ability of anything critical in mainstream institutions is then obviously a long-standing question. In this first section there is a suggestion that universities also have possibilities here. What if anything is non-mainstream in any university you are in or have had recent experience with?

Institutional alternatives, new and old

Alternatives at elementary and high school level

Alternatives outside the state sector have always existed, as was suggested in the historical review earlier. A few schools in some state systems managed (particularly in the 1970s) to establish themselves on similar lines. But present-day manifestations of the "traditional" alternative sector, in the form of modern inheritors of the free school tradition are predominately private. An interesting point for the international language teaching community is that there is an increasing, though still small number of these schools to be found outside of Europe and North America—that is to say, we can find alternative schools in Japan and Korea (at least). My intent here is to draw the attention of potential critical pedagogues to the existence of these entities and to note that they are on the increase, including in countries where they had previously been even rarer or non-existent. Thus a language teacher with a critical pedagogy orientation might do well to seek them out. For a recent international survey, see Woods and Woods (2009).

Turning to the state sector, though it is at a first analysis homogenous[6] and mainstream by definition, from an institutional point of view there is perhaps more variation in what state schools offer than is realized, particularly when an international perspective is taken. Some old, as well as some newer alternatives, might be hospitable to critical pedagogies.

To take one example: Holland is a case where educational variation *is* possible, and this reflects the historically plural nature of this country. For as long as the modern Dutch constitution has been in effect (Swing, 2000, p. 39) "the Dutch constitution guarantees freedom of education, which means establishing a school is free"; parents can propose a school with a particular "profile," and on the basis of an argument that no equivalent profiled school exists, obtain the right to set one up. These schools are state-supported.

Something like this has recently developed in the US. A major change has been the introduction of "charter schools" (Buchanan & Fox, 2004; Fuller, 2000; Rofes & Stulberg, 2004) and there are similar entities in some other countries (cf. "complementary schools" in the UK, usually with a minority or ethnic culture and language orientation (Creese et al., 2006)); also recently called "free schools" in Sweden and the UK,[7] and "designated character" schools in New Zealand). Under new laws in the US, an organization can apply for permission to start a school which is governed by a "charter," which specifies often cultural and or religious grounds for distinguishing its offerings from conventional state schools. These schools are given substantial financial support by the state. Initially this was an option pursued by evangelical Christian groups in the US who wished to have non-secular curricula and co-curricular practices (such as school congregational prayer, bible study, and so on) which are not permitted under a principle of separation of church and state supposedly enshrined in the US Constitution. Subsequently, indigenous groups, such as Native Americans and Hawaiians, took up the same option so as to provide education that embodies, for example, Hawaiian values. Indigenous education increasingly inculcates values that are distinct from those of the "host" nation-state; they may sometimes represent an implicit critique of them, including their materialistic, acquisitive, or exploitative features.

Community schools

Another variant within the state sector is the community school. The idea of community schools has been around for a very long time. Its formal origins include the US settlement house movement of the late nineteenth century, Danish folk schools, and developments of "village colleges" in the UK in the early twentieth century (Gilchrist & Jeffs, 2001; for the US, see M. Williams, 1989)[8]. The US educational ethnographer Carspecken had early field experiences in a UK community school and provides the following background:

> In England the idea of community education goes back at least as far as Henry Morris, who implemented a rural-based programme in Cambridgeshire during the post-World War I period ... It was during the 1960s, however, that the concept began to be considered as a possible solution to urban school problems. Between 1968 and 1971 the Educational Priority Area (EPA) projects, run under the direction of A. H. Halsey, were carried out as experiments on the community school concept. Community schools were developed in the inner-city districts of four British cities with the goals of increasing parental awareness and involvement and adapting curricular practice to better meet community needs .... In their survey of a variety of community schools during their early stages, Hatch and Moyland (1972) found the attempt to blur community-school distinctions to be the essence of the community-schooling principle. They specified two approaches to it: a "moderate" approach and a "radical" one. Schools taking the moderate approach simply make their facilities available to the community after school hours and offer adult education courses. Some moderate approaches offer classes which adults and pupils attend together, and all attempt to get adult input through their governing board. The radical approach aims at introducing a "community curriculum" for all pupils. Learning activities ... which aim at maximizing the presence of the community in the school, are key aspects of the radical version. At the same time, the radical version advocates putting schools under community control. Williams and Robins (1980) make a similar distinction to that

made by Hatch and Moyland in their study of California community schools by aligning the schools they studied along a "community education continuum" having "programme oriented" activities at one end and "process-oriented" activities at the other. The process-oriented end of the pole includes aims of community action, grassroots democracy, and self-actualization, implying a combination of progressive pedagogy with local power similar to Hatch and Moyland's radical approach.

(Carspecken, 1991, pp. 12–13)

Recently the idea has been resuscitated and advocated for, though examples of practice are not common. The basic idea is attractive: schools should be a resource for the entire community in which they are physically located, and thus be open before and after classes, be space shared by community groups, and provide services beyond basic instruction (to children and parents), particularly involving health and welfare. From a critical pedagogy point of view, community schools which are in poor (not middle-class) areas imply teachers who understand community needs and have relationships not just with elementary or high school students but also their parents, care-givers, and so on. This seems to be a situation more likely to lead to appropriate forms of curriculum and possibly action. One of the most sustained and carefully planned recent initiatives in the US has been conducted in New York with support from the Children's Aid Society (Dryfoos et al., 2005). This area seems to have experienced a terminological shift in the 1990s, and newer terms such as "full-service schools" and "extended schools" are in use in the UK and US (e.g., Dryfoos & Maguire, 2002; Cummings et al., 2011; Dyson, 2011). Also to be found is the term "citizen school" (Apple & Gandin, 2002; discussed in Chapter 9) which has much in common with these ideas but is more clearly grounded in local political activism.

Adult education

I turn now to a classic institutional location for critical pedagogy—adult education. Specialists group together or use interchangeably the terms "adult education, continuing education, extension, nonformal education, popular education and lifelong learning" (Knox, 1993, p. xi), so clearly this is a broad category which covers both areas that are familiar to language teachers as well as some that might not be immediately thought of as areas of action (or employment) for them.

Within this area, adult literacy is a regular and common kind of program, and as previously mentioned, adult literacy programs were the original home of Freirean pedagogy when Freire was the coordinator of adult education projects in Recife, Brazil (cf. e.g., Mackie, 1981a, b) under its socialist mayor, Miguel Arraes. Freirean adult literacy programs continue to be run and are occasionally documented in detail (e.g., Purcell-Gates & Waterman, 2000), and I have already drawn heavily on L2 versions of such programs in discussing key elements of critical pedagogy practice. This is where critical language specialists like Auerbach and Wallerstein, not to mention Morgan, have operated, obviously with much more success and less constraint than critical teachers in many other areas. In urban centers, language education takes place in major institutions such as universities and colleges. But it also thrives in smaller locales: community centers, church basements, staffrooms of hospitals, temporary spaces in malls, and so on. However, back in 1998, Morgan (1998, p. 133) was a little pessimistic that adult education would maintain itself in forms hospitable to critical pedagogy:

> I can't overemphasize the fact that these lessons emerged from a set of social and administrative conditions that encouraged flexibility and autonomy at the classroom level. My concern is that these necessary conditions, and subsequently this kind of teaching, are currently in danger of disappearing. In particular, the kinds of critical approaches I advocate for in this book are vulnerable to political and financial pressures for greater standardization in curricula.

Morgan was right to be concerned. In the UK and the US, adult education has shifted under political pressures (and is increasingly referred to as "lifelong learning"). The changes may be unfavorable to critical pedagogy. As Field (2006, p.55) says, the older forms of adult education

> were movements of collective self-improvement and enlightenment, based broadly around collective identities, and pursuing agendas of social change. ... The new adult education not only takes new forms, it also pursues new purposes. Where the WEA [Workers Education Association] and its equivalents elsewhere saw popular enlightenment as the key to social change, the new adult education allows participants to work actively on their identities and renegotiate their place in a complex world.

Field, in passing, refers to another historically important sector within adult education that might on the face of things be relevant to, or hospitable to, critical pedagogy, namely "labor education" or "worker education"; much of this is associated with organized labor and trades unions. Historically, during the twentieth century labor education was a substantial and strong sector. A good example is the UK Workers Education Association which existed to "create a bridge between the universities ... and the labor movement whose members were increasingly taking on the rights and responsibilities of citizenship" (Field, 2006, p. 54). Even today, it continues to offer ESOL courses to refugees and other immigrants, individuals with needs profiles that would be in many cases consistent with a critical pedagogy.[9] And union-based ESL education is still alive in various locations in the US (Licht et al., 2004; Rosenblum, 1996).

At the same time, it is possible to identify continuing examples of adult ESL literacy programs conducted on Freirean and participatory principles. One of the most visible of these is (or was) the *Reflect ESOL* program, operating in London supported by private foundation grant funds (Cardiff et al., 2007). Though as with many of these initiatives, it is and they are not particularly visible in published literature. One of my points in mentioning them here is to suggest that these admittedly marginal operations do exist and that it would be worthwhile for the interested beginning critical language educator to search them out or correspond with them, as a way of beginning to develop practice in this area.

Informal education

Conceptually next door to adult education lies "informal education." The term is very broad, but one way to understand it is as education that takes place outside of institutional contexts. Thus noted Freirean scholar Mayo (1999) reviews a range of non-school sites for education, such as museums, and considers how they can be used for critical pedagogy. This area has some interesting connections with L2 learning. First of all, the beginnings of SLA as a subdiscipline had strong affinities with informal learning. Early SLA empirical investigations into L2 learning backtracked from the expensive failure of investigations into formal L2 education to produce meaningful results (the methods comparison studies of the 1960s) and shifted to the supposed conceptual core of L2 learning: informal interactions between speakers of one language and another ("NS-NNS" studies)—learning a second language "on the streets" (not to mention in bars and in bed).[10] These interactions were initially supposed to be effective in and of themselves. It was hoped that by studying (some of) these informal learning cases, key features could be imported into formal learning contexts which would thereby be improved.

Jumping forward to the present day, technological advances in video-conferencing have actually made these dyadic, informal "NS-NNS" interactions (I suppose we had better say L1-user/L2-user interactions now) even more widely possible, and may perhaps have enhanced this domain's potential for L2 learning. First, because of international imbalances in resources, middle class students of English in the developed world can easily afford to hire trained teachers of English who reside in, for example, India, whose services are made available through entrepreneurial tutoring organizations connecting teacher and student through the web. Slightly more interesting, some such organizations allow participants to learn a language from a tutor and pay for their lessons that way. Much more in the area of informal learning, however, are internet forums in which person-to-person tutoring arrangements are set up on a purely barter, no-money basis. These arrangements are often language exchanges, or "tandem" language learning, in which partners exchange instruction in one language for instruction in another.[11] As uptake of technological advances continues, accessing and implementation of this possibility in virtual reality (e.g., *Second Life*) will become commonplace. The supporters of such projects have a range of interests: private language schools,[12] The British Council (with a teen-oriented Second Life where teens can practice with other teens on a self-access, not teacher-directed basis), and by contrast the Global Kids Digital Media Initiative[13] "examining subjects such as global inequality, the genocide in Darfur" with input from UNICEF (Stevens, 2006).

As just implied, informal education is not an inherently critical form of education, but critical versions can be developed by having the educational interactions grow out of contacts made through an organization with an appropriate philosophy or values. McMahill and Reekie (1996) report a range of options of this kind under the heading of "feminist language education in practice." These range from peer tutoring in which a Japanese and an English-speaker (both feminists) work on their languages together, to "peer language exchange with a facilitator," to "small language study groups." The second of these they exemplify as occurring in connection with a weekend workshop with a feminist focus taking place in Japan; a workshop or mini-conference with a mixed attendance of foreigners and Japanese; and similarly they refer to a group ("Feminist English for Beijing") that ran in preparation for the Fourth UN World Conference on Women 1995. The third they mention as being one of a number of regular activities organized by a Japanese feminist organization. These might be placed in the wider context of the new adult education given the sudden increase in number of reading groups (a long-established informal learning structure) in developed countries. E. Long's (2003) study of such groups in Texas, mostly with a majority of women, indicates that their members are using them "to pursue their own autonomy and assert their own individual position in the hierarchies that matter to them" (Field, 2006, p. 55).

TASK: SHARE EXPERIENCES AND OPINIONS

Have you ever learned any non-language content through one-on-one tutoring or in an informal learning setting? What were the strong and weak points of this experience? How about second language learning— how would a critical orientation play out in a "tandem learning" context?

Online educational institutions

It hardly needs to be said that all forms of education have been affected by the massive change in knowledge accessibility provided by the web. But is a "virtual school" any more hospitable to a critical pedagogy that a bricks and mortar school? Useful features may simply be operating costs and visibility (less, presumably; cf. Berge & Clark, 2005); that is, it costs much less to start a web-only educational enterprise, and it may be able to avoid unwelcome attention. A second has already been alluded to in Chapter 2, namely that "web 2.0" perspectives expect user-generated content and participatory structures for learning. One more that has been touched on in our literature is the ability to operate across national borders and outside of state administrative structures. SL specialists Cummins and Sayers (1995) identified the work of twentieth century educational pioneer Freinet as an important forerunner for technologically supported innovation towards critical education. Among many other forward thinking pedagogical practices that Freinet and his Modern School Movement promoted, the establishing of school-to-school connections, outside of national control and reflecting teacher-to-teacher and class-to-class contact, is particularly interesting. Cummins and Sayers (1990) are optimistic that the cross-cultural questioning that arises from this kind of international inter-school network is a fertile field for the development of a critical pedagogy.[14]

> We would hypothesize … that when networking projects are implemented within a liberal educational context, they do have *the potential* to act as a catalyst for critical analyses by students of societal issues that may pose a challenge to the status quo. This is because the collaborative input into the "construction zone" cannot be pre-scripted to exclude joint critical inquiry on relevant social issues. However, when implemented from within an explicit critical pedagogy perspective (as was the case with the projects initiated by Freinet), learning networks can play a major role in both student empowerment (particularly of minority students) and societal transformation.
>
> (Ibid., p. 25)

Private language schools, aka "conversation schools"

The private language school sector has always played an important role in the field of language teaching, even if it has often lacked respect because of its use of the less-qualified teacher (cf. Howatt, 1984; Crookes, 2009) and primary pursuit of profit. Perhaps its breadth and diversity is one reason for respect issues, because although at one end we have the highly professional (e.g., the partially government-funded enterprises of the British Council or the old US binational centers), at the other end we have fly-by-night enterprises—mere covers for long-stay tourist visa holders and boutique money-laundering outfits staffed by short-stay backpackers.[15] Given its size and importance I still believe the sector is extremely under-researched, although I there is perhaps more research being done in and on this sector than before (e.g., Duff & Uchida, 1997; Richards, 2008).

In some parts of the private language school sector teachers have quite a large amount of freedom, with the main constraint being keeping the students satisfied.[16] (Administrators of such enterprises are often business people without much orientation to language education, primarily focusing on "the bottom line"; teacher turnover may be high and quality low, in which case a dedicated language teacher may quickly be promoted and be asked to develop curriculum, to lead or train teachers.) Few published studies of *any* sort of curricular initiatives that can emerge from these conditions are likely. However, a report that supports this position is McMahill (2001)—a good example of the sort of thing one might hope for in a critical language teaching entity on the margins. McMahill describes a feminist English class in Japan. "The class termed 'Colors of English' started in 1996 and is organized by a women's counseling service and publishing house called Femix. It is held weekly in a meeting room in a women's center in Tokyo" (p. 312). My interest in this case in the present chapter is not so much the content of the course as the fact that this English class was not (even) in a school, and my question is, 'What was institutionally or resource-wise necessary for it to run?' The answer is, among other things, that there was a women's center, a counseling service, and some source of funds, presumably the publishing company, not to mention the students who were middle-class. In a related report (McMahill & Reekie, 1996), the authors discuss both a small private language school, the "English Conversation Terakoya for the Discussion of Environmental Issues and Feminism," and another which was opened in 1988 by Japanese feminists. Both were quite small (the second is described as having twenty students). Besides their orientations as manifested in curriculum content (avoiding use of commercially available textbooks in favor of "authentic material that deal with issues relevant to women and/or Asians in Japan"), the latter school is different from regular private language schools at least "in that they also offer students counselling on personal problems, and when appropriate, steer them in the direction of women's support groups and hotlines" (p. 24)

I have had personal reports of critical language education on an alternative cruise ship, the *Peace Boat*;[17] one also sees ads for language learning in ecological camps (this tends to be of Spanish, and occasionally indigenous languages). One wonders if these circumstances are so basic that syllabi are at the absolute survival minimum, or whether there is any opportunity for basic critical language pedagogy here. I look forward hopefully to the appearance of published reports.

TASK: SHARE EXPERIENCES AND OPINIONS

Readers: Any comments on the private language sector? In the absence of published reports, your anecdotal input on things critical there would be most welcome!

Advocacy

A teacher who is beginning to explore critical language pedagogy is likely to also need to do some "advocacy" for his or her program (cf. Morgan, 1998)—that is, teachers themselves should have an action orientation. A small literature in our field (e.g., Forhan & Scheraga, 2000) encourages and supports L2 teachers as advocates for our programs and for critical perspectives in the profession, and Morgan (2009) discusses how this goal is to be tackled in L2 teacher education. If you think your courses or program are important and valuable then clearly you must not only develop them but also argue for their importance. You need to let others know about them (publicity and recruitment); if you want materials for the courses and there aren't sufficient but could be purchased, presumably you need to think about resources. Extra funds might help improve your salary or preserve your job, too.

So at this point, willy-nilly, you are in the area of fundraising, for which advocacy (which means "raising one's voice") is needed. Yet of course this is not something that most of us were "trained" in; it is not part of ordinary professional education in language teaching. If we are very lucky we may get apprenticed into it. Otherwise we need some basic pointers and some self-help guides, which is what I am going to try to sketch here.

Accounts of advocacy theory and practice in our field have been scarce but are increasing in number. McGroarty (1998) was a path-breaking review and analysis of some aspects of this matter (see also Auerbach, 1996, 2002). Dubetz and de Jong's recent (2011) thorough review of thirty teacher advocacy studies in bilingual education in the US finds (discouragingly) that much of this advocacy is individualistic and confined to the classroom. The work of Anyon (discussed in the next chapter) provides context for social organizing, and also provides some guides to what is needed in advocacy.[18] Based on the above and other work, I move now to present a simple set of headings that represent matters that need to be addressed by practitioners in this area. Before I discuss them, a caveat is in order. The base assumptions here apply primarily to social, cultural, and institutional contexts which are, for want of a better word, "democratic." Yet at the same time, even in less democratic contexts, networking and making a case for an innovative language teaching program is still important and possible within internal, non-public settings.

In Crookes and Talmy (2004), partly as a result of reviewing what wasn't working during an effort by Hawai'i ESL teachers to pressure their legislators for funds, we arrived at some basic ideas concerning individual (critical) teacher capabilities, that would be needed in support of any non-mainstream programs located in democratic environments. Critical language teachers should be able to do the following.

1 Organize (develop institutional networks, develop connections with parents, develop networks in the community; and this generally implies recruitment, as well).
2 Address leadership (but try to see that all are leaders, if provided with the right orientation and skills).
3 Fundraise: there's a literature on fundraising in mainstream education targeting the post-secondary level, but little guidance for the rest of us, with possibly the sole example in our L2 literature being Brady (2008).
4 Engage in action: the old labor slogan "direct action gets the goods" is relevant because in some places conventional politicking will not result in the desired outcomes.[19]

Besides these matters, crucially, shifts in perspective and self-image are needed. Teachers might feel that they are not comfortable or even shouldn't do this sort of thing or shouldn't involve students in their struggles. But some case studies make it clear that these actions, to which citizens are entitled in a democracy, are also part of what critical language teachers may need to engage in (e.g., Ferguson, 1998).[20] It is important for critical practice in our field that teacher education, teacher re-education, and teacher in-service programs place greater attention on these areas as well.

Organizing

Organizing can be understood in various ways, but basically it is a term of practical politics, and refers to means and systems for getting people to act together in support of a cause. Within it, networking is an important element. In our literature, past TESOL President Mary Ashworth drew on her activist roots to provide guidance to TESOLers trying to act on the development of language policy. Within that context, on networking, she had the following to say (Ashworth, 1985, p. 105).

> Networking is an old phenomenon which, as result of the breakdown of some of the established hierarchical administrative structures coupled with the information explosion, has recently gained strength. It is an attempt to solve the problem of how people can exchange information and share ideas

with those they trust ... Networks ... move horizontally. Colleagues in the network system trust each other and look to each other for support rather than to a supervisor. Networks link individuals to individuals, individuals to organizations, and organizations to organizations. The process involves the decentralization of information by providing horizontal access to it.

Two individuals or two organizations can set up a network which they can expand quickly or slowly according to their resources. Networks should guard against becoming too large too quickly: first, because funding the newsletter (or whatever means of information dissemination is used) can become a problem and, second because members of a large organization often feel out of touch, something networking was supposed to cure not cause.

A network should be initiated for a particular purpose, that is, there should be one common denominator which binds all the members together. ... Networks are not self-sustaining. They have to be well organized if they are to succeed. Someone or some group must prepare the newsletter, call meetings, register new members, keep the accounts and plan ahead. Networks should not be seen as permanent structures.

Networking at a very basic level is certainly a practice conducted assiduously by Cowhey (2006), again showing the benefit of a community activist background. She reports:

About two weeks before school starts (as soon as I can get a class list), I send a letter to all of my students' families. I introduce myself and say I would like to meet them, listing the days I will be making home visits. I give them my e-mail address and phone number so that they can contact me if they'd like to schedule an appointment. Some people call and ask to schedule a different time if they will be on vacation then. ... One way or another, I connect with most students and their families before the first day. ... I always ask families about their work and their schedules and what skills they might like to share with us as I invite them to volunteer and visit our class. [p. 68] ... If I do this family and friend work well, I am able to draw on these resources for years to come [p. 70].

I will just mention two other sources that have productively highlighted networking and the network metaphor. Miettinen (1990, cited in Engeström 1991, p. 255) refers to the formation of networks of learning that transcend the institutional boundaries of the school. He describes an advanced network of learning as follows.

It includes educational researchers, researchers of certain fields of science, practitioners, teachers, parents, and pupils. There are several examples of this kind of collaboration. A project called *Art and Built Environment* was carried out in England between 1976 and 1982. In this project, the network consisted of architects, community planners, teachers, and pupils. The idea of the project was to study the surroundings of the school and to give pupils models and instruments to influence their surroundings.

(Miettinen, 1990, p. 24)

Moll and Greenberg (1990) provide a more recent example of such a network in the making. They were working with parents, teachers, and students in a Hispanic community of Tucson, Arizona, looking for new ways of literacy instruction that draw upon knowledge and skills found in local households.

> We build on the idea that every household is, in a very real sense, an educational setting in which the major function is to transmit knowledge that enhances the survival of its dependents … In order to examine the instructional potential of these household activities, we have created an after-school 'lab' within which researchers, teachers, and students meet to experiment with the teaching of literacy. We think of the lab setting, following Vygotsky, as a "mediating" structure that facilitates strategic connections, multiple paths, between classrooms and households.

The theoretical point made by Moll and Greenberg, that the lab setting is a mediating structure, is also a practical one. The resourceful activist teacher needs to consider what entity might be needed (besides the teacher her/himself) to hold together the various elements of the network. A lab, a foundation, some physical or web-based space, might be needed besides the teacher's own classroom, to provide also a fundraising target and an entity that would provide further profile and dignity to the enterprise.

TASK: REFLECT; PLAN

One simple strategy for moving in a critical direction is to establish an informal add-on to an existing class, outside of regular hours. It does obviously involve some volunteer time. In Japan, advanced English classes sometimes occur in "English Speaking Societies," after-school clubs which have English as their focus. Duncan-Andrade and Morrell's work on critical pedagogy in inner city US urban schools reminds us of the importance of co-curricular activities for establishing alternative patterns of student-teacher interaction as the basis for education that really meets the critical needs of marginalized groups of students. So, is there anything in your context that would fit into this "lab" category, as Moll and Greenberg call it?

Leadership

Probably the first place to start here is with yourself. Leadership should be seen, not as a feature of a charismatic individual, but as a set of skills that all can have, or processes all can share in.[21] Can you identify priorities, make a plan, hold a meeting, assign responsibilities to participants, and follow up? Can you work on the social dimensions, build rapport, foster unity and a sense of fellowship (or if not, can you enlist someone who can)? But after that, can you provide a simple workshop in which the idea that everyone has so-called leadership capabilities is pushed? And can you recruit a specialist to tell you all how to talk to the press/ media? What Crookes and Talmy (2004) reported was that when local funding for an ESL program was cut, although teachers were willing to demonstrate on the street, they had no training and no confidence in engaging with the media, and little or no experience of approaching their political representatives. The time for developing these and associated skills is not at the moment of a crisis, but well before that!

Fundraising

This is important. Even if your program, or the critical components of it, are ensconced within a mainstream educational organization, such as a state-funded university, it is quite likely to have financial or resource needs that cannot be provided by regular funding. All state educational institutions are under pressure in the present era. The more visibility your program has, if it is also a challenge to the status quo, the less likely it is to be supported or supportable by higher levels of administration. So it is highly desirable to develop outside sources of support.

A first point to note (from Schneiter & Nelson, 1982) is that a common mistake is to confine the responsibility for fundraising to an administrator. Ideally, all participants in a program should be aware of the need to raise funds and prepared (and trained) to do so, or to participate in fundraising activities.

Relationships are crucial. Sources of support may be grass-roots level individuals, grassroots organizations, NGOs, social service delivery agencies, a teachers' union, a publisher, a foundation, or a wealthy private individual, to name a few categories and types. Regardless of the source, fundraising specialists and the fundraising literature make it clear that developing and maintaining relationships with these groups or individuals is crucial. For that, your own program needs to have a clear mission that can be simply and easily articulated. It needs to have appropriate fliers and publicity materials. And it needs to engage in asking for money, on a systematic and regular basis, in turn based on the development and maintenance of relationships. Of course, language teachers in general are not familiar with the relevant literature; post-secondary education is different from the rest of the field in having specialists working in this area (which they may term "development" or "program advancement") and has a greater range of published sources (e.g., Rhodes 1997); some state high and elementary schools in the US would approach the matter within the context of community organizing (e.g., Shirley, 1997). Almost the only source that discusses fundraising in the context of language teaching programs is the highly useful chapter by Brady (2008). Country and local conditions undoubtedly vary enormously so perhaps this is a case where a critical language teacher should simply seek out a specialist in this area associated with the home institution (that can be trusted); or find a critically supportive fundraiser and consult them. The main point here is to recognize this as an area of importance, one that we are unlikely to have been oriented to in our professional training otherwise, and take preliminary steps to explore it.

Engage in action

Action can be simple and not particularly visible, and it can be consistent with culturally appropriate ways of persuading power-holders. If this means showing up at a party held by the candidate for mayor or town councilor, and many petitioners do it, you should too, preferably with a few of your deserving students in hand. And you must be prepared to answer the question, If I do this for you, what will you do for me? I believe you must be prepared to get your hands dirty if you engage with the political process. Remember, a definition of politics is it's about who gets what, how much, when and where (Lasswell, 1936).

What about other forms of action? Engage in visible action with extreme care. But under some circumstances, as Ferguson's report makes clear, it can be productive. In some countries and cultures, it may be a legitimate part of political engagement. In some countries we can say explicitly that it is not. But where it is, even if students and teachers aren't accustomed to doing it, other people do and they benefit, so why not you.

At the same time, we must not be foolhardy. Above all, it seems clear that horizontal networks of support and power must be engaged first, and lines of communication to publicity and sympathetic media are essential if there is to be any payoff to visible forms of non-violent protest.

Critical administration/administration for social justice

Language teachers engaging with critical pedagogy who are not in the initial phase of their career may wish to think beyond the classroom, about the administrative implications of this work. Because such experienced teachers have, we may hope, with their experience achieved some success (perhaps tenure, their own networks of support, or at least "deviance credits"[22]), so they may have slightly greater freedom of action and can legitimately turn their attention to oversight of other practitioners (and students). If they have some administrative responsibilities they should ask what the critical implications of these are. Beginning teachers should recognize that their career is unlikely to keep them in the classroom, alone, forever. Good language teachers often end up being administrators (of some sort). They should be apprised now of options that exist for a critical orientation in the later phases of their career.

Young professionals in our field are generally trained only to be employees (whether as teachers or researchers). However, we are seeing the rise of programs that also educate our people to be administrators.[23] These courses mainly draw on mainstream practices (e.g., the running of private language schools: White et al., 2008) and mainstream literature (the managerial tradition of educational administration: Christison & Murray, 2009). Recent developments in the private language school literature are highly corporate (more so than in the past) and orient to a mindset that seems unlikely to be complementary to a critical perspective. But certainly, critical pedagogies within applied linguistics do need individuals who can set up, run, maintain, prevent from being shut down, the operations which can sustain the courses we would like to see happen. Our (critical) program administrators will need not only to schedule courses, hire teachers and recruit students; they will also need to network and fundraise. They may not be able to inherit or become part of a pre-existing conventional operation and might have to consider starting a new one. They may have to engage both more fully and sometimes more oppositionally, with existing political and administrative systems.

Despite educational administrators' usual commitment to hierarchies of power,[24] there actually is a line of work in the academic study of educational administration that is sensitive to critical conceptions of society. Initially this was a very small body of work associated with the conceptual analyses of Foster and of Bates (Crookes, 2003b; discussed later). These authors pointed out the inadequacies, theoretical and empirical, of the existing positivist technicist research on educational administration; they pointed to the impossibility of finding administrative techniques that would be effective in a society that was uniformly conflict-ridden and inequitable. And they provided conceptual guidance concerning what might be possible and legitimate for the critical educational administrator; however, they did so in a data-free manner.[25] Encouragingly, in the last decade or so the number of scholars pursuing critically informed perspectives on program administration has grown; the area has shifted its main descriptor from "critical educational administration" to "educational administration (or leadership) for social justice" (Marshall & Oliva, 2006); and there is some empirical work. Overall this is not a well-developed area, and I will depend almost exclusively on US literature and the handful of empirical studies concern principals in US state schools (not language programs, etc., unfortunately) though there is more now than there was even ten years ago.

Critical pedagogues Kanpol et al. (1997) draw implications from the critical pedagogical literature to end up with some advice for sympathetic principals. They suggest that principals focus on developing the "voice" of their students and teachers (that is, the ability of these people to be heard and make a difference); recognize and empathize with "the Other" in their schools (other cultures and values); and finally recognize similarities within difference to nurture citizenship and democracy. And they lay out some common school administrative problems and how these would be addressed, both traditionally and by administrators with a critical perspective. However, they note, "there has been sparse literature directed to principals regarding the role they may play in challenging forms of oppression, alienation, and subordination" (p. 79).[26] Kanpol also comments: "[W]hen we do have some administrators in my graduate foundations courses, we are often met with disdain and/or a numbing coldness, as if critical pedagogy is cancerous" (p. 79). Writing some time ago Marshall (1997, p. 142) claimed of the US that "we know that white males with a bureaucratic maintenance orientation have dominated the ranks of school administration." And Kempner (1991) referred to an earlier interview-based study of 144 Oregon educational administrators to make the following scathing observations:

> [M]ost administrators either lack a level of awareness or do not possess the socialization and language to communicate a democratic vision for their leadership or a philosophy for the schools. Rather than value those administrators who are critically aware of themselves and society, the dominant ideology of administration favors and selects those who subscribe to a rationalistic approach that assumes a science of administration. …The perspective is one of organizational manipulation, not individual empowerment. … It is apparent that women, minorities, and others who do not share the physical, social and cultural attributes of those who currently predominate in educational administration do not find easy access … How individuals are systematically excluded from administration and who is prevented from entering are certainly questions needing further research. From a critical perspective, however, any training programs that simply perpetuate the existing inequalities of who is allowed to lead the schools are unacceptable.
>
> (p. 120)

Given the increased pressures for control that have become apparent in the school systems of most countries, it seems likely that much of Kempner's analysis may still be relevant.

Associated with evidence of the exclusion of those who do not share dominant physical and socio-cultural attributes from the ranks of educational administrators are, I believe, the effects of a disdain of administration and administrators on the part of those involved in critiques of the system. Power, particularly that which appears to accrue to individuals in positions of authority in systems of questionable moral integrity, like schools under critical attack, is seen as undesirable to some critical teachers; administrators in such systems are seen as inherently corrupt. Indeed, the libertarian tradition on the left distrusts "leaders" so much that it goes to great lengths to set up governance systems that will enable, for example, instant recall of delegates, union leaders, and so on. This, coupled with a very low visibility of argument about critical educational administrative structures and practices, may discourage teachers with a transformative orientation from entering the administrative ranks. Finally, in academia, administrative positions are felt to kill off academic careers; in elementary and secondary education, not to mention proprietary institutions (i.e. private language schools) they are positions of high stress and long hours.

Literature relevant to this topic had an early phase in which it went by the heading "critical" and was the province of just a handful of specialists, notably Foster. It subsequently appears to have dropped "critical" in favor of "social justice" (see following sub-section). The early analyses of Foster (esp. 1986; 1989, 1991a, b, 1999; Smyth, 1989) denied that management science can identify universal laws of administrative or managerial behavior. Foster also recognized the darker side of administration. "Educational administration has taken as its goal the structuration and control of institutional life, which forms the autonomous individual but which has formed such individuals within wider structures of domination and inequality" (1999, p. 111). He called on critical educational administrators to see themselves as "an oppositional tendency within structures of control," which he would call "postadministration" (ibid.).

He rejected a conception of "the social life that can be reduced to the cognitions of individual actors" (1991b, p. 114) and accordingly his analysis directs the critical administrator to support the development of meaningful communities that can support practice, and then asks us to understand professionalism in terms of the moral and ethical aspects of our practice.

He remarks that we should "rethink [our] mission in terms of establishing community rather than in terms of individualistic decision-making, for it is really within the community that social problems are addressed" (1991b, p. 120). The critical educational administrator should have a "theory of transformative action" (Fay, 1987), which "involves the critique of current structures" and asks "what particular strategies, viewpoint, and perspectives are important to achieving the kind of social reality which lends itself to more equitable relationships within communities" (p. 122).[27]

For present purposes, Foster's emphasis on the administrator's responsibility for developing critical communities of practice (1991b) is the key point. In this sense, the educational administrator is one who persuades, leads, and above all educates, rather than merely acts as a bureaucrat or timekeeper. This is also Freire's position: "In reality, we cannot even think about gaining teachers' compliance with, for example, a model of teacher/student relationships that is more open, more scientific, and also riskier by imposing our point of view on them. We need, above all, to convince, almost convert" (Freire, 1993, p. 39). Foster's point here is that educational administration must be educative or it becomes only administration and loses its roots, thereby, in school as an educational institution. And leadership here means broad consciousness raising. What should be aimed for in educational administrators are individuals who have a reflective consciousness about their work, as well as a critical and emancipatory conception of it. And what they should aim for is a particular kind of community.

In Foster's last publication he cites Haber (1994, p. 108, in Foster, 1999, p. 111) on the importance of a community of practice which has a critical orientation:

> Since the subject is an effect of multiple community formation, alternative subjects can only be formulated within the discourses of alternative communities. This is to claim that there are no individuals, in the traditional sense and that the traditional autonomous subject must be replaced by the concept of subjects-in-community.

(Here, incidentally, we see the earlier socio-cognitive forms transposed into a discoursal mode reminiscent of Foucauldian analyses.) How is this goal to be achieved? Gradually, undoubtedly. Paulo Freire, when he was an administrator, remarked, "Everything that can possibly be done ... to introduce democratic change in the school structure must be done. There must be, for example, permanent development of educators, without ideological manipulation, but with political clarity, making clear the progressive orientation of the administration." He also referred to "other changes" which are very much part of the alternative education tradition that has resurfaced under the heading of school-community based management: "curriculum reformulation, community participation in school life, parents' associations, school councils, etc." (1993, p. 49). These things exist, have been worked for, in many places. They are not always developed with a fully critical understanding, perhaps.

Speaking to the critical teacher, Foster concludes that "pockets of resistance are both available and viable," but that "the project ... is not the final and ultimate victory over forces of coercion and domination ... In a postmodern world, power and domination will always exist, and pure emancipation is, perhaps, deceptive, but we do what we can" (1999, p. 110). Or, to use an old slogan from a different domain, "politics is the art of the possible." The recognition that school staffs are usually not unitary in perspective and that schools themselves are usually contested sites is realistic and welcome.

More recent work includes valuable empirical studies such as Theoharis (2007) on principals oriented to social justice, as well as the work of Marshall (e.g., 1997, Marshall & Oliva 2006) on introducing a social justice agenda into US educational administration programs (which are the places where principals get their credentialing). Some of the things critical educational administrators can do, according to Brooks and Miles (2008, p. 107) are as follows:

> [O]ptions available to leaders seeking to enact social justice include introducing and supporting democratic and ethical organizational processes, reforming, aligning, and expanding curricula to better meet the needs of a particular population, promoting understanding of multiculturalistic pluralism, practicing difference-sensitive instructional leadership ... Contemporary leaders have a variety of tools and techniques at their disposal that can help them identify social injustice in schools. For example, school leaders can:
>
> 1. Conduct equity audits using aggregate or disaggregated student achievement data ...;
> 2. Examine allocation of instructional and curricular resources among school personnel and programs to determine if traditionally disadvantaged populations are receiving equitable disbursement of goods and services ...;
> 3. Form meaningful and vibrant communications networks that include and validate the perspectives of students, families, and community members in addition to educational professionals who serve the school ...
>
> Leaders who develop this perspective and adopt a social justice stance have been characterized as:
>
> 1. Transformational public intellectuals ...
> 2. Bridge people, who are "committed to creating a bridge between themselves and others, for the purposes of improving the lives of all those with whom they work" (Merchant & Shoho, 2006, p. 86).
> 3. Critical activists, who will deconstruct political, social, and economic inequity and organize school and community resources toward the central aim of providing opportunity for traditionally underrepresented and oppressed peoples ...
>
> Still, numerous resources, innovative options, and outstanding individuals do not guarantee that processes will be implemented faithfully or that educational outcomes will necessarily improve.

In closing

So that we don't get carried away, in conclusion let me refer again to Theoharis's (2007) interview-based analysis of seven social justice-oriented US principals.

They report enormously long work hours, high stress caused by resistance to their efforts, and ever-increasing pressure from the state usually against rather than in favor of their efforts. As ever, the practicalities of swimming against the mainstream are challenging. In non-L2 administrative areas we do now have the advantage of both theoretical analyses and empirically grounded advice, however, as well as solid critiques of the dominant discourses in educational administration and management (the only ones available in the L2 literature). Let us remember that in a hierarchically organized enterprise like most institutional forms of education, critical pedagogy needs people outside the classroom as well as inside. It's a dirty job, but someone has to do it (critically).

Questions for discussion

1 What skills and dispositions do you think are needed to engage in administrative aspects of (language) teaching? What additional skills or extra emphases are necessary in the critical area of administration? If possible, talk to a sympathetic educational administrator and ask them what are the tasks they spend most of their time on. Ask if they are able to manifest their values in some ways through this aspect of their work. Ask, too, about the extent to which their work is rational and logical, as opposed to emergency-driven.

2 Overall, are you at a point in your professional development where you have already taken on some of the responsibilities addressed in this chapter, or not? Do you shrink from the possibility, or do you address it with some enthusiasm? What additional experiences or support would be valuable for you in this area?

3 Have you ever engaged in mentoring, or been mentored? Supposing you were going to take on organizational responsibilities, is there anyone in your vicinity you could shadow, or go to for advice? How would you begin to locate such resources?

Notes

1 This wasn't always the case; at the time of Proudhon, anarchist educators in France thought that they could reform the state sector from within using syndicalist methods—that is, depending on the strength of organized labor (M. P. Smith, 1983).

2 "I personally prefer to work with the social, popular movements in the periphery of the cities, instead of working in schools" (Shor & Freire, 1987, p. 38). Interviewed in 1970, Freire commented: "Look, I think that Ivan Illich is absolutely right when he describes the schools ... as instruments of social control. Really, schools themselves are domesticating institutions" (Davis, 1981, p. 66). His institutional location for his main Brazilian literacy programs was a provincial university extension program, prior to getting national government backing. "The Cultural Extension Service

(SEC) of what was then called the University of Recife was born of a dream of [the university] president and mine … We talked about the possibility of breaking through the university's walls and extending its presence into nonacademic areas among such schooled populations as pre-college students and public school teachers; and extending it to potential clients in popular areas—for example, offering educational program with union leaders or (why not?) facing challenges like literacy" (Freire, 1996, p. 13).

3 For a recent review of the institutional inability of school to fulfill even basic liberal democratic aspirations, see Schrag (2006).

4 Though in her first years as a teacher she had many hostile colleagues; and she says: "There's something to be said for staying, for quietly doing what you do, however strange it may seem to skeptical colleagues" (Cowhey, 2006, p. 217)

5 Cowhey is aware of the differences:

"Still, when I visit schools in other countries, I am struck by the number of resources we take for granted. I visited a rural senior primary school (grades 4–7) in Kwa-Zulu Natal, South Africa, similar in size to my school. There was no electrical power, no running water, and no phone line. There were no computers or copy machines. There were some old textbooks and a small cabinet of science materials. There was no library."

6 In countries where a common school tradition has been strong … as opposed, say, to Germany and the UK.

7 A confusing usage. These are state schools, and different from institutions like Summerhill.

8 See also http://www.infed.org/schooling/b-comsch.htm

9 http://www.wea.org.uk/news/esolearlydaymotion.aspx

10 References suppressed to protect early SLA researchers.

11 See http://schoolofeverything.com/

12 E.g., *Avatar Languages,* http://www.avatarlanguages.com

13 Financial support from the MacArthur Foundation.

14 "When attention is centered on the making of mutual meanings and the gradual taking of new perspectives by specific classes engaged in concrete joint projects, teachers can propose, test, reject, and refine hypotheses on a range of research questions concerning each of the cultures involved. In so doing, teacher-researchers can make valuable contributions to the elaboration of a critical pedagogical theory of cross-cultural inquiry" (Cummins & Sayers, 1990, p. 22).

15 I would like to take this opportunity to thank these entities, my past employers when I was actually capable of shouldering a backpack.

16 This was my own experience thirty years ago; my current students confirm this is still the case.

17 http://kyotopeaceevents.blogspot.com/2011/01/opportunities-for-students-to-travel.html

18 See also the recent special issue of *Educational Policy, 23*(1), 2009.

19 Popularized by the anarcho-syndicalist trades union, the Industrial Workers of the World.

20 A comparable and more recent case is the public demonstrations by ESOL students in London against funding cuts for ESL programs. These students had participated in Freirean and participatory L2 classes. http://www.youtube.com/watch?v=ZWBvNhNHww0; <reflect-action.org/reflecttesol>

21 This old idea, originally stemming from a political commitment to egalitarian participation, is now the cutting edge position in cognitive studies of leadership (cf. Lakomski, 2005; Hartley, 2007).

22 Shor and Friere (1987, p. 66): "If you take part in a variety of small tasks, you begin slowly to root yourself in the life of the institution. The recognition you get for doing this is like an account of credits that allows you more room to deviate."

23 Most obviously, the International Diploma in Language Teaching Management (IDLTM) < http://www.idltm.com>

24 These days often referred to as entrepreneurial governance or The New Public Management (Boston et al., 1996; Fusarelli & Johnson, 2004).

25 Having reviewed the literature on critical approaches to education from an organization standpoint, Earle & Kruse (1999, p. 170) commented that this work "tend[s] to focus on broader societal patterns ... and tend[s] to have underdeveloped discussions of the detailed particularities that constitute school organizational processes. ... Although some critical education scholars have focused on school organizations as the primary unit of analysis ... these efforts have not been built on and expanded nearly to the extent that they might be. New critical work has been done in looking at business organizations ... but little has been done recently regarding schools."

26 They do not cite any such literature, though one obvious source would be the one work in which Paulo Freire himself talks about his administrative experience as a superintendent of schools for the city of Sao Paulo (Freire, 1993).

27 And if it comes to the matter of key aspects of a community, Wenger's (1998) three definitional terms—joint enterprise, mutual engagement, and shared repertoire—suggest useful subgoals.

8

CONCERNS AND OUTCOMES

What is to be done?

The "imposition" question

When language teachers (researchers, academics, applied linguists, etc.) put our professional skills into practice, we are engaged in a moral enterprise. We can help, or harm, our students (and society). Language professionals with a critical orientation undoubtedly believe that their work has significant individual and social implications; many adopt or acquire a critical orientation because of their ethical analysis of society or societies, and intend their professional action to improve society. So values-based or ethical analyses of our practice are crucial to its actual applicability and relevance.

In the case of critical, radical, alternative, and emancipatory pedagogies (of language and of any other content area), there is a longstanding ethical issue that needs to be considered. For me, it often comes up when I speak to audiences who aren't familiar with the general critical enterprise. Regularly, at the end of my talk, someone will ask if teachers are *entitled* to do whatever it is the inquirer thinks we are doing in critical language teaching. Sometimes this is an honest, open question; on other occasions the inquirer's implication is actually that we are not so entitled, and s/he is likely to use the word "imposition" in making such an assertion. Teachers new to critical pedagogy may also pose a similar question: "Are we perhaps imposing our views on our students?" they wonder. And obviously the choice of the word "imposing" goes hand in hand with a sense that such a thing would be wrong—i.e., unethical. This is a very important question, one that is posed by beginners in this field and also by their potential opponents, so it is equally important that we have answers to it.

Discussion of this matter has been engaged in by curriculum specialists and educational philosophers, going back well before the term critical pedagogy came into use. The discussion has often used a term stronger than imposition: "indoctrinate." Under this heading the topic was addressed in the US during the 1930s in connection with reconstructionist views on the social studies curriculum (Watras, 2003). The topic continued to be of interest in the period just after World War II because by the 1940s the term "indoctrination" had become related to the use of education in totalitarian regimes; not only the ones that had just been overthrown, associated with the Nazi movement, or fascism in general, but also those prominent at the time associated with totalitarian state socialism.

A fairly comprehensive review which dates from just after that period is Nagai ([1952]/1976). Nagai was a Japanese scholar who completed doctoral studies in the US in the immediate post-war period. His research was stimulated by the many cases of indoctrination that had taken place in various sites during World War II; in addition, during his doctoral studies in the US he encountered idealizations of the US presented by his professors and also the beginnings of the McCarthy era which "eventually had important bearings on public school education through the country" (Nagai, 1976, p. vi). His exposition begins by recognizing three senses of the word "indoctrinate." In religious education, the older sense of the word "indoctrinate," as in the passing on or teaching of "doctrine," was still understood in a positive or legitimate sense. Possibly extending from this sense, at that time (but probably not now), there was a sense in which to indoctrinate was taken as synonymous with instruction; in this sense it does not have any derogatory implications. Then, on the other hand, there was the meaning by which indoctrination is used derogatorily related to the expression of a "partisan point of view." As Nagai summarizes, a debate had taken place in the US in the 1930s between the reconstructionists and the progressivists. For the former, Counts (1932, p. 6), claimed that "All education contains a large element of imposition ... [and] the existence and evolution of society depend upon it." By implication, since society was in the grip of the Great Depression at that time, it was legitimate to explicitly teach certain matters—we might call them doctrines—that would be likely to cause a general improvement of society that would bring it back from the brink of destruction that it faced. Anticipating a standard Freirean position, Counts argued that it was not possible to be neutral in education. Even apparently neutral positions merely articulated and promoted the status quo in society. As Nagai points out, Counts was by no means the only person to advocate along these lines. The title of one other example is indicative: *Indoctrination for American democracy* (Pittenger, 1941). Against Counts, however, Dewey weighed in for the progressive movement in a carefully balanced formulation: "Instead of recommending an imposed indoctrination, we are striving to challenge all the indoctrination of conscious dogma and of the unconscious bias of tradition and vested interest which already exist" (Kilpatrick et al., 1933, p. 72[1]). To me, this sounds like an attempt to cast aspersions on both left and right. Dewey's progressive colleague Kilpatrick nevertheless agreed with Counts and condemned neutrality as an abdication of responsibility, and though Dewey argued that primarily they were seeking to promote intelligence among individuals "to take part in the management of conditions under which they will live" (p. 71), at the same time "we frankly accept the democratic tradition in its moral and human import" (p. 72) which presumably accepts some transmitting of democratic values.

A formulation that seems close to how the matter has subsequently been taken up by criticalists is that advocated by one of the last reconstructionists. Brameld (who was actively publishing well into the 1970s, by which time society had actually caught up with his views) produced the term "defensible partiality" (1950, p. 87). Here, the word "partiality" is a recognition that any viewpoint must be partial, meaning both incomplete and tending to favor a particular stance (as in, "I am partial to ice-cream"); and "defensible" alludes to the point that ideas must stand up against "open, unrestricted criticism and comparison." After criticism, a person can still have a partiality to a particular view, clearly. Thus as Nagai says, "What determines whether teaching becomes indoctrination is not so much the points of view a teacher wants to stress as the ways in which he expresses his views" (1976, p. 12).

The area was surveyed yet again during the 1960s by educational philosophers using the techniques of analytic philosophy, with its probing of what "we" really mean when we[2] use a term like "teach" (or "indoctrinate") to explore the topic (Snook, 1972a, b). The intention of the teacher is taken to be crucial by Snook, and a criterion of inquiry (similar to Brameld's analysis) is advocated. This is a topic that reappears in the literature of philosophy of education over and over again.[3] Critical pedagogy specialists do not seem to cite these arguments, but write in a way consistent with them, based on their own experience. Criticalists, too, tend to say that so long as the chance is given to answer back, we are fairly safe from the charge of imposition. One of the more extended treatments of what this answering back might take, which itself further defends against the charge of indoctrination, is provided by Shor (1992). Here he first divides syllabus content into three categories: "generative themes," which "make up the primary subject matter ... [and] grow out of student culture and express problematic conditions in daily life"; second, "topical themes ... [such as] a social question of key importance locally [etc] ... raised in class by the teacher." And third, "academic themes ... material brought to the discussion by the teacher [with] ... roots in formal bodies of knowledge" (p. 55). Then he goes on to make needed space: "Critical teachers are willing to take the risk of introducing topical themes because student conversation and thought often do not include important issues in society." He nevertheless identifies the risk that this may change:

democratic relations into unilateral authority, replacing mutual inquiry with one-way teacher-talk [p. 56]. ... A topical theme, to be critical and democratic, cannot be an isolated exercise or unchallenged lecture by the teacher. ... The topical theme is part of a syllabus students can reject or amend as they exercise their democratic rights ... Critical teachers offer students a topical thematic choice which they can accept or reject.

Clearly Shor is implying that the ethically correct position is to be professional, critical and democratic. First of all, as a trained teacher (or in this case a professor), the instructor has a legitimate right to express and present a theoretical position on the content of curriculum, the material that is formally to be taught. In addition, a teacher is also a citizen:

Introducing a topical theme is a teacher's professional and moral right as long as it is appropriate for the subject matter of the class and for the age and level of the students, situated inside a participatory process, and not framed as a sermon or a harangue. A teacher has [this] right ... because she or he is a thinking citizen, a professional educator, and a moral human being with freedom of speech to present important issues to others.

(Ibid., p. 56)

On the matter of balance, Shor (like others, especially feminists) says that because various important issues or perspectives are underrepresented in mainstream syllabuses or the media, "it is the critical teacher's special responsibility to present them." Most rational people would surely agree that it is bad for "democracies" if the citizens being prepared in educational institutions never have the opportunity to consider global and local problems in connection with their role as citizens in a democracy, and all that follows from that.

Shor reports cautiously on an occasion when he introduced into one of his classes an anti-individualist "topical theme" as an adjunct to one generative theme (personal growth); he states that he was unable to convince the students that his position on the matter was correct and so dropped the topic. He states:

Students cannot be thought of as a captive audience. If they don't want to discuss a topical theme, they must not be forced to do so. Forced discussion is wholly contradictory to critical-democratic education; it is just another version of the authoritarianism of the traditional school system. No ideals justify indoctrinating students. Their right of refusal must be equal to the teacher's right of presentation. That is what it means for authority to be democratic and mutual instead of authoritarian and unilateral.

(Ibid., p. 57)

He concludes by saying:

> I want to mention that the democratic side of a critical pedagogy means not ignoring, silencing, or punishing unhappy students but rather inviting them to make their criticisms public for deliberation.
>
> (Ibid., p. 57)

For second language specialists, the most substantial treatment of this topic is that of Benesch (2001, pp. 67–85). In this discussion, Benesch reviews a critique (Santos, 2001) of an earlier report she produced on balancing a psychology curriculum that ignored women with an assignment (by her) of the topic of anorexia for a three-week part of a semester-long course. Writing specialist Santos questioned this, partly on the grounds that composition teachers should no longer "assign" topics as if they were the only person who knows what must be studied, and also because she identified the topic of anorexia as conforming to Benesch's "socio/political consciousness raising."

Benesch's detailed analysis of the issues includes several key points. One is that the whole discussion ignores any "notion of student agency and resistance balancing teacher authority" (p. 70). Those charging teachers with imposition seem to assume that "students are susceptible to the unquestioning absorption of critical teachers' political agendas, not possibly active participants in dialogic teacher-student relationships. The coexistence of power and resistance in those relationships is not recognized" (ibid.).[4]

Also, in terms of practical pedagogical techniques, Benesch asked the students to maintain a journal and submit entries to her (of course, a standard technique in an EAP class with a writing or content learning focus) and in them, several students who were not sympathetic to the topic of anorexia expressed their resistance to the topic (as well as, on occasion, in class). Benesch suggests that this shows the students' willingness to engage in dialogue and indeed express resistance, rather than passively absorb what was "impositionally" taught, or silently resist a "monological" curriculum. It hardly needs to be said that joint student and teacher participation in the construction of curriculum is characteristic of critical pedagogy. Benesch concludes by saying:

> The most effective way to engage students might be to try a mix of teacher and student choice with whole-class selection of a theme as a third alternative. Each possibility has its benefits:
> 1. teacher-generated themes allow students to fulfill externally imposed requirements, an essential component of an EAP class whose students are in or will be in content classes where no choice is offered;
> 2. individual student choice allows for a wider selection of research areas and sharing of findings with others; and

3. whole-class selection of a shared topic requires democratic decision-making, an important component of community building in a critical classroom.

(2001, p. 82)

Critical whole language specialists Edelsky and Johnson (2004, p. 137) come to much the same conclusion when they remark that a critical curriculum is more visible than a regular one, because of its difference, but go on to say that it is "not propagandistic":

> Critical whole language practice does not tell students *what* to think. But it does pose some new things to think *about*. Attempts to prohibit critical practice, by contrast, impose barriers; such attempts tell teachers and students what *not* to think about. Bigelow and Peterson (2002, p. 5) distinguish between biased practice and partisan practice. The former ignores multiple perspectives and does not allow interrogation of its own assumptions. "Partisan teaching, on the other hand, invites diversity of opinion but does not lose sight of the [critical] aim of the curriculum."

The topic, as I indicated earlier, is a perennial one. Its most recent substantial manifestation in the US came about only a couple of years ago, when the National Council for the Accreditation of Teacher Education programs was found to have a statement, buried a long way down in a guidance document, that identified a disposition towards fostering social justice as a desirable feature of teacher education programs. There was discussion, both academic and popular, concerning whether this was an example of imposing values, and the statement was removed. Hare (2007) provides a careful and thorough analysis of this event, for much of his exposition tending to sympathize with the critics, perhaps, but concluding firmly:

> None of this is to say that teacher educators should not try to persuade prospective teachers that certain views, practices, and policies with respect to social justice and other controversial matters are justifiable. Setting an example of critical thinking and open-mindedness does not preclude taking a stance and defending a particular point of view with respect to an issue of social justice [Hare, 1985]. Everything depends upon the manner in which this is done. The general criteria are clear: Rival views must be given a fair hearing; reasons and evidence must be provided to support favoured positions; questions and challenges must be encouraged and given due consideration; and there must be no requirement or expectation (stated or implied) that student teachers come to share the substantive views defended by their professors. In the

absence of these conditions, defensible partiality will degenerate into ideological propaganda.

Hare's remarks bring this continuing discussion up to date with yet another careful presentation of a position vis a vis a possible charge of imposition. A truly hostile school administrator will not listen to our protestations of democratic dialogue if anything has come up which s/he disapproves of. But we may find some supporters inside or outside our school administration (if we have cultivated our networks) and we must provide them with whatever ammunition we can should there be a confrontation. Criticalists, and social reconstructionists earlier, have faced such charges (Evans, 2006). Given the importance of the matter, and the danger of the charge, criticalists of all orientations must be well prepared to deal with it.

TASK: SHARE EXPERIENCES AND OPINIONS

As a language teacher, do you have a right to your opinion about the nature of language? Do you explain to your students some aspects of how language works, how it changes, the nature of, say, a standard language and dialects? In doing so, do you allow for alternative understandings to be expressed by students? Do you feel that you run the risk of "imposing" your views? How about if we take culture (the culture of the L2) as the focus—are you entitled to express (to profess) your professional understanding of the L2 cultures you are engaged with? What practices would put you at risk of a charge of indoctrination?

Compromise

> We all try to keep from compromising on the big things while we compromise on the minor matters. To me the big thing in life is my work, and I shall compromise always enough to keep that work from being stopped.
> A. S. Neill writing to Wilhelm Reich, 1945 (Placzek, 1982, p. 133)

"It's a tricky business to organize an untraditional class in a traditional school," says Shor (1987, p. 128), and among other things he means that we may not always get as much as we want, may not be able to go as far as we would like with our critical projects, quite possibly because of administrative or other external pressures. Indeed, teachers starting out to craft a radical language pedagogy should certainly not be allowed to think that critical pedagogy is easy and that all they are aiming for can be achieved, in curriculum and practice, in their first efforts. On the contrary, it is quite possible they will be opposed, directly or indirectly, and they may be unable to deliver what they had hoped for. They may be disheartened by the difficulties they encounter and lack of sympathy they face at the outset. Frankly, this is actually to be expected. The mainstream is not so called for no reason. We can go back to Gramsci (e.g., 1971) and ask why it is that people don't see what their best interests are (and in the present era we can answer in terms of the hegemonic power of the media, and in terms of who owns the media). In any case, dominant perspectives dominate, either numerically or by covert or overt force. The radical is often taken as a synonym for what is both outside the mainstream and likely to be opposed by it. Perhaps if you say you are implementing a radical pedagogy and experience no opposition you are not doing it right! But assuming you do experience opposition, certainly in the short run you are likely to have to compromise; and as the above quote from A. S. Neill suggests, we should choose to compromise rather than give up altogether. Being prepared to compromise and seeing this as a strategic move rather than an admission of failure is going to be important in the work of a critical language educator.[5, 6]

I do not want to leave the discussion of compromise at that commonsense, unresearched level. There has been some (though surprisingly little) philosophical work on compromise which might further comfort us or give us ammunition. The main philosophical argument for compromise concerns the need to see such action within a longitudinal context of a life. It is of course always a matter of judgment concerning how far one can compromise on what points, but the idea is that a temporary maneuver preserves one's capacities and capability for action in the long run. Here are some central points derived from Benjamin's (1990) book-length analysis of the topic.

First of all, why are we worried about compromise? The answer is because there is a widespread valuing of an alternative concept, that of integrity, and in particular, because of the idea that a life (and a self) which has integrity is coherent, and thus makes sense. But, argues Benjamin, being all of a piece, or unitary, is a positive feature of the form or shape of something; consequently, you or your life can have the characteristic of integrity but yet not be moral. Benjamin then takes up and accepts a common idea about the nature of life in a changing world: "The world is complex, and ... internal conflict is a feature of human life" (p. 56). There are often gaps between duty and desire. "We add or accumulate values and inclinations without fully extinguishing those that preceded them and that, for the sake of integrity, we may now consciously disavow" (pp. 56–57). This philosopher thus prefers the term "wholeness" (of a life) to integrity. And then Benjamin moves on to make observations which are consistent with my own observations of life:

> Conventional wisdom says that in cases of conflict one's moral values and principles are of overriding importance. This however, may be profoundly alienating and destructive of overall integrity. ... The claims of morality,

if omnipresent, unremitting, and overriding, may force us to relinquish commitments to develop certain morally unobjectionable skills or talents or to complete certain similarly unobjectionable undertakings and in some instances, our reason for living.

(Benjamin, 1990, p. 58)

Taking up the views of another prominent philosopher Benjamin (p. 72) draws on MacIntyre:

What the agent is able to do and say intelligibly as an actor is deeply affected by the fact that we are never more (and sometimes less) than the co-authors of our own narratives ... We enter upon a stage which we did not design and find ourselves part of an action that was not of our making.

(MacIntyre, 1981, p. 199)

In summary remarks, Benjamin comments:

To acknowledge this feature of the human condition is to make room in one's outlook for a certain amount of mutual accommodation. ... Those who categorically reject all such compromise with high-minded appeals to integrity often fail to appreciate the limitations and complexities of integrity ... We must regard our integrity as a matter of degree and not all or none [p. 73]. ... Compromise in such circumstances, when incorporated into a true and coherent narrative ... does not threaten integrity but rather preserves it [p. 74].

(Benjamin, 1990)

Since the topic is rarely treated in the philosophy or philosophy of education literature, it is even more unlikely to get dedicated attention in literature closer to our disciplinary home(s). However, there are occasional passing mentions. Edelsky and Johnson (2004) jointly present an account of the critical whole language teaching practice of one of them (Johnson). They note that while Johnson often used her school's existing non-critical materials in an adaptive critical way, she also played safe given the highly constrained working conditions in her US ESL high school class; taught test-taking; and

also compromised with her principles; she still taught the ten-minute daily phonics lessons/exercises in sounding out multi-syllabic words ...

(p. 130)

The authors note also that as a still new teacher she didn't go all the way towards the standard critical pedagogy position of generating work or lesson content just from what students could bring in or articulate. Partly because of the issues arising from large-scale state-mandated standardized testing, she felt a need to have a more clearly determined curriculum. So here again was a compromise:

> The compromise she was able to work out was one between content and form. This is, it was she who determined "forms" to be learned but the students offered the content.
>
> (p. 131)

TASK: SHARE EXPERIENCES AND OPINIONS

List a few of the things you have compromised on in your life (let's *not* choose really big matters here, for this exercise). How did you justify them? Specifically, did you look at trade-offs in the moment, or did you take a long-term view? What are some compromises you make in your language teaching (or learning) roles?

Actually participating and taking action

For Freire there was a direct link between a Brazilian adult literacy student completing a sequence of "culture circles" (thereby acquiring Portuguese L1 literacy and thus the right to vote) and political action. That man or woman could now vote (being able to pass the literacy test associated with voting) and it was assumed that s/he would. In the older traditions that flow into critical pedagogy, too, it is clear that an educated citizen is the goal of, for example, a Deweyan progressive pedagogy; an educated, informed citizen, capable of making critical judgments and actively socialized into citizenship from his or her school days on, was and indeed remains the target. In the English-speaking world we can trace this line back at least to the US president Thomas Jefferson, who attempted to legislate universal primary education in his home state of Virginia. It is clear that he linked the matter to citizenship and presumably would have promoted it nationally as President had conditions allowed (cf. Heater, 2004).

Citizenship goes beyond merely voting once every few years. But staying for a moment with a narrow understanding of citizenship, look at the voting participation rates—in most democracies, they are surprisingly low. It is interesting that Dewey became pessimistic about the usability of the dispositions he had hoped to see fostered in schools: "What assurance is there in the existing system that there will be opportunity to use their gifts and the education they have obtained?" (Dewey, 1939/1988, pp. 318–19, cited in Schutz, 2001, p. 261). A casual glance at social change in the twentieth century might suggest that though in some democracies, the vote has allowed social and political change, it has often followed such changes rather than led them, and that those changes have been associated with mass movements along with conventional political initiatives (like voting).

Part of the background to this is the presence or absence of education for active citizenship in regular schools. This is quite varied across countries (cf. Hahn, 1998); in some cases it is avoided (or was until recently, viz., the UK). Young people have little interest in participation and many have negative attitudes towards politicians. Many high school students feel they are unlikely to be able to have an effect on the political and social issues of the day and also feel little confidence in their elected representatives, the political class. Thus, a revitalized citizenship education would apparently have a role to play in critical pedagogy.

Turning now to the teachers, it should be noted that Freire (and Dewey) did not believe that schools alone or the implementation of a critical pedagogy within classrooms alone could change society. Freire stressed that teachers should participate in social movements, which he obviously thought were as important as schools in social change. Within the Freirean tradition, "social movements" is a term referring to "collective efforts to promote some type of change in power" (O'Cadiz et al., 1998, p. 42).[7] After World War II, in his home city of Recife, Freire was a member of the Movement for Popular Culture (MCP), organized by city politicians, union leaders, and artists (Freire, 1996). He states that teachers "should expose themselves to the greater dynamism, the greater mobility you find inside social movements" (Shor & Freire, 1987, p. 38).[8] He also notes that critical pedagogy has to focus on what is taking place "today" in social movements, and refers to them in general as creating a pedagogy of resistance. Mayo (1995, p. 372) summarizes, saying that "There is therefore evidence in Freire's work, particularly in his later 'talking books', that he supported the view that regards "Cultural Action for Freedom" as being more effective when carried out within the context of a social movement or movements." As Schutz (2001, p. 279) similarly states, Freire argued that his approach to schooling was important because it could be connected with … 'the general march of events.'"

But the action component of our critical pedagogy materials to the extent we have seen them so far, and their relation to social movements, is not very substantial. Perhaps it cannot be, since so much depends on local circumstances. But still it might be asked, what is needed, pedagogically or in and around schools, to foster a truly active citizenship? Relatedly, it seems we need to ask, "What is the role of social movements in the implementation of a critical (language) pedagogy, and/or associated educational change?" The person who has most seriously inquired into the matter among scholars associated with critical pedagogy is Jean Anyon (looking, it must be said, exclusively at the US and with urban schools in mind; Anyon, 2005; 2009a, b). Her understanding of forms of citizenship[9] and action for social change are closely tied to the concept of a social movement. Anyon's empirical data is extensive and both historical (personal narratives of the US Civil Rights movement, present-day interviews with young activists in US inner cities; surveys of the many social movements in the US that have affected education) and personal (her own family and friends). A central finding from her studies of the Civil Rights movement in the US is that merely being informed about injustice or inequity, even affecting oneself, does not necessarily lead to any form of action even when conditions are relatively favorable. Rather, it is through being socialized into forms of active citizenship that a disposition and an understanding of what is involved comes into being; there is a change in identity, one might say.[10] It is notable that she does not cite theories of social learning or identity shift. Yet the details from personal narratives of activism she describes conform repeatedly (in my reading) with the structures of Lave and Wenger's social learning theory with its emphasis on legitimate peripheral participation leading to group membership and identity shift as a form of learning.

What are the implications of this for critical pedagogy? It seems that the action phase becomes particularly important. Ferguson's (1998) account of how she actually not only involved her community college ESL students in writing to legislators but also brought them to the legislators' offices to press for the funding of their program—this would appear to be the sort of thing we need to hear much more of. Cowhey (2006) has an entire chapter on "learning through activism" (see also e.g., Oyler, 2011). In it she describes a range of actions, some undertaken outside the classroom, that few elementary teachers would engage in and which few elementary teachers would get extensive parental support for (though of course she did).[11]

> Learning through activism is powerful because the need to use vital academic skills for social justice motivates their acquisition. These skills include reading, writing (reports, letters of thanks or inquiry, news articles, speeches, etc.), speaking, singing, listening, researching (asking good questions, finding people with answers), gathering and representing data, noting observations, making posters and banners, raising money, getting to know political leaders and how to access them, or more specific skills, such as how to organize a voter registration drive. The most important skill that can and must be developed through activism is critical thinking. ... It also empowers children and their families in concrete, authentic, replicable ways. It is not just about feeling good in the moment. Learning through activism recognizes and honors "everyday activists," which in turn cultivates more activism among students.
>
> (p. 103)

During Cowhey's voter registration drive,

> We got voter registration materials from the city registrar. Our class parent volunteers sent home a notice to the families and scheduled the family volunteers. We ran the voter registration drive at a table in the school lobby for a half hour on each of three mornings and afternoons, as staff and parents were coming and going. Each table had an average of four parent volunteers. A total of twenty parents volunteered ... After completing the drive, the students rode the city bus downtown to deliver the completed voter registration cards to the registrar's office at city hall. Students were asked to prepare an exhibit for the mayor's office and wrote captions for a collection of drawings they had done titled "How to Register Voters". ... Most students and many parents have never been to the mayor's office. After visiting there twice, having their artwork exhibited there, organizing a vigil there, and receiving letters from the mayor and her staff, my students feel like they belong there, that they have access. [This action won a Women's League of Voters national award.]
>
> (p.105)

Similarly, Duncan-Andrade and Morrell (2008, p. 13), as mentioned in earlier chapters, report on an extended intervention motivated by critical pedagogy ideas into the curriculum of an urban high school in the US. This had a strong action orientation and, like Cowey's, connected with established legislative politics. Students in one of their classes investigated inequities in education. This led them to call for action to alter educational policy in their state, and they were able to reach out to legislators and press for new legislation concerning student rights in California. At a somewhat different level, their students who were heavily engaged in school sports took the action of organizing basketball "clinics" for younger girls who did not have sporting facilities.

Of course, this is within a country with established, indeed legally protected traditions of civic participation, ranging from lobbying legislators to organized protest, in which not only adults but also minors are entitled to engage in social action (cf. Lewis, 1991). Critical pedagogy emerged from South contexts (e.g., Brazil) in which such traditions were not always protected, yet social movements were nevertheless active in those contexts. Recent international events (at time of writing) make it clear that popular protest is an option, though admittedly a dangerous one, even in countries and cultural regions where it has not been so visible of late. But this also suggests the importance of locating social movements in a wider international context and that is also provided by the wider scholarship on this topic, which I will now briefly reference.

Probably because of their massive historical and socio-political importance in the last few decades in developed nations, social movements have been the subject of an extensive scholarly literature. The term was apparently first used in the mid-nineteenth century, by German sociologists studying the French revolution. It encompasses the development and activities of organized labor (the "labor movement"), the many politically oriented organizations that continue to struggle for political change (e.g., the "socialist movement"), and more recently "single-issue" (i.e., supposedly non-political) movements such as those for women's rights, gay rights, of course the US Civil Rights movement, and so on. These are all international in reach, scope, and membership; and the more recent ones have sometimes been termed "New Social Movements." Of course, not all social movements promote democratization. Some social movements have clearly anti-critical aims. And social movements can be coopted or repressed. According to Tilly (2003, p. 37; see also 2004), the foremost historian and theorist of social movements, they are effective when they promote three classes of democracy-promoting mechanisms:

> by broadening and equalizing collective political participation, [by] insulat[ing] public politics from existing social inequalities, and [by] reduc[ing] insulation of trust networks from major political actors. To the extent that social movement activism promoted establishment of recognized but autonomous collective political actors involving heterogeneous members and integrating their own distinctive trust networks, its democratizing effects increased.

A sub-category of social movements is "educational movements," which have apparently been effective in various countries in recent times. Swain (2005) has collected case studies of such movements (with an overall ethnic minority orientation) from Bosnia/Herzegovinia, Colombia, India, Malaysia, Peru, South Africa, and the US drawing on the work of the United Nations Research Institute for Social Development (UNRISD) which has a particular interest in social movements. Overall, he finds that

> the social initiatives in the educational domain have originated either when states have failed to fulfill their role in providing facilities and opportunities for their citizens to receive basic education and/or when a certain section of the society feared losing its identity due to nation-building projects of the state through educational curriculum machination.
>
> (p. 209)

However, in all cases, the role of the state is great. Some social movements work with it against local problems; if the state is hostile to social movements, in this set of cases the movements make little progress at a national level though may create their own ethnic educational institutions. Swain is, however, encouraging concerning the ability of educational social movements to benefit from networking and support beyond national borders.

To some extent this leaves the matter of participation in social movements open. Just as creating a critical pedagogy in the classroom alone will not result in social change, participating in social movements alone will clearly not result in social change. However, if one of the goals of critical pedagogy is to foster active citizenship, one of whose most obvious forms might be participating in social movements, it would behoove a teacher to speak from experience. Thus Freire's suggestion (to teachers, that they participate in such movements) remains an important one, and Anyon's position on the role of socialization into action has clear implications for this aspect of critical pedagogical practice.

TASK: SHARE EXPERIENCES AND OPINIONS

Have you ever participated in any political activity or social movement? Was it formal (voting), or informal (writing to a representative, taking part in a march or protest)? Was it within an institution (complaining about a teacher or course) or a political entity (a city, a county, a state)? Were you in any way socialized into such forms of action?

In closing

We have been considering a somewhat disparate group of issues in this chapter. The matter of "imposition" is important. If you are trying out critical language pedagogy, I promise you it will come up—either for you, in your own thinking, or against you, as a challenge from others. Compromise is a more slow-burning matter, potentially something that might nag at you, gradually, over time, from the inside. For some of us, it may have to be radical pedagogy at the weekends and a straight "day job" during the week; for others it may be that, with a different approach to compromise or more favorable circumstances, we can integrate our values and our practice … but one usually has to add "… to some extent." At least with this discussion of compromise, I feel that a matter usually confined to the shadows has been subjected to inspection and analysis, and in a positive way. And as for action … yes … it's important, and what I've put down here only scratches the surface of an area for further investigation. Much more exists under the heading of political socialization. I hope some readers will have a chance to explore this area more, and report back.

Questions for discussion

1 Obviously there is a hypothesis (or two) to be tested here. How could one establish whether or not a critical pedagogy (seen here as related to citizenship education) resulted in the forms of action or thought that it intended? What would be some problems faced in trying to establish a causal relationship? Does it make sense to think in terms of a causal relationship here? How about some indirect or multi-causal connection?

2 Try taking the opposite position on compromise, as a way to think things through. Start a short exposition by saying "Compromise is always wrong. It is always something to be ashamed of ..." and follow this up with some examples and argument.

3 Writing this question today, I can tell you that yesterday a visiting professor said to me "Education should be neutral" (while complaining about the weakening of her university system by government action reflecting economic problems). This position may be behind some of the concerns about "imposing" views and values. What do you think are some of the connections between this view and a concern about any values being transmitted? And why is this position probably wrong?

Notes

1 This was a jointly authored work, but Dewey with Childs had responsibility for the chapter from which this quote is taken.

2 Despite the complacent assumption that the texts and writers of that now far-distant period made, that "we" are a unitary reading public.

3 See also Huttunen (2003), who takes Snook's work as central. The topic is not confined to language teaching, needless to say, and interesting historical pieces on indoctrination in the curricula of fascist, communist, colonial and more democratic states exist. There is also active work on indoctrination in its original non-pejorative sense of religious instruction, which has received new emphasis recently both in the US and in Europe.

4 This refers to the important analysis of power by Foucault (e.g., 1980), now part of the theoretical apparatus that can be brought to bear on this ancient topic.

5 Generally it is only in passing remarks, such as that quoted above from A. S. Neill, that one finds reference to compromise by educators. But also, Hyslop-Margison and Dale (2011, p. 68) comment on Freire's early work: "In the early 1960s, two opportunities presented themselves to Freire ... In an era when funds were scarce, the Alliance for Progress [funded by the US to oppose communism in South American] made educational programs available to many people. Freire was given an opportunity to oversee these education programs and he was not naïve about the source or intent of the funds."

6 Janks (1991): "In state-controlled schools which proscribe the teaching of politics as is the case in South Africa, it is particularly difficult to implement a critical approach in education. It is nevertheless possible to introduce much of what has been described here, particularly if one is clever about reading the spaces that can be opened in one's own particular context. In repressive States, a critical approach to

teaching language is more risky for teachers. Such an approach is perhaps also more necessary" (p. 199).

7 Compare the definition of Tilly (2003, p. 23): "a sustained challenge to powerholders in the name of a population living under the jurisdiction of those powerholders by means of repeated public displays of that population's worthiness, unity, numbers, and commitment."

8 Mayo (1995, pp. 371–72) brings together several places where Freire touches on this point.

9 Note that at this point we are also in the realm of citizenship education or political education.

10 And this is consistent with the general findings in the area of political socialization which support a broadly Deweyan position (e.g., Andolina et al., 2003).

11 Or am I too pessimistic here? This sort of thing, within citizenship education, was at least *advocated* by the US National Education Association as early as 1918, and "the extra-mural feature was the recommended application of classroom learning to social action in the local community whereby pupils might advocate, for instance, more parks or railroad or post offices or pure food law" (Heater, 2004, p. 115).

9

IMAGINATION AND TARGETS

Critical pedagogy specialists have had less than one might expect to say about the social and political formations that a critical pedagogy is in search of. [1] This may be part of a general problem in which "progressive currents lack both a coherent vision of an alternative to the present order and also a plausible scenario as to how such a vision, if one existed, could conceivably be realized" (Fraser, 2009, p. 143). Or, less negatively, it could be: (a) because it is impossible to predict the outcomes of social change; or (b) to avoid being accused of an unrealistic "utopianism" (P. B. Smith, 2009). More pragmatically, it could also be: (c) if the targets are specified explicitly, and in forms that some unsympathetic readers find hostile, it might provide ammunition for attacks (as happened to the reconstructionists). Yet one can still ask, "Would students and teachers perhaps be more motivated, or be able to facilitate more useful forms of critical pedagogy, if they knew to what ends this developed critical capacity, and capacity for action, was intended?", beyond merely addressing problems with students' immediate life and work. It might even improve the effectiveness of this form of language education for appropriate social actions. After all, successfully using one's second language to get the landlord to fix a leaky roof doesn't actually change the problems caused by inequities in land ownership.

In this chapter I work towards some specifications of goals in this area of societal change. I first glance at the role of the imagination, since being able to imagine alternatives is a first step towards attaining them; then I consider the specification of economic alternatives; then political alternatives; and finally, I return briefly to the matter of educational alternatives that was opened in Chapter 7.

Goals, imagination, and the imaginary

One intermediate step towards specification of the outcome of social critique is to use one's imagination; this can perhaps create such targets for a new world, or just a new school, newly imagined, even without their being pre-specified by theorists. Presumably there would at least be motivational benefits from some such exercises of the imagination; to the extent that these imaginary institutions, practices, and social structures were not too unconstrained or unreasonable, there could be benefit in establishing targets and goals that reflected them. The basic idea I am advocating here could be summed up in the popular advertising slogan "think different"!

The imagination and an associated term, "the imaginary," were theorized in ways that may be helpful for this discussion by Sartre (1940). From a Sartrean point of view, the imaginary adds the concept of ontological freedom on to our capacity to imagine things. It is because of the imaginary that we can imagine that we can reconstitute the world. This philosophical version of the imagination has been taken up by philosophers and radical social theorists (to some extent Althusser, e.g., 1971; Castoriadis, 1974/1987; Costa Lima, 1984/1988). Noted critical pedagogy theorist Roger Simon has consistently talked about a pedagogy of possibility (e.g., Simon, 1987, p. 372) and also uses the term "the imaginary" when he says (1992, p. xv; cf. p. 37) that

> education might be understood as a practice of cultural production whose effects influenced not only the distribution of material goods and available opportunity structures but as well, the social imaginary through which people defined both what was possible and desirable.

The term will reappear throughout this section; it is a term of art found useful by many of my sources.

Within critical pedagogy, Freire has often referred to the role of hope. "The idea that hope alone will transform the world ... is an excellent route to hopelessness ... But the attempt to do without hope, in the struggle to improve the world ... is a frivolous illusion" (Freire, 1994, p. 8). A practical critical pedagogy manifestation of a specific form of hope, or the imaginary, is found in the work of Shor, who in several books (e.g., 1987, 1996) has discussed his long-standing community college course on "Utopia." As a writing teacher, working in the curriculum tradition of US freshman composition but also sometimes teaching remedial writing courses, Shor has had fairly wide latitude to explore issues which would be stimulating for student writing. Choosing topics of interest to his working-class students allowed Shor to engage them in "writing our own reality," critiquing the social mainstream as well as writing about alternatives. In addition, he comments (1987, p. 60, citing Freire, 1970, pp. 40–42) that

Future-making or Utopian consciousness, as features of critical thinking, have been emphasized by Freire as fundamental to liberatory culture.

The curriculum tradition of US freshman composition allows for "teaching" literary texts. That is, the instructor is at liberty to select parts or all of literary works which have content relevant to a course on—in this case a course on writing. Shor reports using works such as Thomas More's *Utopia* as well as other literature on utopian themes and the general idea of a utopia, as a concept to promote students' analyses of their present-day situation and their speculation about a future better world.

Critical pedagogues (such as Giroux, Shor, and Apple) mostly put all their political vision (and hopes) into the term "democracy." As Hytten (2008, p. 337) has pointed out, this is a noble or aspirationist version of democracy in which

> democracy is more than just a political system; it is a way of life that involves a balance between individual rights and social responsibilities, a concern for the common good, a commitment to cooperation and problem solving, and ongoing work "to promote human dignity, equity, justice, and critical action" [Apple & Beane, 2007, p. 5]. In this vision of democracy, citizens work together to address social problems, challenge inequities, provide equality of opportunity, and cultivate economic justice. Such citizens are engaged in the world around them, informed, and civically and politically active. Yet rarely is this justice-oriented, participatory vision of democratic citizenship the dominant one we cultivate and pass on in schools. … Democracy is taught as if it is a fixed, static system passed on to younger generations. For example, we teach classes in government, yet rarely engage the meaning of citizenship in an ongoing and sophisticated fashion. Is it any surprise then, that so many people conceptualize democracy in naïve, self-interested, and vulgar ways?

Taking this one step further towards the imagination of political alternatives, she says (p. 340):

> We need citizens who can ask critical questions of our current system and who can imagine possibilities for humane social arrangements that do not involve the increasing accumulation of wealth in the hands of fewer and fewer people, while others suffer needlessly.

In our field, Norton has made productive and repeated use of the phrase "imagined communities"[2] and imagined identities (e.g., 2000, pp. 163–64, Kanno & Norton, 2003). She believes that imagination is important in the "creative process of producing new images of possibility and new ways of understanding

one's relation to the world that transcend more immediate acts of engagement";
she and her colleagues have documented the effects of imagined identities in
several case studies (such as those collected in Kanno & Norton, 2003).

I think that the actual state of one's, our, our students' "imaginary" is not
good. Our students have good facilities of imagination, but the realm they can
imagine has been colonized by, let's say, hostile forces, and so what they have
access to is limited. Critical pedagogy needs the imaginary back, or, we need one
that will better serve our purposes.

Resources for critical educational imaginaries have been available for some
time, and critical pedagogues should not ignore both the old and the newly arising
material. Historically, speculative writing has played an important role in the
development of education. Rousseau's *Emile*, a fictional account of the upbringing
and education of a boy,[3] stirred the imagination of parents and teachers and was
a best seller in Europe at the end of the seventeenth century. Its ideas were taken
up by educators, of whom Pestallozzi is a good case. Pestallozzi ran schools (with
interruptions, between 1798 and 1825) implementing some of the ideas Rousseau
had articulated.[4] Within his first few years, he wrote fictional treatments of
education based on his experiences (1781, 1801), which greatly contributed to the
fame of his schools, which were visited by intellectuals and educational innovators,
and further promoted what would later be called progressive education. He was
opposed to many of the mainstream educational trends of his day.

During the nineteenth century, the ideas of "integral education" (mentioned
in Chapter 4) were promoted in novelistic form (Beach, 2008), and to some
degree, this pattern continues even now. The role of the utopian imagination
in education has recently been discussed by Halpin (2003); a handful of
specialists are using creative literary works in professional education (e.g.,
Nussbaum, 1995; Florio-Ruane, 2001). Kurth-Schai and Green (2006)
interestingly combine an entirely fictional narrative about school reform and
charter schools with academic essays; particularly relevant to my point here
is their chapter on the role of intuition and vision in the education of young
teachers with school reform in mind. The practice is continuing and being
used closer to the main content area under consideration in this book, as SL
specialist Murphey has placed his critique of English examination problems
in Japan in front of the public in the form of a novel, reasoning that decades
of scholarly effort to reform this part of the L2 education system there have
failed, so an alternative approach, appealing to the popular imagination, should
be tried (Murphey, 2010).

For these exercises to be of maximum use, I think that the "new school" has
to be imagined not just with regard to its internal, pedagogical characteristics,
but also other aspects as well. These would be its internal governance features,
its economic character, and its networks of connections and relationship to the
host society and political entity it might be part of (or working in opposition to).

TASK: REFLECT

Do you agree that your ability to imagine alternatives is limited by the options provided by mainstream society? In trying to imagine how things could be different, what holds you back? Consider schools, language teaching, and society as a whole.

And some analysts (e.g., Apple, 2009) would say it has to be imagined within a program of getting there from here. There is also the matter of its wider economic and political contexts. I will return to this matter after the next sections.

Socio-economic options

Taking the overall importance of "thinking different" as established (for critical pedagogy), there is still the question of what targets and options are available, desirable, particularly appropriate, as putative conceptual long-term goals for critical language pedagogists. Because I think it is interesting and stimulating to think about options for schools as institutions, not just "society," I will begin by taking up alternative economic enterprise options, before moving on to where political thought has gone, post-critical theory and after the era of Freire.

But first let it be noted that the importance of vision was also there in the precursors to critical pedagogy, for example social reconstructionism. Counts (1971, pp. 172–73, cited in Gutek, 2007, p. 37) referred back to his *Dare the school build a new social order?* pointing out that at the time of its publication he had emphasized the importance of promoting an alternative vision of society:

> We should … give to our children a vision of the possibilities which lie ahead and endeavor to enlist their loyalties and enthusiasms in the realization of the vision. Also our social institutions and practices, all of them, should be critically examined in the light of such a vision.

During this time, when class was the primary term of analysis in critical social theory, a political system based on freeing the working class from oppression was the primary expression of the goal of critical action. The goal was almost certainly to be expressed using a totalizing term like socialism, which refers primarily to public, cooperative or national ownership of the means of production. It was a more widely accepted position in many countries including the US at that time than now. Its acceptance among educators is indicated by the fact that Dewey, though not a social reconstructionist, expected the US to move towards socialism given the exigencies of the Depression. But socialist theorizing was and is so broad that the term itself does not imply a single perspective on state governance. As it turned out, the most famous apparent manifestations of socialism historically came to be governed using authoritarian, non-democratic political mechanisms and were inhospitable to diversity, dialogue, and many other features of critical pedagogy. But against the authoritarian regimes of past USSR and China can be set, in opposition, the ideas of libertarian socialism, with their rejection of the state in favor of worker-managed democratic workplaces, direct democracy in local governments, and networks of cooperatives. There is also the ambiguous inheritance of the social democratic welfare states of Europe; a negotiated (im)balance between the demands of business and of the less advantaged, in which economic pluralism of a limited kind persists under the governance of a political system of representative democracy within the borders of nation-states. In some cases this is formally agreed to by leaders of both major sides of opinion and power (Germany); in others it seems that only a temporary truce exists between perpetually warring factions (UK).

As a number of theorists have recently argued, in attempting to conceive (or discuss) political, economic and/or social formations consistent with the attributes and desires of critical pedagogies, social and economic pluralism and cultural diversity within or in association with these seems to be necessary (e.g., Day, 2005). Thus it is not a matter of thinking about a unitary structure or future form of society. Also, it has been claimed that some aspects of global society are now distinctly different from the previous era of modernity. That is, some say that current times are those of postmodernity.[5] If we are in a condition of postmodernity, it is said that we are likely to recognize and value diversity and non-homogeneity and we will not assume some linear and terminal form of progress. On the basis of the history we have so far, a continuing struggle seems most likely, with local and temporary successes rather than final solutions everywhere. So at the political level, instead of saying that critical pedagogies are likely to lead to or be consistent with one single term out of a set consisting of liberalism, socialism, anarchism, or other specific political -isms, inquiry should consider a range of local socio-political formations, which could possibly involve local instantiations of a diversity of mixes; socio-political and economic "mash-ups" (to use a current term).

TASK: REFLECT

Do you agree that the world is different now? Are current conditions so different from those of the twentieth century as to justify the term "postmodernity"? (Note that the term is rather different from "postmodernism".) Are you ok with the possibility that different imaginaries could apply to different locations and contexts, or do you think that in any case globalization is working to homogenize all such arrangements?

Post-capitalism

My discussion continues then, not with politics, but with economics,[6] by summarizing work by Gibson-Graham (2006).[7] The authors,[8] whose disciplinary home is economic geography, present a set of reports on regions around the world where "businesses" and "capitalism" as generally understood are not the dominant economic form of association. They are helping us understand non-capitalist exchange systems by emphasizing the non-homogenous nature of international political economy. They too stress the role of imagination and call for a "feminist imaginary of possibility" (p. xxvii). They deliberately offer an encouraging analysis, because they say that the lack of an imagined alternative is itself an obstacle to change.[9] In addition, they devote some attention to the way that capitalism is constructed by discourses (or discourse processes), in such a way that we see it as universal when upon closer inspection that may not be so. They intend to subject it to a form of critical discourse analysis—a position that critical language specialists should find appealing. Thus they emphasize the *diversity* of "the economy" (another totalizing and obscurantist term, like capitalism), in terms of different kinds of transactions, different types of labor and compensation, and different types of enterprise and ways of producing a surplus, not all of which are capitalist.[10] To take the matter of enterprise types, for example, they list communal, independent, feudal, slave (all non-capitalist); family firm, private unincorporated firm, public company, multinational (capitalist); and state enterprise, green firm, socially responsible firm, nonprofit, producer and consumer cooperative (alternative capitalist) (see Gibson-Graham (2006, p. 65, figure 15).[11]

One of their first moves is to analyze how many hours a typical individual (in the US) spends in capitalistic enterprises in a day, and how much they spend on other forms of economic activity (exchange, barter, voluntary work, unpaid childcare, etc.). In their analysis, the hours associated with capitalism are in the minority, at 40–45 percent. That is, about half of our work takes place in non-capitalist contexts.

Another move is to question the capitalisticness of "the firm." The firm (the business enterprise) is an entity that critical pedagogues should definitely know more about, because according to critical social theory it constitutes one of the most important mechanisms for oppression. In this analysis, the structure of the firm and the circumstances it places its employees in, acts to extract "surplus value" from the products produced by employees, and transfers this either to the owner-manager-entrepreneur, or to the shareholders. It thus makes possible concentrations of capital in the hands of business owners, at the expense of the workers in the firm; this is often referred to as exploitation (cf. Reeve, 1987; Liu et al., 2010). However, Gibson-Graham suggest that many firms do not actually behave as if they wished to maximize the extraction of surplus value, or profits, and there is thus considerable diversity even within this sector. These include less conventional firms which attend to the welfare of their workers, those fostering "fair-trade" prices of commodities; this also extends more generally to differences of opinion concerning the actual behavior of firms by questioning economists (e.g., Anderson & Ross, 2005; Asplund, 2007; Gudeman, 2008).

Perhaps more importantly, they go on to describe a small set of empirical cases around the world (located in Mondragón, Spain; Bohol, Philippines; Kiribati, the Pacific; and Kerala, India), of non-capitalist economic enterprises, or networks of diverse economic enterprises, to persuade us "that the world is not governed by some abstract, commanding force or global form of sovereignty" (p. xxxiii). They refer to these cases as community economies, which support (they claim) spaces of "political decision." Some of their key features (p. 87) are that they are "small scale, cooperative … culturally distinctive … [have] local ownership … [are] oriented to local market … [and involve] communal appropriation and distribution of surplus."

One of their choices is far more well-known than the others. That is the cooperative network of Mondragón, Spain, which has been in existence for almost one hundred years. Cooperatives are economic enterprises which are owned and run by their workers. In them, the shareholders of conventional limited liability firms, entirely distant from and not interested in the business, do not exist. Shareholders in a cooperative are usually the workers themselves. In the case of Mondragón, the share of the cooperative that each worker owns must itself be held collectively until retirement. This effectively provides the cooperative with working capital, which it does not distribute on an annual basis, but rather uses to invest, often building up other cooperatives in the network. So here it is clear that generating and then handling a surplus, and doing so differently from the typical capitalist firm, is a central strategic feature of this alternative economic form.

An interesting extension of this point, to the globalized and developing world, is the redirection of "surpluses" from migrant contract workers. Countries like Mexico, the Philippines, etc., derive a lot of their income from remittances sent back by migrants; these usually go straight to family members. But Gibson-Graham report several initiatives in different countries (Hong Kong, the Philippines, India) in which part of these remittances are being directed to somewhat alternative enterprises. In their report on the Indian case (Kerala) they also emphasize the role of local government, which in some parts of Kerala has a history of supporting development. In this case another network of producer cooperatives is under construction, with funding from both poor cooperative members and local government. Several of their other examples depend on the concept of "the commons." Prior to the industrial revolution in Europe, large tracts of land surrounding villages were held in common, and the products of their use allocated by law or tradition, to villagers. The accumulation of private capital in the hands of the rich was partly facilitated by political action (by the rich) to legally eliminate the commons (the enclosure movement). These monies were then part of what drove the investments behind railway building and development in general, which did not necessarily benefit the villagers who had lost their access to common land. Gibson-Graham point to several initiatives (Kiribati; Massachusetts; Mexico) in which commons are being reinstituted, to the benefit of those who share in access; the commons will be used for productive purposes (growing food, fishing, etc.) but the labor and the distribution of surpluses produced are, once again, not in the "conventional" capitalist mode. In several of these cases, the interpenetration of economic localities is important. Kiribati, the Mexican case (a forestry project), and the migrant worker cases, all show how international flows of financing and sales (such as fair trade agreements) affect, in these cases positively, the feasibility of community economies. (The benefits of flows of international financing may be obvious to those who work in private language schools.) Summarizing some shared aspects of these projects, Gibson-Graham (p. 193) identify four principles:

> Though there will be many other ways of framing the issues for decision, we have specified four coordinates that can be (and are being) used to orient the development of community economies—*necessity, surplus, consumption,* and *commons.* In the examples we presented, communities are pursuing alternative routes to development by various means:
> - choosing to meet local *needs* by delivering increased well-being directly (rather than relying on the circuitous route of capitalist industrialization) and recognizing and building on the diversity of practices that support subsistence and sustain livelihoods
> - using *surplus* as a force for constituting and strengthening communities—defining the boundary between necessary and surplus labor, monitoring the production of surplus, tracking the ways in which it is appropriated and distributed, and discussing how it can be marshaled to sustain and build community economies
> - recognizing *consumption* as a potentially viable route to development rather than simply its end result, and defining and making decisions about consumption versus investment on a case-by-case basis, rather than privileging the latter as the "driver" of development
> - creating, enlarging, reclaiming, replenishing, and sharing a *commons,* acknowledging the interdependence of individuals, groups, nature, things, traditions, and knowledges, and tending the commons as a way of tending the community.

TASK: INQUIRE

Does second language teaching merely prepare students for work in conventional (exploitative) enterprises? How could your curriculum orient students to alternatives? What economic alternatives exist in your vicinity?

Post-socialism, post-liberalism, post-nation-state

I turn now to political theory (and to some extent, political practice) as another place in which alternatives might be found or from which they might be derived and imagined. Quite a lot of preliminary points and reminders are going to be needed. To start with, I believe that we should initially direct our interest to options and discussions that reflect the many changes in the world almost fifty years after Freire's first writings—that is, *current* political theory. As in the above discussion of economic options, some of the political options discussed even by the latest theorists have been in existence for a long time, perhaps for ever, and the question is, which to focus on, in what theoretical frameworks? At the same time, despite their longevity, perhaps one or two key concepts really do need to be reformulated or called into question. It is no good setting up goals or options that don't do justice to changed circumstances. (The question of how to get there from here remains, of course.) At the same time, the discussion should continue lines of political thought consistent with, or at least not totally opposed, to those of Freire. As has been documented by various scholars (Taylor, 1993, Mackie 1981b, Holst, 2006), Freire's influences were many, though two often identified are liberation theology and various aspects of the socialisms of the 1960s. He himself made clear his disapproval of authoritarianism, or oppression, of all kinds. Thus one would expect a Freirean politics to be in the direction of libertarian socialism or a social democratic position.[12] On the other hand, we know that early Freirean political thought was weak on the subject of gender and largely ignored race, as indeed did socialism, both in its original forms and subsequently in the latter half of the twentieth century (cf. critical pedagogy expert Aronowitz [1996], who proposed that the term "socialist" be replaced by "radical democracy" because social movements and non-class related struggles, had supplanted it as the locus for active social change). This weakness is one of the reasons advanced for the need for "post-socialism" in a post-socialist world (cf. Fraser, 1997). The question then becomes: What political forms follow in the lines originally advocated by critical pedagogy specialists, which are nevertheless reflective of current socio-cultural and political conditions?[13]

My next preliminary move is simply to provide a couple of *recent* definitions of politics: "processes by which a group of people with initially divergent opinions or interests reach collective decisions generally regarded as binding on the group, and enforced as common policy" (Miller, 1987, p. 390). "'Politics'... indicates the ensemble of practices, discourses and institutions which seek to establish a certain order and organize human coexistence in conditions that are always potentially conflictual" (Mouffe, 2000, p. 100). Note that a political system can be distinguished from governance, its administrative and processual features.

Democracy everywhere

The definitions above emphasise groups of people and institutions, and notably, practices and discourses. They do not immediately refer to national politics or the state. This allows us (paralleling Gibson-Graham), to think in terms of a diversity of sites for kinds of politics and kinds of governance that might be consistent with or encouraging to critical pedagogy. In making this point I am suggesting we need to work against a kind of blinkeredness about the political similar to that identified in the previous section concerning the economic. In the economic realm, Gibson-Graham argued against the dominance of a single idea of the economic, and identified different economic forms in networked diverse locations. In the case of politics, current understandings would suggest that it is not something that occurs in a single location (the house of representatives, the parliament), and probably should not be associated merely with the state, but should rather be seen as something that occurs in all institutions, and in some non-institutional realms, such as civil society and in inter- or supra-national spaces. Most of us are located simultaneously within diverse institutions (family, school, firm, cooperative, nation-state, federation, world), and systems for determining who gets what, when, and to what degree operate in all of them. The question is whether those systems are democratic. What guidance is available concerning these matters that is current and consistent with the present situation in the world of the early twenty-first century, as opposed to being implicated in past failures?

In moving to provide some suggestions in answer to these questions, I would like to lead off from political suggestions made by critical pedagogy specialists, which are not by any means uniformly stated in terms of political theory. I will then go on to some recent political theory identified as useful by a couple of critical pedagogy specialists, and conclude with some reference to empirical studies and actual practice.

First, I want to acknowledge some concrete proposals, as opposed to critiques, from critical pedagogues. Apple (2009 *inter alia*) has done empirical (as opposed to theoretical) work analyzing the means by which the Right in the US has taken over state education, because he thinks that the Left should learn from these organizing techniques. And Anyon (2005, 2009a) has analyzed social movements in the US because she believes that the only way to improve state education is to have a new social movement for education. These are useful lines of work, and they are motivated by a desire to get "there" from here, from the present very unfavorable situation of state education in the US as viewed by critical pedagogists.[14] In light of my previous review of the diversity of educational institutions, and given the emphasis I am placing on diversity of economic and political formations, the work of Anyon and Apple has the weakness of only focusing on state education.

Critical literacy specialists Bomer and Bomer (2001) identify participatory democracy as a target. This is a form of democracy, they say, which is distinct from what generally exists in the US (which they call liberal democracy); they suggest that we should be educating students who can engage in a participatory democracy even if one is not possible at a national level. They review the words of social reconstructionist Rugg (cited earlier in this book) and conclude that most of the targets (equality, justice etc.) that he identified are ones they would want too. And they critique their past teaching for failing to produce writers who could develop texts that "carry an image of a good society" (p. 18). This discussion (rare in critical literacy writings) is useful because even though the authors don't specify a form of politics, they are identifying political principles associated with critical pedagogy (equality, justice, etc.) and could lead to a specification of kinds of politics and governance that will instantiate them.

McLaren, the well-known and prolific critical pedagogy theorist, having flirted with post-structuralist understandings of society, has adopted (e.g., 2005a, b) as his main political frame of reference a very traditional conception of Marxism. Perhaps consistent with Marx's own reluctance to go into detail concerning the final outcomes of the progress of society he predicted, McLaren's position doesn't enable him to say exactly what the target would look like. He has stated[15] that critical pedagogy is about the negation of existing matters (such as the idea that the teacher is a wage-slave; the negation would be that the teacher is a professional); thus he says that critical pedagogy doesn't put forward a positive target.[16]

However, earlier he and Kanpol (Kanpol & McLaren, 1995, p. 7) identified the work of Laclau and Mouffe (often described as post-Marxist)[17] as among the most promising political theorizing for critical pedagogy:

> Laclau and Mouffe's (1985) description of the "democratic imaginary" best depicts our own notion of democracy: democracy exists not in all places at one time but in many places, instances, and events where people struggle to undercut and alleviate the oppression, alienation, and subordination they and others experience.

The work of Laclau and Mouffe from this period is presented for educators by educational philosopher Peters (1995)[18]. I focus on his detailed consideration of the work of Mouffe (1988, 1992; drawing on Bobbio, 1987, 1990):

> Mouffe ... argu[es] that it is not possible to find more radical principles for organizing society than those of freedom and equality: they have provided the symbolic resources to wage democratic struggles in the past and democratic advances have occurred as new groups have claimed rights on the basis of them. The notion of radical democracy is simply a recognition of this state of affairs. ... [This] depends upon a reformulation of the liberal tradition. It depends, in the first instance, upon breaking the connection between the political project of liberal democracy and economic liberalism so as to free modem democracy from its highly rationalistic and individualistic premises, while rehabilitating the notions of citizenship and community as the basis for a more participatory and pluralistic conception. Radical democracy thus defined, Mouffe argues, is the only hope for the renewal of the left-wing project. Yet this deceptively simple outline of the project for radical democracy leaves unanswered a vitally important question: How is it possible to rehabilitate notions of community and citizenship without succumbing to an ideology of individualism or falling back on some notion of an organic sociocultural unity? In other words, how is it possible to reinvent notions of citizenship and community that recognize the increasing degree of differentiation characterizing pluralistic societies in the West without privileging either the liberal notion of individual or the Marxist notion of class?
>
> (Peters, 1995, p. 47)

If we can in fact find a political theory that favors democracy, freedom, equality, justice, but does so without conforming to the liberal idea of the person (or the overemphasis on class), then we will have kept many of the valuable theoretical concepts that socialism shared with liberalism, but will have moved into the twenty-first century and a post-socialist political theory that does justice to post-structural conceptions of the individual. Since present-day critical pedagogy also reflects post-structural views of the person (discussed in Chapter 6), this would seem to be important. Peters advocates that critical educators take up the ideas of Mouffe amplified somewhat by incorporation of those of Young (1990), yet another political analyst who emphasizes (as does Freire) the significance of new social movements. These have led Young to question liberal theories of justice (based on the general, unencumbered individual). Justice, she says, should start by recognizing the reality of domination and oppression (rather than starting from some free, imaginary state of nature). After this, five concepts likely needing to be addressed by justice are identified: "exploitation, marginalization, powerlessness, cultural imperialism, and violence." Older ideas about social justice deal with injustices through a process of redistribution of resources, but it will turn out that this alone is not sufficient, and instead recognition and acceptance of difference will turn out to be essential. Mouffe[19] has continued her inquiries (2000, see also 2005) with a focus on "deliberative democracy." She rejects earlier analyses of democracy emphasizing values and discourse (of Rawls and Habermas), because they imply a consensus of values in a polity. She claims this cannot be achieved and trying to make it happen weakens certain democratic values. In her most recent work she calls for an "agonistic" democracy (or "agonistic pluralism," 2000, p. 101), one in which there is a pluralism of values but enough deliberation that agreements are not mere compromises. She is particularly scathing about the actual model of democracy in existence in most cases, which she refers to as "aggregative democracy," in which citizens are discouraged from active participation and instead encouraged to vote for one or another tendency among an elite of leaders. "Deprived of the possibility of identifying with valuable conceptions of citizenship, many people are searching for other forms of collective identification ... the growth of various religious moral and ethnic fundamentalisms ... is a direct consequence of [this] democratic deficit." In summary she emphasizes several main points:

> Democratic individuals can only be made by multiplying the institutions, the discourses, the forms of life that foster identification with democratic values [p. 96].

> Taking pluralism seriously requires that we give up the dream of a rational consensus which entails the fantasy that we could escape from our human form of life [p. 98].

> If we accept that relations of power are constitutive of the social [presumably following Foucault], then the main question for democratic politics is not how to eliminate power but how to constitute forms of power more compatible with democratic values [p. 100].

> By warning us against the illusion that a fully achieved democracy could ever be instantiated, it forces us to keep the democratic contestation alive [p. 105].

> [Because of] the primary reality of strife in social life [p. 113] ... the specificity of modern democracy lies in the recognition and legitimation of conflict and the refusal to suppress it through the imposition of an authoritarian order. ... In modern democratic politics, the crucial problem is how to transform *antagonism* into *agonism*.

> (Mouffe, 2000)

Perhaps this seems a bit hair-splitting and not leading to or representing much of a change. Would aligning oneself with the reformulation of the liberal elements in Mouffe's post-socialist political theory make any difference? Perhaps it is easier to conceptualize using the last phrase of Peters, "an identity politics." Whatever practices and institutions might be used to obtain a certain order, and whatever governance procedures might be used to deliver it, they would have to reflect diversity and difference far more than is presently the case. This means (in the formulation of Fraser) that both redistribution and recognition are the necessary targets: not only the redistribution of surpluses to address the principles of equality and justice, against poverty and class, but also the recognition of identities that were previously ignored by the liberal state (gender, ethnicity, sexuality, etc.), again with the intention of promoting equality and justice. However, we would also have to give up youthful hopes of a complete and comprehensive change:

> We had therefore abandoned the idea of a need for a radical break with the previous society—the idea of revolution. We began to understand our politics as a radicalisation of ideas and values which were already present, although unfulfilled in liberal capitalism. I think there is nothing more radical than asserting liberty and equality for all. The problem was that these ideas were not put into practice in the societies which claimed to follow them. What a left-wing project should do is to try to force those societies to really put those ideas into practice.
>
> (Mouffe, in Castle, 1998, n.p.)

So one development of the line originally favored by prominent critical pedagogy theorists results in seeking to continue democratic developments and potentials inherent in the existing ideas of the more progressive political formations of the present time. This is consistent with the many very vague calls in critical pedagogy for just "more democracy."

Laclau (as opposed to Mouffe) has worked on the topic of social movements. In an interview, he commented: "The plurality of modes of oppression is counterbalanced by processes which can bring people together. Any group's identity and struggle can be transformed by changing its relationship with other groups" (Castle, 1998, n.p.). So he would probably specify, as an intermediate target, starting or joining social movements (which is what Anyon says, too). This would be consistent with the position that civil society, rather than the nation-state, is the place in which to push for change, or the location in which change can be imagined.

TASK: INQUIRE

Is there anything like a social movement in your vicinity? Have you ever engaged in or been part of one? What would it take for you to check one out? Do you think that the amount of democracy in any institution you are part of could be increased? How?

Not (just) the state

A further step in the argument can be taken by bringing together the emphasis on "identity politics" with Mouffe's reference to what the entities are ("those societies") that are going to "really put those ideas into practice." In the early twenty-first century, "globalization" (whatever else this ambiguous term implies) includes a weakening and calling into question of the nation-state. Is the nation-state capable of putting these ideas into practice—and can it be trusted to?

Questioning the nation-state is consistent with the way we've come to realize how people are. You never get a unitary polity, with everyone agreeing about moral and political beliefs. A defining feature of the classical nation-state is unity; but if we value diversity we cannot be thinking in these terms. The power of social movements these days is very often that they cut across national boundaries, so that "international opinion" is brought to bear on domestic injustice. At the same time, not only do international business enterprises intervene (as they always have done) to bend small nation-states to their will, the vast masses flow increasingly in and out and over the ever-porous borders of the nations, rendering them plural and at times weakening them.

Nation-states are heterogenous and always have been, though they have often been reluctant to acknowledge this. People have different ethnicities and religions, and yet they live side by side and sometimes work out their differences peacefully. However, the singular, unitary liberal conception of the person (and the polity) that underlies both economic liberalism and socialism is one that post-structuralism and arguably the present condition of the social world (post-modernity?) would lead many to reject. If so, political theory that is based on this misconception must also be rejected. Both of these theories, in addition, have been attached to the form of the state; if a unitary conception of the individual is no longer satisfactory, this would correspond with arguments (such as those of Day, 2005, that):

> despite their many historical and theoretical differences, classical Marxism and liberalism share a belief that there can be no "freedom" without the state form (Leviathan or dictatorship of the proletariat), and therefore also share a commitment to political (state-based) rather than social (community-based) modes of social change.
>
> (p. 14)

The emphasis on plurality and diversity militates against a unitary polity, particularly one implicated in domination, whether by liberal or Marxist tendencies.

This questioning of the nation-state ought to be taken further. I have just referred to the values that Mouffe sees as implying that the radical project begun with liberal democracy is not yet finished: democracy, freedom, equality, justice. Political theories of justice had proved a sticking-point for radicals the last time I looked (Crookes, 2009), because this work had drawn on extremely unrealistic forms of theorizing (e.g., that of the nevertheless highly respected Rawls). A prominent new investigator of political justice, Fraser (2009), takes up the burden of showing what justice needs to do to deliver for radical hopes, but in turn asks us then to turn to broader conceptions of what entities can put this idea into practice.

A point of departure for Fraser is not a wholesale condemnation of the state (as we would find in anarchism or libertarianism), but a consideration of the nation-state at recent times versus in the present and near future. She often refers to the "national-Keynesian welfare state" (e.g., Fraser & Honneth 2003, p. 90), which she contrasts to the "post-Westphalian" state[20]. The former assumed territorial integrity and a homogenous membership; it also attempted to provide justice mostly in the form of recognizing distributional inequities (rich and poor) and correcting them (taxes, welfare services including mass and supposedly meritocratic education). The latter is a version of the nation-state that has been weakened by the international forces of capitalism (no control over the movement of capital in and out of the national economy, no tariff barriers), by supranational institutional bodies with economic focus (the International Monetary Fund or the World Trade Organization placing constraints on a government's domestic economic measures), and supranational bodies with political focus (e.g., the UN Human Rights commission, or e.g., the European Community on a range of social and even familial concerns). It is also a state which has porous borders and struggles to control the flow of indigent migrants, narcotics dealers, political exiles with links to international terrorism, sex workers and sex tourists, and grapples with incursions in the form of attacks by drones (or hijacked aircraft) and the snatching and covert rendering of citizens by armed groups of soldiers or private militias associated with other militaristic nations or even non-state, extraterritorial groups.

> The cumulative weight of transnational processes is calling into question an underlying premise of that system, the premise of exclusive, indivisible citizenship, determined by nationality and/or territorial residence ... globalization is currently decentering the national frame that previously delimited most struggles for justice, whether focused on status [i.e., identity] or class (ibid., p. 91) ... Under these conditions it is imperative to pose questions at the right level ... national, local, regional, global (p. 92).

In slightly later work, Fraser's emphasis comes closer to my theme. Summarizing a now widely-accepted position ("we are seeing the emergence of a new multi-leveled structure of governmentality, a complex edifice in which the national state is but one level among others," 2009, p. 126)— she addresses herself to meta-level political injustices, which arise as a result of the division of political space into bounded polities. An example is the way in which the international system of supposedly sovereign states gerrymanders political space at the expense of the global poor. Channeling the latter's claims into the domestic political arenas of relatively powerless, if not wholly failed states, this system denies them the mean to confront the offshore architects of their dispossession—and thereby shields transnational malefactors from critique and control.

She calls for (more) "transnational courts or arbitration bodies. … If such powers are to be legitimate … they must be accountable to everyone potentially affected" (p. 149). Referring to the need to get beyond the frame of the nation-state, she says that in abstract terms, the form of political progress implied here requires a continuing cycle of critique of the established political entities and frame of reference, followed by reframing, and likely then further cycles of critique and reframing, as no single final best structure is likely to be arrived at while the world continues to change.

These transnational entities can be located in what political theorists call "the public sphere." But Fraser is not optimistic about the potential of this entity to be the site of efficacious action at present. She finds at least six reasons for worrying about the power of this entity as what she calls a "critical category." Three relate to the already-stated weaknesses of the state: (1) that its laws are subject to intervention by supranational entities; (2) that citizens reside outside the national territory and the national territory is inhabited by multiple nations as well as non-citizens; and (3) and that its economy is notably not under state control. But the other three interestingly relate to matters of language and communication.

First, there is " the denationalization of communicative infrastructure" in the direction of "market-driven, corporately-owned … niche media," in some cases operating in a range of minority or exterior languages. Also, a more classical nuance is the idea that the public sphere depends on a shared social imaginary "rooted in national literary cultures," which themselves no longer exist in the face of cultural hybridity, world literature and on the other hand, "global mass entertainment" with its US stylistic dominance. Finally, more substantively for us, the matter of an increasing absence of national languages.

[E]xisting states are *de facto* multilingual, while language groups are territorially dispersed, and many more speakers are multilingual. Meanwhile, English has become the *lingua franca* of global business, mass entertainment, and academia. Yet language remains a political faultline, threatening to explode countries like Belgium, if no longer Canada, while complicating efforts to democratize countries like South Africa and to erect transnational formations like the European Union. These developments, too, pose threats to the critical function of public opinion. Insofar as public spheres are monolingual, how can they constitute an inclusive communications community of all those affected? Conversely, insofar as public spheres correspond to linguistic communities that straddle political boundaries and do not correspond to any citizenry, how can they mobilize public opinion as a political force? Likewise, insofar as new transnational political communities, such as the EU, are multi-linguistic, how can they constitute public spheres that can encompass the entire *demos*? Finally, insofar as transnational publics conduct their communications in English, which favors global elites and Anglophone postcolonials at the expense of others, how can the opinion they generate be viewed as legitimate) For all these reasons, and in all these ways, language issues compromise both the *legitimacy* and *efficacy* of public opinion in a postwestphalian world.

(Fraser, 2009, p. 91)

It would seem that there is a role for the L2 specialist and L2 education in fostering justice in a postwestphalian world.

Most recent discussions of this line of theorizing, including criticisms, are to be found in Little and Lloyd (2009), who identify two main lines of post-socialist theorizing, those of critical theory radical democrats, and that of post-structural radical democrats. They focus on the post-structural line. Little and Lloyd (2009, p. 2) quote Young (2000, p. 183) as saying that the goal of this sort of politics is a "project of democratizing the state, civil society and the 'corporate economy,'" and that "radical democrats ... favor participation and enhanced popular control (self-government) over the limits of representative democracy." Even within the existing nation-state framework, it is possible to introduce more levels of deliberation, and it is possible to move towards more radical and participatory democracy practices overall and at specific institutional levels or contexts. European countries have moved to "devolution" of metropolitan power to regions; there is talk and writing of the "new localism," with mayors (and cities) playing a larger role in public policy making than before. The question of whether "the firm" can have democratic procedures is a question with more than one hundred years of struggle associated with it. Cooperatives usually have democratic forms of governance, though not always direct democracy as in Mondragón. It is certainly possible to democratize school governance (and the questionable School-Community Based Management initiative had some positive qualities in this area). It is possible to shift patriarchal practice within the family as a result of media content, programs for women (or fathers), and so on. It is certainly possible to work against racial, gender, and sexual orientation discrimination.

TASK: INQUIRE

Are you attached to the idea of the nation-state? Are you a patriot? Does your vision of change conform to the boundaries of a nation? From your particular geographic location, would holding on to the nation-state be a good idea or not? How do you imagine the future of the nation-state?

I have been picking up lines of development in political theory which align themselves with highly visible developments in the real world. Identity politics, social movements and civil society are favored over the state as the principal site of struggle. One way to capture this development is to say that in turning to the personal and away from the state we are also turning to the local, but a local that is interconnected globally as never before. We have arrived, some say, at the network society. Far from being an entirely new concept, this metaphor was central to a body of older political theory that also disfavors the nation-state and emphasizes the local, namely anarchism. Some of the things we could take from this body of political theory are its complete distrust of representative democracy (it prefers immediately recallable delegates) and its emphasis on federations of similar productive enterprises (cooperatives) linked in mutually supportive networks, and its aim for radical democracy within the enterprise itself. When focused on the city, this line of analysis has been called libertarian municipalism (Biehl & Bookchin, 1998). Other important trends within this body of thought and practice were some aspects of syndicalism, implying again, a disfavoring of the state as the site of politics, and instead a turn to the local worksite, with such places being linked together in a non-hierarchical (network) form. The main point here is that we can integrate the concern for justice, equality, and radical democracy with the local, the workplace and the town or city and region, without needing to focus on the nation-state. Teachers are not likely to be political actors on the national stage; perhaps we can more easily conceptualize ourselves as having a voice in the local community and being a real influence on the way our own schools are run.

The local: The municipal and the regional, as opposed to the national

A number of applied linguists, in discussing globalization as it applies to our field, have noted that the intensification of connections internationally has, paradoxically, made it easier to know about and communicate about localities, including linking localities that are in some ways different from or at odds with national and international entities. The forces of globalization will nevertheless attempt to coopt or appropriate localisms of all kinds, hybridizing them and through contact changing them. At one level of analysis, local knowledge will be commoditized, though it is also a site and a means of resistance. Canagarajah (2002) suggests that local knowledge not be considered as a static entity, but rather as a process.

> Celebrating local knowledge refers to adopting a practice. We treat our location (in all its relevant senses: geographical, social, geopolitical) as the ground on which to begin our thinking. Local knowledge is not a *product* constituted by the beliefs and practices of the past. Local knowledge is a *process*—a process of negotiating dominant discourses and engaging in an ongoing construction of relevant knowledge in the context of our history and social practice. What is important is the *angle* from which we conduct this practice—that is, from the locality that shapes our social and intellectual practice.
>
> (pp. 251)

And he concludes, "This is nothing new" (p. 251); which is a fair point and enables me to move to the history of local politics and some discussion of actual political practice.

At various times during the history of civilization, it has been the city which has been the dominant political and cultural entity. For the Western tradition, the city-states of Greece were the original theoretical basis for democracy; some cities of the late middle ages, particularly those of Italy developed a renewed republican democracy and the beginnings of modern humanism, and were the basis for the municipalism that characterized the industrial revolution in Europe. That era, too, saw a swing towards political decentralization in some cases, notably France (Hazareesingh, 1997, 2001). Strong regional cities grew up and were not isolated entities; important for the present discussion were periods of "municipal internationalism" in Europe, before WWI and just after WWII.

> The first burst of activity, beginning in the late 19th century and peaking in 1913 with the formation of the first internationally representative organ for municipalities ... laid the basis for networks that still exist and flourish today, networks that antedated the first permanently organised cooperative action between modern nation-states. The second, symbolised ... by ... town twinnings since the late 1940s, was a practical manifestation of the embryonic movement for supranational unification within postwar Europe.
>
> (Ewen & Hebbert, 2007, p. 327; cf. Gaspari, 2002; Hebbert, 2007)

Being aware of the considerable history of this concept makes it more likely that one would recognize that, as one major analyst of local government has observed, "local self-government ... is in any case the practice implicit in urbanism as a way of life" (Magnusson, 2005, p. 96); and of course, current population and geographical trends mean that urbanism is actually the dominant way of life of the early twenty-first century. Something like municipal internationalism has revived in a range of city-level organizations.[21] Even though "political theory focused on the state and urban analysis focused on the city ... there are many other structuring principles in the world besides state sovereignty, and the practices by which we are governed do not all emanate from the state" (ibid., p. 97). Magnusson continues,

> We need to open ourselves up to the extensiveness and messiness of urban life and to take the politics and government of it more seriously. Hobbes proposed the sovereign state as a simple solution to all our political problems, and we have been enthralled by that simple solution for much too long. Urbanism as a way of life demands a multiplicity of authorities of different types and on different scales, a variety of practices of self-government and endless adaptability in face of changing circumstances. ... Federalism need not be a model of negative government, in which each level of government works to prevent the others from doing things. It can be a model of multiple centres of initiative. In such a model, local authorities can play an especially important part, not only in organizing whatever is most immediate but also in laying the ground for a cosmopolitan order. ... Every space of opportunity is a venue for local self-government, which can be nurtured or stifled by public administrators. ... [P]ublic administrators have a particular responsibility to nurture these spaces of opportunity, since elected governments generally want to stifle them in the vain hope of enhancing their own power. People generally do want to govern themselves in their own way, and the public administrator's responsibility is to this democratic aspiration rather than to the desires of particular groups or individuals for sovereign authority.
>
> (Magnusson, 2005, p. 119)

A variety of prerequisites and also targets for action come to mind given this emphasis on local government, such as the role of public space for fostering democracy in urban locations, not to mention indeed in schools, and then, as we are in the internet era, the technological equivalents of this.

One positive recent example of the success of political engagement at the local level is the city of Porto Alegre in Brazil. Brazil itself is a country that has experienced a degree of decentralization following political reform over the last twenty years, and away from the centralized dictatorships it experienced during much of the post-WWII period (Montero & Samuels, 2004). Partly reflecting this, but also reflecting sustained organizational efforts, the city of Porto Alegre and its surrounding area have been "governed by a coalition of leftist parties" since

1989, report critical pedagogy specialists Apple and Gandin (2002). Of particular interest, and indeed a matter of world fame, is the participatory budgeting that the municipal administration brought in. Direct citizen involvement in the budget development process of a city is becoming popular; around the world more than 1000 cities use some form of this including even one in the US: Chicago.[22] Going beyond this (but building on it) has been the establishment of highly participatory structures for the development of new schools badly needed by the impoverished neighborhoods of Porto Alegre. In this case, the discourses of autonomy and responsibility that manifested in the short-lived efforts for School-Community Based Management mentioned earlier appear to have been taken up and creatively redirected (according to Apple and Gandin) by the local Porto Alegre administration. They have established "the Citizen School" (*Escola Cidadã*) by way of a "democratic, deliberative, and participatory forum … the Constituent Congress of Education" (p. 30), which specified "democratization of management … access to the school, and democratization of access to knowledge" (p. 31). The mechanisms for achieving these goals were a structure for progression up the grades without repeated exam-based expulsion of students, a curriculum which reflects critical pedagogy principles of themes derived from "the interests or worries of the community" (ibid.), and Schools Councils, with substantial parent participation and votes, which advise the principal and the school management.[23] Strikingly,

> In Porto Alegre's schools, the entire school community elects the principal by direct vote. Thus, the person responsible for implementing School Council decisions is elected on the basis of the program she or he articulates. This enhances administrative legitimacy in the community. Hence, the principal does not represent the interests of the central administration inside the School Councils, but instead has attained majority support within a particular educational community.
>
> (p. 34)

And schools have autonomy in the management of their share of the participatory budget. This is an example of a degree of democracy that is rare. It would not actually support a critical pedagogy if there had not already been decades of organizing, theorizing, and practicing that could be drawn upon by the activists involved. Presumably the persistence of such a structure also depends on a degree of radicalization among the communities involved as well as the availability of activists to mobilize participation. And the Municipal Secretariat of Education is reported to be aware that mere decentralization can result in power being devolved to units that are *not* "accountable by criteria … based on democratic decisions" (ibid., p. 35). For that reason it provided support and advice to citizens and parents concerning how and why to participate in Schools Councils.

Writing in 2002, Apple and Gandin cautioned that it remained to be seen whether this initiative could withstand larger political forces both inside and outside Brazil. The municipality of Porto Alegre at least took steps to strengthen its support by establishing a *Network of Educating Cities*, joining forces with a number of other cities in signing up to a manifesto of principles. It had earlier benefited from inter-city contacts about education with the city of Barcelona, located in a region (Catalonia) of which Flecha (2009, p. 335) writes:

> Catalonia has a long and profound libertarian tradition … Many people do not respond to the proposals of participation made by governmental institutions and political parties, but they engage in intense activity when the initiatives come from themselves. This approach connects to the grassroots spirit of an increasing number of current social movements.

It presumably has helped that the mayor of Porto Alegre became Minister of Education in the Brazilian national administration. Local politics changed in 2005 when the Workers' Party lost control of the municipal administration, but Gandin (2009, p. 341) states that the policies and practices mentioned above were "already organic to the life of Porto Alegre."

The example of Porto Alegre has been of interest to many specialists. To provide one more point of departure that the reader may wish to pursue, let me note that Porto Alegre is also cited in Fung's extended analysis (2004) of "urban democracy" and the Chicago Public Schools. Fung points out the great need for actual empirical studies of how (indeed, whether) participatory democracy theory can work out in actual practice in contemporary environments, and the comparative rarity of such analyses which include educational systems as well.

The identification of local and diverse sites as places which we might imagine differently, and locations to which our efforts might also be directed, implies and requires, to repeat, the network both as a metaphor and as a reality. We will always need help—that is to say, we will need to be part of a network or federation of similarly politicked and governed entities—networks of localities, of economic enterprises, of municipalities, and probably, ideally, networks of schools. Which leads me to my final section: a return to the matter of language schools themselves.

TASK: INQUIRE

What level of democracy is there in your locality? Could it be different? Could you imagine yourself choosing to be in a place that had more, rather than less democracy?

Options for a critical educational institution

It is an enormous job to imagine alternative socio-political and economic structures, so let me draw back now, also as a way of concluding, to alternative educational institutions. Perhaps critical (language) teachers should attempt the less challenging task of imagining alternative (critical language) schools or programs. Within this same frame, the importance of one's imagination, I would encourage critical language teachers to begin imagining their ideal school, then, as an entity manifesting alternative values and acting as a model institution with a mandate to assist critical (or radical) change in society.[24] (Though as well as starting with an ideal, in some cases, their own schools might be sites for their critical work, or places that their students could use to develop their own action plans that might improve their living and learning contexts.) I surveyed a range of administrative alternatives in Chapter 7, and I do not want to zero in on just one form here. Let us see if a set of elements, some taken from those alternatives, could be combined in a form that is productive for motivational effects here.

As a preliminary remark, let me mention that although this imaginary educational institution has language as its central focus or driving force, it will be part of the mandate of this school to address culture as well. It would be a base for various forms of community outreach, sponsoring cultural festivals, support to poorer communities, and fostering study in other countries

To begin, we could think small and consider the second language-focused instructional entities that serve an immigrant community. Perhaps, given the Auerbach and Wallerstein tradition, this is a natural first structure to consider. These entities can be extremely small; merely one or two classes, a handful of teachers, and thus could have democratic administrative structures.[25] They also allow democratic, participatory means of curriculum and program development. A weakness is they can be very dependent on local and national government funding for immigrant service support.

We might take some inspiration from the private language schools that do not only handle the power languages of the world but also the languages of the countries they are located in; these are more common than before. Where these countries or cultures have alternative or resistant political and cultural traditions they might be hospitable to critical pedagogies. I am thinking of a number of cases of Spanish language teaching programs that serve mainly an adult visitor population in places such as Guatemala; these sometimes manage to combine Spanish language teaching with instruction concerning indigenous communities and ecosystem support activities. They may be dependent on an international market but equally are then independent of government support and perhaps insulated from local pressures.

In general, one might choose to be optimistic about the free-standing private language school as having potential for critical practice. A balance may need to be struck between forms of cultural action involving second languages, on the one hand, and on the other hand delivering a high quality product for instrumental purposes (including exam preparation) along with providing access to connections (local and international, NGO, foundations, and governmental). Building out the program in its conventional direction will allow the school to establish a large clientele that could then be interested in other matters as well. Ideally, such an entity could be engaged in educational work across national borders, integrating language teaching with, say, ecological projects and developmental studies.

What about non-free-standing institutions? A range of higher education institutions has shown itself moderately hospitable to critical pedagogies. Adult education institutions and community colleges have explicit missions to serve disadvantaged sectors of society, and as mentioned before, the adult education sector is the *locus classicus* of Freirean literacy programs, of course. But size and the highly contested nature of some such institutions remain as problems.

State universities at various times and in various locations have found themselves influenced either by broadly drawn mandates for social development or have responded to the viewpoints of their professors and students, such that social change goals have been adopted. This does not mean that they naturally also had critical pedagogies; here I am thinking of parts of the US, European, and Latin American university sectors during the 1960s and 70s.[26] At the present time, one might consider a range of much smaller private universities and colleges in certain locations. A few small private colleges and universities around the world (both in the US and in Korea and perhaps Japan) have variations on the theme of peace and global education as part of their mission statements. Some of the elite private liberal arts colleges in the US (and perhaps elsewhere) also have missions and orientations that would lend themselves to some forms of critical pedagogy. Entities that have established and maintain Women's Studies programs are living testament to the extent to which originally radical program development initiatives were able to take root and maintain themselves; one would certainly expect feminist pedagogies still to be found in such places. There are clearly tensions to be found, however, when the strategy is to establish programs in a host institution when the overall mission of the institution is mainstream and that of the program is not.

Finally, perhaps we could take some, though by no means all, elements from the concept of the community school. At very least, our school or program would not only be open to elements of the community but could also be a physical base for community organizing. It might also be a site which cooperates with other agencies and deliverers of local services, so that connections could be made to local issues in our curricula but also so that coalitions of potential actors could be built.

All of these entities should be seen as not located only in geographic space but also partly located in cyberspace. We cannot ignore the highly connected future that is anyway already with us. I have not developed the online possibilities of critical pedagogy much in the present work (besides a gesture towards user-generated content in Chapter 2), partly because the possibilities change and increase on an almost day-to-day basis. But clearly all aspects of our school should be looked at with a view to enhanced communication through online capacities. This might particularly be advantageous for the implementation of a radical administrative philosophy certainly involving direct democracy of teachers, students, and staffers and connected to supportive federations of like-minded institutions, probably cooperatives.

TASK: INQUIRE

Where to start? I admit that language schools operating for profit alone may not be the best place to start. Maybe only volunteer work or internships will be initiatives consistent with this vision. Share any ideas you might have for places to get relevant experience in your environment. Draw up a list of programs you could inquire into, to develop your vision of an alternative language teaching program or an alternative, critical, educational entity.

In closing

"You may say I'm a dreamer" (Lennon, 1971)—but my objective in this chapter, remember, has been to push back against the colonization of the imaginary by mainstream conceptions of society. I assert that the sketch of the last few pages is not entirely a work of free-flying fiction, but rather, as the extensive referencing earlier may have indicated, grounded in both other imaginative individuals' work as well as actual empirical practices, found in the history of education as well as in plans for the future. ("So I'm not the only one," ibid.)

No one is saying that change is easy. Also, no one is saying that there would be some unitary path to a terminal point of progress. On the contrary, it is increasingly clear that different modes of life coexist. I would be happy with a little more space and time for things tagged with the term "critical," and I am sure that most readers of this book recognize that there can be no conclusion to the efforts that are needed to maintain those places. There can be no end to our enterprises; the struggle will continue.

Notes

1 "Progressive educators have always been better at critique than at possibility" Shapiro (2009, p. i); more strongly: "The romantic possibilitarian rhetoric of some of the writers on critical pedagogy is not sufficiently based on a tactical or strategic analysis of the current situation" (Apple, 2009, p. 36).

2 Originally from Anderson (1991) and from a rather different discourse, on the history of the development of the nation-state.

3 Rousseau himself, as opposed to this literary work, is a rather ambiguous source. *Emile* was written by a man who had no teaching experience, didn't marry, and produced four illegitimate children that he gave away to orphanages. His comparable work on the education of girls was quite opposed to modern ideas about the equality of the sexes. And note also that "Rousseau was not ready to call for equality: [since he wrote:] 'Remain in the place which nature assigns to you in the chain of being. Nothing will be able to make you leave it.' [And that] for the poor he offers no benefit from education: 'The poor man does not need to be educated. His station gives him a compulsory education. He could have no other'" (Rousseau, 1979, p. 83 & p. 52, in Sworowski, 1995, p. 324).

4 According to de Guimps (1904, p. 95), he also tested and discarded other ideas of Rousseau's.

5 Harvey (1990), Bauman (1997), radical modernity (Giddens, 1990).

6 Whether politics arises from economics, or vice versa, has apparently been the subject of long-standing debate.

7 Drawing also on an analytic review of their work (Tonkiss, 2008).

8 Two individuals, Gibson, and Graham, chose to write their major academic works under the single authorial pen-name Gibson-Graham.

9 And one they ascribe to Laclau & Mouffe (1985; see also Laclau, 1991, p. 97).

10 Cf. Gunn & Gunn (1991).

11 In discussing economic associations, we are addressing a kind of entity that is assumed to contribute to the continuing oppression of people on a class basis. But what about racism, sexism, etc.? Back to imagination—there is a need to imagine non-racist societies, and there is a need for indigenous and working-class students to imagine themselves differently, and teachers to imagine those students differently as well (cf. Bishop, 2010).

12 When Freire returned to Brazil, he aligned himself with the political party of Lula, the Workers Party, which indeed pursued this line.

13 Not all critical pedagogy theorists would accept the idea that present conditions imply the use of newer political theoretical developments (e.g. McLaren).

14 It remains to be seen if there is any equivalent non-US work (see Apple et al., 2009).

15 http://joshuajkurz.wordpress.com/2010/10/17/critical-pedagogy/

16 McLaren (2005b, p. 94): "Revolutionary Critical Pedagogy is not in the business of presaging as much as it is preparatory … decidedly more praxiological than prescored." But see also McLaren & Jaramillo (2009).

17 In later publications they no longer articulate a joint position (Wenman, 2003).

18 http://illinois.academia.edu/MichaelPeters

19 http://www.westminster.ac.uk

20 This refers to the Peace of Westphalia, treaties between European nations signed in 1648 that are considered to establish the political and diplomatic order of nation-states.

21 The *World Mayors Summit*, the *Global City Forum*, the *Sister Cities International Congress*, the *Asia Pacific Cities Summit*, the *World Congress of Metropolis*, and so on.

22 http://wphr.org/2011/qdtruong/participatory-budgeting-empowers-citizens/

23 These reflect initiatives made by Freire during his time as Secretary of Education Sao Paulo (Flecha, 2009). For another example of direct democracy in education in Brazil, see McCowan (2003).

24 Besides the myriad of actual examples, Schutz (2001, pp. 296–98) does a similar sort of three-paragraph thought experiment as a way of exploring Dewey's vision

and then coming up with one of his own in a specific area where he is questioning Dewey's version of democracy.

25 Depending, to some extent, on the students' own backgrounds.

26 Consider reports on Cuban education after the revolution (Bowles 1971; Kozol, 1978) and discussion of socialist pedagogies in Small (2005).

APPENDIX

In this appendix, I have gathered three sets of materials extracts. First, pages from Auerbach and Wallerstein, second from Norton's source materials (the Mphahlele autobiography as a graphic novel), and third, extracts from Janks's work.

Part 1: Extracts from *ESL for action*

Here are some of the classic pages from the first unit of Auerbach & Wallerstein (1987a). The discussion in Chapter Two takes you through the key sections of the unit. Here you can also see the careful depiction of the classroom situation by the illustrator. The teacher is in a responsive, facilitator role—it is the students who (in a circle) are actively sharing and dictating their names to the teacher, who is writing them down. And careful inspection of the illustration suggests that these students are mostly women of color.

UNIT **1**

Introducing Ourselves

Lesson 1 Introductions: What's Your Name?

INTRODUCTORY ACTIVITY: Getting started

1. Make a circle with your chairs. Go around the circle and introduce
yourselves:

"My name is _____. What's yours?"

2. Tell the teacher one name you remember. He or she will write it on the
board:

"This is Mario."
"That is _____."

3. Is everyone's name on the board? Ask each other questions until all the
names are written correctly.

1

2   UNIT I / Introducing Ourselves

CODE

Supervisor: Stella, this is Duc Nguyen. Please show him the job.

American worker: Sure. What's your name again?

Vietnamese worker: Nguyen Duc.

Stella: What was that?

Duc: It's Duc.

Stella: (laughing) It sounds like Duck. I guess I'll call you Doug. My name is Stella.

Duc: Tella?

Stella: No! STELLA. S-T-E-L-L-A.

Duc: OK.

Questions for discussion:

1. What is the Vietnamese worker's name?
   What does the supervisor call him?
   Can Stella say Duc's name?
   Can Duc say Stella's name?

2. What does Stella call Duc?
   How do you think Duc feels about this?
   What does Duc call Stella?
   How do you think Stella feels about this?

3. Do Americans ever have trouble with your name?
   What do they call you? Do you like it?
   Do you have trouble with American names?

4. In your country, are family names first or last?
   In your country, who do you call by their first name?
   In your country, who do you call by a title (Teacher, Sir, Grandmother, Doctor)?
   Do you think immigrants should take English names? Why or why not?

5. What can you say if Americans have trouble with your name?
   What can you say if you have trouble with a name?

THINKING ACTIVITIES

A. NAMING SYSTEMS: Getting information

In pairs, find out about each others' names. Ask these questions; ask your teacher, too.

1. What is your name?
2. What is your *family name* (or *last name*)?
3. What is your *first name*?
4. What is your *middle name*?
5. (For married women): What is your *maiden name*?
6. In your country, do you keep your parents' name when you get married?
7. In your country, what do you call your teacher?
8. What do you want to be called?

Discussion: You feel comfortable calling your teacher "Teacher" or
Mr. _____, but he wants to be called by his first name. What should
you do?

B. NAMING SYSTEMS: Chart

Make a class chart of name differences in your countries.

Country	Names
U.S.	First, Middle, Last
China	Last, Middle, First

Grammar Practice (simple present tense—*to be*): Make sentences like these
about your chart:

    In the U.S., the family name is last.   In China, the family name is first.

ACTION ACTIVITIES

A. COMPETENCY: Asking for help with names

What does Stella say when she doesn't understand Duc's name?
What other questions can you ask to get help with names?
Practice asking for help with other students' names.

        Example: Student #1: This is Nicholas.
                 Student #2: I'm sorry. What was that?

B. COMPETENCY: Polite ways to keep your name

Do Americans sometimes change your name? What do they call you? What do
you want to be called? What can you say to keep your name? Add to this list:

        I'd rather be called _____.   I prefer _____.

Practice this conversation, using each others' names:

Stella: What's your name again?
Nguyen Duc: Nguyen Duc. Duc.
Stella: Can I call you Doug?
Duc: I prefer Duc.

4   *UNIT 1 / Introducing Ourselves*

C. STUDENT INTERVIEWS

CLASS QUESTIONS: What would you like to know about each other? Make a list of questions to ask each other using *what*, *where*, and *why*. Then ask the questions in pairs.

Examples: What country are you from?
What kind of work do you do?

Where do you work?
Where do you live?

Why do you want to learn English?
Why did you come to the U.S.?

INTRODUCTIONS: Introduce your partner to the class.

Example: This is Duc. He is from Vietnam. He works at the Marriott Hotel. He came here because of the war in his country. His brother is here.

CLASS CHART: After you've introduced each other, make a chart about the students in class.

Name	Where are you from?	What do you do?
Duc	Vietnam	Housekeeping/hotel
Hien	Vietnam	No job

Grammar Practice: Make sentences like this:

Duc and Hien are from Vietnam.

CLASS CHART: Make another chart about your class. What is the same about the students? What is different?

Same	Different
all women	countries
no English	jobs

STUDENT ACTION RESEARCH

Ask three friends about name problems:

1. What do Americans call you?
2. What do you want to be called?
3. Do you think immigrants should keep their names or take American names? Why?

Discuss your interviews in class: Why do some people want American names? Why do others *not* want them?

Part 2: Extracts from *Down Second Avenue: The comic*

There are two extracts: (1) The first page of the story; (2) a section after the story, which speaks directly to the reader exhorting him or her to become a writer, and goes on to encourage multiple readings of the text, direct contact between reader and publisher, and many other things that Norton Pierce points out as early manifestations of critical L2 literacy in support of a political struggle.

What are the lessons we can learn from this? L2 teachers can't usually write autobiographies of political struggle nor illustrate comic books. So this particular variant of critical language pedagogy is dependent on well-produced preexisting materials. The original material autobiography was banned in South Africa; these kinds of materials are still hard to find for the regular L2 teacher today.

However, the second half of the book (see extract 2) could be a model for the critical L2 teacher, since it is basically a commentary on the first half. If you had some appropriate content, you could comment on it. This still requires a good sense of critical language awareness, though; perhaps this is not for the beginner.

As for "content"—see my list of books on page 29; however, consider the cost and the difficulty of obtaining them in many international locations.

I wonder about the availability of equivalent L1 materials in EFL countries; if found, could they be translated into the L2 or used to assist students to design their own materials?

Down Second Avenue

I have never known why we —
my brother and I — were taken
to the country when I was five.
We went to live with our grandmother. My father and mother
remained in Pretoria where they
both worked. That was in the
autumn of 1924.

My grandmother was not the smiling type.

YOU'RE NOT FROM SCHOOL TODAY, ESKI AND I CAN SEE IT IN YOUR EYES.

I AM FROM THERE GRANNY.

I hated school, and I swore to myself I would loathe it to the end of my life.

F-O-X, FOKOS
B-O-X, BOKOS
F-I-X, FIKIS

Fox
Box
fix

We learnt a great deal from the communal fireplace — history, tradition, communal responsibility, social living and so on...

WHEN THE SWAZIS CLASHED WITH BAPEDI...

AS THINGS WERE UNDER BOER RULE...

Often the crops failed us. Often we ate practically dry, boiled corn. Some moon-light nights we went out to hunt hares. Sometimes we caught stray pigs.

One day our mother arrived to fetch us. We were going back to Pretoria to live with my parents.

ARE WE GOING ON A TRAIN?

YES ESKI AND YOU MUST LOOK SMART AND NEAT FOR THE CITY.

1

Become a writer like Es'kia Mphahlele .... Use the next 10 pages to brush up on your writing and reading skills.

Before you start here is a short note about the activities:

- Work with a friend if you can — it's more fun.
- The instructions will tell you what to do.
- Sometimes there are answers to refer to. Lots of times you'll have to work it out yourself!

How well can you copy?

Do you recognise these pictures from the comic? The difference is that these pictures have missing sentences. See how accurately you can copy what is missing.

IMPROVE YOUR VOCABULARY, TRAIN YOUR MEMORY AND PRACTISE FINDING THE WORDS YOU NEED.

WHAT IS ZEPH SAYING ? LOOK BACK TO PAGE 5 OF THE COMIC AND WRITE DOWN WHAT HE SAYS.

WHAT IS ES'KIA SAYING ? LOOK BACK TO PAGE 9 OF THE COMIC AND WRITE DOWN WHAT HE SAYS.

WHAT IS ES'KIA'S SON SAYING ? LOOK BACK TO PAGE 12 AND WRITE DOWN WHAT HE SAYS.

Now, ask a friend to check that you have copied each word accurately and that you have put in the punctuation marks. Give yourself 2 marks for each sentence you copied accurately.

If you got 6 marks .... you are a shining star as a copyist!
If you got 5 marks .... you can improve.
If you got 3 marks or fewer .... you need lots more practice!

13

Here is the second extract from *Down Second Avenue*:

How well do you read?

Look carefully at the following pictures. How much information can you get from them? Answer the questions about each one.

COMICS ARE MADE UP OF WORDS AND PICTURES.

Look back at page 1 of the comic to see where this picture is in the story.
- What is happening in this picture?
- How many people are sitting at the fireplace?
- What are they learning about?
- Do you think that Es'kia was also there?

Look back at page 5 of the comic to see where this picture is in the story.
- What is happening in this picture?
- Why did the photographer take a photograph of some pupils in blazers at St. Peter's Secondary School?
- Why were these pupils wearing blazers?

Look back at page 6 of the comic to see where this picture is in the story.
- What is happening in this picture?
- Why was the school building burning?
- Why was the missionary throwing water at the school building?
- Why were the students not helping to put out the fire?

Compare your answers with a friend's. Pictures can be interpreted in different ways and so your ideas may differ. That is why we have not given you any answers to refer to.

Part 3: Extracts from *Language and position*

Finally, here are some pages from Janks (1993a). Although not all follow the same pattern, many do use a sample of language which is physically dissected on the page.

THE WRITER'S POSITION AND THE READER'S POSITION

We have seen how a person's view of reality leads him or her to construct what he or she says in particular ways, from a particular point of view. On page 4 we saw that the writer of the article has a different point of view from the map maker and he thinks that South African maps should be drawn differently. What we need to think about now is the relationship between the writer's point of view and the reader's. Obviously writers hope that their readers will come to share their perspective, their position, otherwise there would be no point in writing.

In the poem **Streemin** written by Roger McGough, the poet disapproves of educational streaming. Streaming separates students into different classes according to how clever they are. He has an anti-streaming position. He wants his readers to share this position so he uses language to position his readers against streaming. Let's see how this works in practice. Read the poem aloud and answer the questions in bubbles.

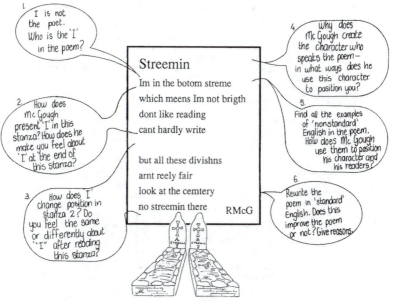

1. I is not the poet. Who is the 'I' in the poem?

2. How does McGough present 'I' in this stanza? How does he make you feel about 'I' at the end of this stanza?

3. How does 'I' change position in stanza 2? Do you feel the same or differently about "I" after reading this stanza?

4. Why does McGough create the character who speaks the poem — in what ways does he use this character to position you?

5. Find all the examples of 'nonstandard' English in the poem. How does McGough use them to position his character and his readers?

6. Rewrite the poem in 'standard' English. Does this improve the poem or not? Give reasons.

Streemin

Im in the botom streme
which meens Im not brigth
dont like reading
cant hardly write

but all these divishns
arnt reely fair
look at the cemtery
no streemin there

RMcG

By examining the language of any text carefully, we can often uncover how the writer uses language to create points of view or positions for the reader. Sometimes writers do this deliberately. At other times they unconsciously choose language which best expresses their position. Readers are usually not conscious of how they are positioned by the writer.

HOW WE USE LANGUAGE TO POSITION OTHER PEOPLE

Imagine that you and your sister (or brother) have just had a fight. Your mother is very angry with both of you. She asks each of you to tell her what happened. You both agree on the facts (you both tell her essentially the same story) but each of you will use language to position your mother so that she sides with you.

In groups of three role-play the scene: there are three characters, the mother and the two children.

Remember that you have to agree on the facts. Work these out together first. Then work out what language to choose to present each child's position. The aim of the exercise is for each child to try and win the mother over to his or her position. If you script the play the choice of language is deliberate. If you decide to improvise, then when you imagine yourself into the role, the character's choice of language will be less conscious.

Once you have finished your role plays, some groups should act them out in front of the class.

A job for the audience to do
While you are watching the performances you need to concentrate very carefully on the language used by the two children. Think about how the children are using language to position their mother. These questions will help you to notice the language.

1. Did the children choose different vocabulary? Write down examples.
2. Did the children present the information in the same order?
3. What tone of voice did the two children use?
4. What other techniques did either of the children use to win their mother over to their position?
5. If one child convinces the mother that she or he was justified, try to work out how the child did so.

Compare your answers afterwards with the audience and the actors.

Because **values are often a part of the language we speak,** in choosing words we are not fully conscious of their effects. Even words referring to space such as 'up', 'down', 'high', 'low', 'rise', 'fall', are not neutral. In English 'up' words have a positive value or connotation whereas 'down' words have a negative value.

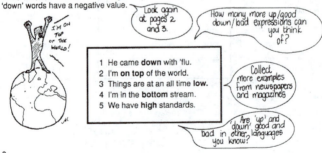

I'M ON TOP OF THE WORLD!

Look again at pages 2 and 3.

How many more up/good down/bad expressions can you think of?

1 He came **down** with 'flu.
2 I'm **on top** of the world.
3 Things are at an all time **low**.
4 I'm in the **bottom** stream.
5 We have **high** standards.

Collect more examples from newspapers and magazines

Are 'up' and 'down' good and bad in other languages you know?

8

DO NEWSPAPERS USE LANGUAGE TO POSITION READERS?

In 1990 *The Star* ran the advertisement on the opposite page as part of their *The Star tells it like it is* advertising campaign. Cover the writing below the picture. Look at the picture and the caption written on the picture. How are they trying to position you, the reader? What do they make you think? What is the writer assuming about the reader?

The words in the box below are the same as the words under the picture. Read them and then answer the following questions. This can be done in writing, either individually or in pairs.

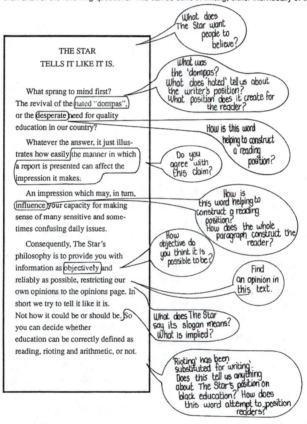

THE STAR

TELLS IT LIKE IT IS.

What sprang to mind first?
The revival of the hated "dompas",
or the desperate need for quality
education in our country?

Whatever the answer, it just illustrates how easily the manner in which
a report is presented can affect the
impression it makes.

An impression which may, in turn,
influence your capacity for making
sense of many sensitive and sometimes confusing daily issues.

Consequently, The Star's
philosophy is to provide you with
information as objectively and
reliably as possible, restricting our
own opinions to the opinions page. In
short we try to tell it like it is.
Not how it could be or should be. So
you can decide whether
education can be correctly defined as
reading, rioting and arithmetic, or not.

Annotations around the image:

What does The Star want people to believe?

What was the 'dompas'? What does 'hated' tell us about the writer's position? What position does it create for the reader?

How is this word helping to construct a reading position?

Do you agree with this claim?

How is this word helping to construct a reading position? How does the whole paragraph construct the reader?

How objective do you think it is possible to be?

Find an opinion in this text.

What does The Star say its slogan means? What is implied?

'Rioting' has been substituted for 'writing'. Does this tell us anything about The Star's position on black education? How does this word attempt to position readers?

11

REFERENCES

Akyea, S. G. & Sandoval, P. (2004). A feminist perspective on student assessment: An epistemology of caring and concern. *Radical Pedagogy, 6*(2). Unpaginated, online http://radicalpedagogy.icaap.org/

Althusser, L. (1971). *Lenin and philosophy.* London, UK: New Left Books.

Alvarez, S. (1990). *Engendering democracy in Brazil: Women's movements in transition politics.* Princeton, NJ: Princeton University Press.

Anderson, B. (1991). *Imagined communities: Reflections on the origin and spread of nationalism.* New York: Verso.

Anderson, W. L. & Ross, R. L. (2005). The methodology of profit maximization: An Austrian alternative. *The Quarterly Journal of Austrian Economics, 8*(4), 31–44.

Andolina, M. W., Jenkins, K., Zukin, C. & Keeter, S. (2003). Habits from home, lessons from school: Influences on youth civic engagement. *Political Science and Politics, 36*(2), 275–280.

Anyon, J. (2005). *Radical possibilities: Public policy, urban education, and a new social movement.* New York: Routledge.

Anyon, J. (2009a). Critical pedagogy is not enough. In M. Apple, W. Au & L. A. Gandlin (eds), *Routledge handbook of critical education* (pp. 389–395). New York: Routledge.

Anyon, J. (2009b). What is to be done? Toward a rationale for social movement building. In S. Shapiro (ed.), *Education and hope in troubled times* (pp. 47–63). Taylor & Francis.

Apple, M. (1985). *Education and power.* Boston, MA: Routledge & Kegan Paul.

Apple, M. (1988). *Teachers and texts: A political economy of class and gender relations in education.* New York: Routledge.

Apple, M. (2009). Is there a place for education in social transformation? In S. V. Shapiro (ed.), *Education and hope in troubled times* (pp. 29–46). New York: Routledge.

Apple, M. W. & Beane, J. A. (eds). (1999). *Democratic schools: Lessons from the chalk face.* Buckingham, UK: Open University Press.

Apple, M. W. & Beane, J. A. (eds). (2007). *Democratic schools: Lessons from the chalk face* (2nd edn). Portsmouth, NH: Heinemann.

Apple, M. & Gandin, L. A. (2002). Can education challenge neo-liberalism? The Citizen School and the struggle for democracy in Porto Alegre, Brazil. *Social Justice, 29*(4), 26–40.

Apple, M. W., Au, W., & Gandin, L. A. (eds) (2009). *The Routledge international handbook of critical education*. New York: Routledge.

Appleton, M. (2000). *A free range childhood: Self regulation at Summerhill School*. Brandon, VT: Foundation for Educational Renewal.

Aronowitz, S. (1996). Towards radicalism: The death and rebirth of the American left. In D. Trend (ed.), *Radical democracy: Identity, citizenship, and the state* (pp. 81–101). New York: Routledge.

Ashworth, M. (1985). National policies and language teaching. *Beyond methodology: Second language teaching and the community* (pp. 85–113). New York: Cambridge University Press.

Asplund, M. (2007). A test of profit maximization (CEPR discussion paper no. DP 6177). Available at http://ssrn.com/abstract=1133821

Auerbach, E. (1995). The politics of the ESL classroom: Issues of power in pedagogical choices. In J. Tollefson (ed.), *Power and inequality in language education* (pp. 9–33). Cambridge University Press.

Auerbach, E. (1996). *Adult ESL/literacy from the community—to the community: A guidebook for participatory literacy training*. Mahwah, NJ: Lawrence Erlbaum.

Auerbach, E. (2000). Creating participatory learning communities: Paradoxes and possibilities. In J. K. Hall & W. G. Eggington (eds), *The sociopolitics of English language teaching* (pp. 143–164). Clevedon, UK: Multilingual Matters.

Auerbach, E. (2001). "Yes, but ...": Problematizing participatory ESL pedagogy. In P. Campbell & B. Burnaby (eds.), *Participatory practices in adult education* (pp. 267–305). Mahwah, NJ: Lawrence Erlbaum.

Auerbach, E. (ed.). 2002. *Community partnerships*. Washington, DC: TESOL.

Auerbach, E. R. & Wallerstein, N. (1987a). *ESL for action*. New York: Prentice-Hall.

Auerbach, E. R. & Wallerstein, N. (1987b). *ESL for action: Teacher's guide* New York: Prentice-Hall.

Auerbach, E. R. & Wallerstein, N. (2004). *Problem-posing at work: English for action*. Edmonton, Canada: Grassroots Press.

Auerbach, E. & Wallerstein, N. (2004). *Problem-posing at work: English for action*. Edmonton, Canada: Grassroots Press.

Austin, J. L. (1962). *How to do things with words*. Oxford, UK: Clarendon Press.

Avrich, P. (1980). *The modern school movement: Anarchism and education in the United States*. Princeton, NJ: Princeton University Press.

Bailey, C. R. (1998). Municipal government and secondary education during the early French revolution: Did decentralization work? *French History, 12*(1), 25–42.

Bailey, J. P. (1977). Consciousness raising groups for women: Implications of Paulo Freire's theory of critical consciousness for psychotherapy and education. *Dissertation Abstracts International* 38, 164–65A. Ed.D. dissertation, University of Massachusetts.

Banks, J. A. (ed.). (2009). *The Routledge international companion to multicultural education*. New York: Routledge.

Barber, C. (1997). *The English language: A historical introduction*. Cambridge, UK: Cambridge University Press.

Bartlett, L. (1990). Teacher development through reflective teaching. In J. C. Richards & D. Nunan (eds), *Second language teacher education* (pp. 202–214). Cambridge, UK: Cambridge University Press.

Bartlett, L. (2005). Dialogue, knowledge, and teacher-student relations: Freirean pedagogy in theory and practice. *Comparative Education Review, 49*(3), 344–364.

Bartolomé, L. (2010). Daring to infuse ideology into language-teacher education. In S. May & C. E. Sleeter (eds), *Critical multiculturalism: Theory and praxis* (pp. 47–60). New York: Routledge.

Bauman, Z. (1997). *Postmodernity and its discontents*. New York: New York University Press.

Beach, C. (2008). Savoir c'est pouvoir: Integral Education in the novels of André Léo. *Nineteenth-century French studies, 36*(3–4), 270–285.

Benesch, S. (1996). Needs analysis and curriculum development in EAP: An example of a critical approach. *TESOL Quarterly, 30*(4), 725–738.

Benesch, S. (1999). Rights analysis: Studying power relations in an academic setting. *English for Specific Purposes, 18*(4), 313–327.

Benesch, S. (2001). *Critical English for academic purposes: Theory, politics, and practice*. Mahwah, NJ: Erlbaum.

Benesch, S. (2009). Theorizing and practicing critical English for academic purposes. *Journal of English for Academic Purposes, 8*, 81–85.

Benjamin, M. (1990). *Splitting the difference: Compromise and integrity in ethics and politics*. Lawrence, KS: University Press of Kansas.

Bentley, T. (1998). *Learning beyond the classroom*. London, UK: Routledge.

Bernstein, B. (1961). Social class and linguistic development: A theory of social learning. In A. H. Halsey, J. Floud & C. A. Anderson (eds), *Education, economy and society* (pp. 288–314). New York: Free Press.

Bernstein, B. (1971–1975). *Class, codes and control*. London, UK: Routledge & Kegan Paul.

Berge, Z. L. & Clark, T. (eds). (2005). *Virtual schools: Planning for success*. New York: Teachers College Press.

Bhatti, G., Gaine, C., Gobbo, F. & Leeman, Y. (2007). *Social justice and intercultural education*. Stoke-on-Trent, UK: Trentham Books.

Biehl, J. & Bookchin, M. (1998). *The politics of social ecology: Libertarian municipalism*. Montréal, Canada: Black Rose.

Bigelow, B. & Peterson. B. (eds). (2002). *Rethinking globalization*. Milwaukee, WI: Rethinking Schools.

Billig, M. (2006). *Critical psychology and the rhetoric of critique*. Unpublished manuscript.

Bishop, E. (2010). An ethic of engagement: Qualitative learning in the 21st century. *International Journal of Critical Pedagogy, 3*(2), 47–58.

Block, D. (2007). *Second language identities*. London, UK: Continuum.

Blunden, A. (2010). *An interdisciplinary theory of activity*. Leiden, Netherlands: Brill.

Boal, A. (1974). *Theatre of the oppressed*. London, UK: Pluto Press.

Bobbio, N. (1987). *The future of democracy* (R. Griffin, trans., R. Bellamy, ed.). Cambridge, UK: Polity Press.

Bobbio, N. (1990). *Liberalism and democracy* (M. Ryle & K. Soper, trans.). London, UK: Verso.

Bomer, R. & Bomer, K.(2001). *For a better world: Reading and writing for social action*. Portsmouth, NH: Heinemann.

Boomer, G. (1978). Negotiating the curriculum. *English in Australia, 44*, 16–29.

Boomer, G. (ed.). (1982). *Negotiating the curriculum: A teacher–student partnership*. Sydney, Australia: Ashton Scholastic.

Boomer, G., Lester, N., Onore, C. & Cook, J. (eds). (1992). *Negotiating the curriculum: Educating for the 21st century.* London, UK: Falmer Press.

Bösche, S. & Hansen, A. (1983). *Jenny lives with Eric and Martin.* London, UK: Gay Men's Press.

Boston, J., Martin, J., Pallot, J. & Walsh, P. (1996). *Public management: The New Zealand model.* Oxford, UK: Oxford University Press.

Botha, K. (n.d.) *The ideological and methodological challenges facing language textbook writers: Towards creating a new research model.* Unpublished manuscript.

Boulding, E. (2000). *Cultures of peace: The hidden side of history.* Syracuse, NY: Syracuse University Press.

Bowers, B. & Godfrey, J. (1985). *Decisions, decisions.* Agincourt, Ontario, Canada: Dominie Press.

Bowers, F. B. & Gehring, T. (2004). Johann Heinrich Pestalozzi: 18th century Swiss educator and correctional reformer. *Journal of Correctional Education, 55*(4), 306–319.

Bowles, S. (1971). Cuban education and revolutionary ideology. *Harvard Educational Review, 41*(4), 472–500.

Bowles, S. & Edwards, R. (1993). *Understanding capitalism: Competition, command, and control in the U.S. economy* (2nd edn). New York: HarperCollins.

Bowles, S. & Gintis, H. (1976). *Schooling in capitalist America: Educational reform and the contradictions of economic life.* New York: Basic Books.

Brady, B. (2008). Development, a.k.a. fundraising: A neglected element of professional development. In C. Coombe, M. McCloskey, L. Stephenson & N. J. Anderson (eds), *Leadership in English Language Teaching and Learning* (pp. 154–166). Ann Arbor, MI: University of Michigan Press.

Bragaw, D. H., Loew, H. Z. & Wooster, J. S. (1981). Global responsibility: The role of the foreign language teacher. In T. H. Geno & H. Z. Loew (eds), *Foreign languages and international study: Towards cooperation and integration* (pp. 47–58). Middlebury, VT: Northeast Conference on the Teaching of Foreign Languages.

Brameld, T. (1950). *Ends and means in education: A midcentury appraisal.* New York: Harper & Brothers.

Breen, M. P. (1987). Contemporary paradigms in syllabus design, Part II. *Language Teaching, 20*(3), 157–174.

Breen, M. P., Candlin, C. N. & Waters, A. (1979). Communicative materials design: Some basic principles. *RELC Journal, 10*(2), 1–13.

Breen, M. P. & Littlejohn, A. (eds). (2000). *Classroom decision-making.* Cambridge: Cambridge University Press.

Bremer, J. (2005, Oct. 16). Our diplomats' Arabic handicap. *Washington Post.* Retrieved January 5, 2012, from http://www.washingtonpost.com/wp-dyn/content/article/2005/10/15/AR2005101500104.html

Britton, J. N., Barnes, D. & Rosen, H. (eds). (1969). *Language, the learner and the school.* London, UK: Penguin Books.

Brookfield, S. (1999). *Discussion as a way of teaching.* San Francisco, CA: Jossey-Bass.

Brooks, E. & Fox, L. (1995). *Making peace: A reading/writing/thinking text on global community.* New York: St. Martin's Press.

Brooks, J. S. & Miles, M. (2008). From scientific management to social justice ... and back again? Pedagogical shifts in the study and practice of educational leadership. In A. H. Normore (ed.), *Leadership for social justice* (pp. 99–114). Charlotte, NC: IAP Publishing.

Brown, H. D. (1994). Teaching global interdependence as a subversive activity. In J. E. Alatis (ed.), *Educational linguistics, cross-cultural communication, and global interdependence* (pp. 174–179). Washington, DC: Georgetown University Press.

Buchanan, N. K. & Fox, R. A. (2004). Back to the future: Ethnocentric charter schools in Hawai'i. In E. Rofes & L. M. Stulberg (eds), *The emancipatory promise of charter schools* (pp. 77–106). Albany, NY: SUNY Press.

Bucholtz, M. (1999). "Why be normal?": Language and identity practices in a community of nerd girls. *Language in Society, 28*(2), 203–223.

Bunting, E. (2004). *Fly away home.* Boston, MA: Houghton Mifflin.

Burningham, J. (1994). *Hey! Get off our train.* New York: Dragonfly Books.

Busnardo, J. & Braga, D. B. (1987). Language and power: On the necessity of rethinking English language pedagogy in Brazil. In S. J. Savignon & M. S. Berns (eds), *Initiatives in communicative language teaching II* (pp. 15–32). Reading, MA: Addison-Wesley.

Busnardo, J. & Braga, D. B. (2001). Language, ideology, and teaching towards critique: A look at reading pedagogy in Brazil. *Journal of Pragmatics, 33*(5), 635–651.

Butler, J. (1987). *Subjects of desire: Hegelian reflections in twentieth century France.* New York: Columbia University Press.

Camara, H. (1969). *Church and colonialism.* London, UK: Sheed & Ward.

Caldwell, B. (2008). Reconceptualizing the self-managing school. *Educational Management & Leadership, 36*(2), 235–252.

Cameron, D. (1995). *Verbal hygiene.* London, UK: Routledge.

Campbell, J. K. (1967). *Colonel Francis W. Parker: The children's crusader.* New York: Teachers College Press.

Canagarajah, A. S. (1999). *Resisting linguistic imperialism in English teaching.* Oxford, UK: Oxford University Press.

Canagarajah, S. (2002). Reconstructing local knowledge. *Journal of Language, Identity, and Education, 1*(4), 243–259.

Canagarajah, S. (2005). Critical pedagogy in L2 learning and teaching. In E. Hinkel (ed.), *Handbook of research in second language teaching and learning* (pp. 931–950). New York: Routledge.

Candlin, C. N. (1984). Syllabus design as a critical process. In C. J. Brumfit (ed.), *General English syllabus design* (ELT Documents, 118, pp. 29–46). Oxford: Pergamon Press and The British Council.

Candlin, C. N. (1989). Language, culture and curriculum. In C. N. Candlin & T. F. McNamara (eds), *Language learning and community: Festschrift in honour of Terry Quinn* (pp. 1–24). Sydney, Australia: National Centre for English Language Teaching and Research.

Cardiff, P., Newman, K. & Pearce, E. (2007). *Reflect for ESOL resource pack.* London, UK: Reflect. Retrieved January 4, 2012 from http://www.reflect-action.org/reflectesol

Carrillo, H. (2004). Sexual migration, cross-cultural sexual encounters, and sexual health. *Sexuality Research and Social Policy, 1*, 58–70.

Carspecken, P. F. (1991). *Community schooling and the nature of power: The battle for Croxteth Comprehensive.* London, UK: Routledge.

Casanave, C. P. & Yamashiro, A. D. (eds). (1996). *Gender issues in language education.* Tokyo, Japan: Keio University (ED 425652).

Castle, D. (1998, June 1). Hearts, minds and radical democracy (interview with Ernesto Laclau and Chantal Mouffe). *Red Pepper.* Retrieved June 30, 2010 from http://www.redpepper.org.uk/article563.html

Castoriadis, C. (1987). *The imaginary institution of society* (K. Blamey, trans.). London, UK: Routledge. (Original work published 1974.)

Cates, K. (1990). Teaching for a better world: Global issues in language education. *The Language Teacher, 14*(5), 3–5.

Christensen, L. (2000). *Reading, writing, and rising up: Teaching about social justice and the power of the written word.* Milwaukee, WI: Rethinking Schools.

Christison, M. A. & Murray, D. E. (2009). *Leadership in English language education.* New York: Routledge.

Chouliaraki, L. & Fairclough, N. (1999). *Discourse in late modernity: Rethinking Critical Discourse Analysis.* Edinburgh, UK: Edinburgh University Press.

Chun, C. (2009). Critical literacies and graphic novels for English-language learners: Teaching *Maus. Journal of Adolescent & Adult Literacy, 53*(2), 144–153.

Coelho, E., Winer, L. & Olson, J. W-B. (1989). *All sides of the issue.* New York: Alemany Press.

Cohn, D. (2002). *Si, Se Puede! Yes, We Can!* El Paso, TX: Cinco Puntos Press.

Cohen, R. (2005). Learning English and democracy in Mongolia. *Essential Teacher, 2*(4), 24–26.

Cohen, T. (2004). Critical feminist engagement in the EFL classroom: From supplement to staple. In B. Norton & A. Pavlenko (eds), *Gender and English Language Learners* (pp. 155–117). Washington, DC: TESOL.

Cole, M. & Engeström, Y. (1993). A cultural-historical approach to distributed cognition. In G. Salomon (ed.), *Distributed cognitions: Psychological and educational considerations* (pp. 111–138). New York: Cambridge University Press.

Comber, B. (2006). Critical literacy educators at work: Examining dispositions, discursive resources and repertoires of practice. In K. Cooper & R. E. White (eds), *The practical critical educator: Critical inquiry and educational practice* (pp. 51–65). New York: Springer.

Committee for Children. (2002). *Second Step®: A violence prevention curriculum, grades 1–3.* Seattle, WA: Committee for Children.

Contu, A. & Willmott, H. (2003). Re-embedding situatedness: The importance of power relations in learning theory. *Organization Science, 14*(3), 283–296.

Cook, T. D. (2007). School based management: A concept of modest entitivity with modest results. *Journal of Personnel Evaluation in Education, 20*, 129–145.

Cooke, M. & Simpson, J. (2008). *ESOL: A critical guide.* Oxford, UK: Oxford University Press.

Cope, B. & Kalantzis, M. (eds). (2000). *Multiliteracies.* London, UK: Routledge.

Costa Lima, L. (1988). *Control of the imaginary: Reason and imagination in modern times* (R. W. Sousa, trans.). Minnesota, MN: University of Minnesota Press. (Originally published 1984.)

Counts, G. S. (1932). *Dare the school build a new social order?* New York: John Day Company.

Counts, G. S. (1971). A humble autobiography. In R. J. Havighurst (ed.), *Leaders in American education: The seventieth yearbook of the National Society for the Study of Education* (pp. 151–174). Chicago, IL: University of Chicago Press.

Cowhey, M. (2006). *Black ants and Buddhists.* Portsmouth, NH: Stenhouse.

Cox, M. I. P. & de Assis-Peterson, A. A. (1999). Critical pedagogy in ELT: Images of Brazilian teachers of English. *TESOL Quarterly, 33*(3) 433–51.

Crawford, L. M. (1978). *Paulo Freire's philosophy: Derivation of curricular principles and their application to second language curriculum design* (Unpublished doctoral dissertation). University of Minnesota, Minneapolis, MN.

Crawford-Lange, L. M. (1981). Redirecting second language curricula: Paulo Freire's contribution. *Foreign Language Annals, 14*(4), 257–268.

Creese, A., Bhatt, A., Bhojani, N. & Martin, P. (2006). Multicultural, heritage and learner identities in complementary schools. *Language and Education, 20*(1), 23–43.

Crookes, G. (1997a). SLA and teachers: a socio-educational perspective. *Studies in Second Language Acquisition, 19,* 93–116.

Crookes, G. (1997b). What influences how and what second and foreign language teachers teach. *Modern Language Journal, 81*(1), 67–79.

Crookes, G. (1998). On the relationship between S/FL teachers and S/FL research. *TESOL Journal, 7*(3), 6–10.

Crookes, G. (2003a). *A practicum in TESOL: Professional development through teaching practice.* Cambridge, UK: Cambridge University Press.

Crookes, G. (2003b). Critical conceptions of "professional" knowledge for the EF/SL teacher, and their implications for administrative orientation. In Z. Syed, C. Coombe & S. Troudi (eds), *TESOL Arabia 2002: Critical reflection and practice* (pp. 42–79). Dubai, UAE: TESOL Arabia.

Crookes, G. (2009). *Values, philosophies, and beliefs in TESOL: Making a statement.* Cambridge, UK: Cambridge University Press.

Crookes, G. & Talmy, S. (2004). Second/Foreign Language program preservation and advancement: Literatures and lessons for teachers and teacher education. *Critical Inquiry in Language Studies, 1*(4), 219–236.

Cumming, A. (ed.). (1990). An annotated bibliography of Canadian ESL materials. *TESL Canada Special Issue 2.*

Cummings, C., Dyson, A. & Todd, L. (2011). *Beyond the school gates: Can full service and extended schools overcome disadvantage?* London, UK: Routledge.

Cummins, J. & Sayers, D. (1990). Education 2001: Learning networks and educational reform. *Computers in the Schools, 7*(1–2), 1–29.

Cummins, J. & Sayers, D. (1995). *Brave new schools: Challenging cultural illiteracy through global learning networks.* New York: St. Martin's Press.

Curtis, A., & Romney, M. (eds). (2006). *Color, race, and English language teaching: Shades of meaning.* Mahwah, NJ: Erlbaum.

Davis, R. (1981). Education for awareness: An interview with Paulo Freire. In R. Mackie (ed.), *Literacy and revolution: The pedagogy of Paulo Freire* (pp. 57–69). New York: Continuum.

Day, R. J. F. (2005). *Gramsci is dead: Anarchist currents in the newest social movements.* London, UK: Pluto Press.

de Guimps, R. (1904). *Pestalozzi: His life and work.* New York: D. Appleton & Co.

de los Reyes, E. & Gozemba, P. (2002). *Pockets of hope.* Westport, CT: Bergin & Garvey.

Dendrinos, B. (1992). *The EFL textbook and ideology.* Athens, Greece: N. C. Grivas.

Denman, B. R. (2007). *Step forward: Language for everyday life.* Oxford, UK: Oxford University Press.

Deng, P. (1997). *Private education in modern China.* Westport, CN: Praeger/ Greenwood Press.

Dewey, J. (1938). *Experience and education.* New York: Kappa Delta Pi Publications.

Dewey, J. (1988). The economic basis of the new society. In J. A. Boydston (ed.), *John Dewey: The later works, 1925–1953* (pp. 309–322). Carbondale, IL: Southern Illinois Press. (Original work published 1939.)

Dewey, J. & Dewey, E. (1915). *Schools of to-morrow.* New York: E. P. Dutton.

Discussion Collective No. 6 of the Toronto Women's Liberation Movement. (1974). *Women Unite! An anthology of the Canadian Women's movement.* Toronto, Canada: Canadian Women's Educational Press.

Donnelly, K. (2010). The ideology of the National Curriculum. *Quadrant, 54*(5), 26–31.

Dowsey, S. J. (1970). *Zengakuren: Japan's revolutionary students.* Berkeley, CA: Ishi Press.

Dryfoos, J. G. & Maguire, S. (2002). *Inside full-service community schools.* Thousand Oaks, CA: Corwin Press.

Dryfoos, J. G., Quinn, J. & Barkin, C. (eds). (2005). *Community schools in action: Lessons from a decade of practice.* New York: Oxford University Press.

Dubetz, N. E. & de Jong, E. J. (2011). Teacher advocacy in bilingual programs. *Bilingual Research Journal, 34,* 248–262.

Du Bois, W. E. B. (1996). *The souls of black folk.* New York: Penguin. (Original work published 1903.)

Duff, P. & Uchida, Y. (1997). The negotiation of teachers' sociocultural identities and practices in postsecondary EFL classrooms. *TESOL Quarterly, 31*(3), 451–486.

Duffy, C. B. (1995). *Peace education.* Special issue of *Language and Civil Society.* Retrieved September 1, 2010 from http://eca.state.gov/forum/journal/index.htm

Duisberg, D. V. van (2005). Authentic assessment: praxis with power. *International Journal of Learning, 12*(6), 141–150.

Duncan, K. & Stasio, M. (2001). Surveying feminist pedagogy: A measurement, an evaluation, and an affirmation. *Feminist Teacher, 13*(3), 225–239.

Duncan-Andrade, J. M. & Morrell, E. (2008). *The art of critical pedagogy: Possibilities for moving from theory to practice in urban schools.* New York: Peter Lang.

Dyson, A. (2011). Full service and extended schools, disadvantage, and social justice. *Cambridge Journal of Education, 41*(2), 177–193.

Earle, J. & Kruse, S. D. (1999). *Organizational literacy for educators.* Mahwah, NJ: Lawrence Erlbaum.

Edelsky, C. & Johnson, K. (2004). Critical whole language practice in time and place. *Critical Inquiry in Language Studies, 1*(4), 121–141.

Edge, J. & Wharton, S. (1998). Autonomy and development: Living in the materials world. In B. Tomlinson (ed.), *Materials development in language teaching* (pp. 295–310). Cambridge, UK: Cambridge University Press.

Elliott, J. (1973). "Discrimination Day": An experience in moral education. *People Watching, 2*(2), 17 – 21.

Elsasser, N. & Irvine. P. (1992). Literacy as commodity: Redistributing the goods. *Journal of Education, 174*(3), 26–40.

Engeström, Y. (1987). *Learning by expanding: An activity theoretical approach to developmental research.* Helsinki: Orienta-Konsulnr.

Engeström, Y. (1991). *Non scolae sed vitae discimus:* Toward overcoming the encapsulation of school learning. *Learning and Instruction, 1,* 243–259.

Engeström, Y. (1999). Activity theory and individual social transformation. In Y. Engeström, R. Miettinen & R.-L. Punamäki (eds), *Perspectives on activity theory* (pp. 19–38). New York: Cambridge University Press.

Engeström, Y., Miettinen, R. & Punamäki, R.-L. (eds). (1999). *Perspectives on activity theory.* Cambridge, UK: Cambridge University Press.

Evans, R. (2006). "Social Studies vs. the United States of America": Harold Rugg and teaching for social justice. In K. L. Riley (ed.), *Social reconstruction: People, politics, perspectives* (pp. 45–68). Greenwich, CT: IAP Publishing.

Ewen, S. & Hebbert, M. (2007). European cities in a networked world during the long 20th century. *Environment and Planning, C: Government and Policy, 25*, 327–340.

Fairclough, N. (1990). Critical linguistics, new times and language education. In R. Clark, N. Fairclough, R. Ivanic, N. McLeod., J. Thomas & P. Meara (eds), *Language and power* (pp. 7–20). London: CILT/BAAL.

Fairclough, N. (1992). *Discourse and social change.* Cambridge, UK: Polity Press.

Fairclough, N. (1995). *Critical discourse analysis: The critical study of language.* London, UK: Longman.

Fairclough, N. (2000). Multiliteracies and language: Orders of discourse and intertextuality. In B. Cope & M. Kalantzis (eds), *Multiliteracies: Literacy learning and the design of social futures* (pp. 162–181). London, UK: Routledge & Kegan Paul.

Falkenstein, A. T. (2003). *Critical literacy in an EFL (English as a Foreign Language) context.* (Unpublished doctoral dissertation). Indiana University, Bloomington, IN.

Farias, M. (2005). Critical language awareness in foreign language learning. *Literatura y Lingüítica, 16*, 211–222.

Farrell, T. S. C. (2008). *Classroom management.* New York: TESOL.

Fay, B. (1987). *Critical social science.* Ithaca, NY: Cornell University.

Febvre, L. (1962). *Pour une histoire a part entière.* Paris, France: École Pratique des Haute Études.

Ferguson, P. (1998). The politics of adult ESL literacy: Becoming politically visible. In T. Smoke (ed.), *Adult ESL: Politics, pedagogy, and participation in classroom and community programs* (pp. 3–16). Mahwah, NJ: Lawrence Erlbaum.

Field, J. (2006). *Lifelong learning and the new social order* (2nd edn.). Stoke on Trent, UK: Trentham Books.

Fieldhouse, R. (1989). Great Britain: The Worker's Educational Association. *Landmarks in international adult education: A comparative analysis* (pp. 74–95). London, UK: Routledge.

Fisher, S. & Hicks, D. (1985). *World Studies 8–13: A teacher's handbook.* Edinburgh, UK: Oliver & Boyd.

Flecha, R. (2009). The educative city and critical education. In M. W. Apple, W. Au & L. A. Gandin (eds), *The Routledge international handbook of critical education* (pp. 327–340). New York: Routledge.

Fletcher, M. & Birt, D. (1979). *Newsflash!* London, UK: Edward Arnold.

Florio-Ruane, S. (2001). *Teacher education and the cultural imagination: Autobiography, conversation, and narrative.* Mahwah, NJ: Lawrence Erlbaum.

Flowerdew L. (2005). Integrating traditional and critical approaches to syllabus design: The "what", the "how" and the "why?" *Journal of English for Academic Purposes, 4*, 135–147.

Foley, G. (1999). *Learning in social action: A contribution to understanding informal education.* London, UK: Zed Books.

Forhan, L. E. & Scheraga, M. (2000). Becoming sociopolitically active. In J. K. Hall & W. G. Eggington (eds), *The sociopolitics of English language teaching* (pp. 195–218). Clevedon, UK: Multilingual Matters.

Foster, W. (1986). *Paradigms and promises: New approaches to educational administration.* Buffalo, NY: Prometheus.

Foster, W. (1989). Towards a critical practice of leadership. In J. Smyth (ed.), *Critical perspectives on educational leadership* (pp. 39–62). London. UK: Falmer Press.

Foster, W. (1991a). The administrator as a transformative intellectual. *Peabody Journal of Education, 66*(3), 5–18.

Foster, W. (1991b). A model of agency for postgraduate education. In W. G. Tierney (ed.), *Critique and ideology in higher education: advancing a critical agenda* (pp. 106–125). New York: Praeger.

Foster, W. (1994). School leaders as transformative intellectuals: Towards a critical pragmatism. In N. A. Prestine & P. W. Thurston (eds), *Advances in educational administration. New directions in educational administration: Policy, preparation, and practice* (pp. 29–51). Greenwich, CN: JAI Press.

Foster, W. (1999). Administrative science, the postmodern, and community. In P. T. Begley (ed.), *Values and educational leadership* (pp. 97–113). Albany, NY: SUNY Press.

Foucault, M. (1971). Orders of discourse (R. Swyer, trans.). *Social Science Information, 10*(2), 7–30.

Foucault, M. (1977). *Discipline and punish: The birth of the prison.* Harmondsworth, UK: Penguin.

Foucault, M. (1980). *Power/knowledge: Selected interviews and other writings, 1972–1977.* New York: Pantheon.

Fowler, R. (1991). *Language in the news: Discourse and ideology in the press.* London, UK: Routledge.

Fowler, R. & Kress, G. (1979). Critical linguistics. In R. Fowler, B. Hodge, G. Kress & A. Trew (eds), *Language and control* (pp. 185–213). London, UK: Routledge & Kegan Paul.

Fox, D. R., Prilleltensky, I. & Austin, S. (eds). (2009). *Critical psychology: An introduction* (2nd. edn.). New York: Sage.

Fox, L. (1980). *Perspectives: An intermediate reader.* New York: Harcourt Brace Jovanovich.

Franklin, T. & Harmelen, M. van. (2007). *Web 2.0 for content for learning and teaching in higher education.* York, UK: Franklin Consulting.

Fraser, N. (1997). *Justice interruptus; Critical reflections on the "postsocialist" condition.* New York: Routledge.

Fraser, N. (2009). *Scales of justice.* New York: Columbia University Press.

Fraser, N., & Honneth, A. (2003). *Redistribution or recognition?: A philosophical exchange* (J. Golb, J. Ingam & C. Eilke, trans.). London, UK: Verso.

Freebody, P. & Luke, A. (1990). Literacies programs: Debates and demands in cultural context. *Prospect: Australian Journal of TESOL, 5*(7), 7–16.

Freiberg, J. (ed.). (1999). *Beyond behaviorism: Changing the classroom management paradigm.* Boston, MA: Allyn & Bacon.

Freire, P. (1970). Cultural action for freedom. *Harvard Educational Review Monograph Series, 1.* Cambridge, MA: Harvard Educational Review.

Freire, P. (1973). *Education for critical consciousness.* New York: Seabury Press. (Originally published in English 1969; originally published in Portuguese 1967.)

Freire, P. (1976). *Education: The practice of freedom.* London, UK: Writers and Readers Publishing Cooperative.

Freire, P. (1982). Creating alternative research methods: Learning to do it by doing it. In B. Hall, A. Gillette & R. Tandon (eds), *Creating knowledge: A monopoly?* (pp. 29–37). New Delhi, India: Society for Participatory Research in Asia. (Originally published 1972.)

Freire, P. (1985). *The politics of education.* Hadley, MA: Bergin and Garvey.

Freire, P. (1993). *Pedagogy of the city.* New York: Continuum.

Freire, P. (1994). *Pedagogy of hope.* New York: Continuum.

Freire, P. (1996). *Letters to Christina.* New York: Routledge.

Freire, P. (1998). Cultural action and conscientization. *Harvard Educational Review, 68*(4), 480–498. (Originally published 1970.)

Freire, P. (2000). *Pedagogy of the oppressed.* New York: Continuum Press. (Originally published 1970.)

Freire, P. & Macedo, D. (1987). *Literacy: Reading the word & the world.* South Hadley, MA: Bergin & Garvey.

Friedman, S. S. (1985). Authority in the feminist classroom: A contradiction in terms? In M. Culley & C. Portuges (eds), *Gendered subjects* (pp. 203–208). London, UK: Routledge & Kegan Paul.

Fuller, B. (ed.). (2000). *Inside charter schools: The paradox of radical decentralization.* Cambridge, MA: Harvard University Press.

Fung, A. (2004). *Empowered participation: Reinventing urban democracy.* Princeton, NJ: Princeton University Press.

Fusarelli, L. D. & Johnson, B. (2004). Educational governance and the New Public Management. *Public Administration and Management, 9*(2), 118–127.

Gandin, L. A. (2009). The Citizen School project: Implementing and recreating critical education in Porto Alegre, Brazil. In M. W. Apple, W. Au & L. A. Gandin (eds), *The Routledge international handbook of critical education* (pp. 341–353). New York: Routledge.

Gardner, P. (1984). *The lost elementary schools of Victorian England: The people's education.* London, UK: Croom Helm.

Gaspari, O. (2002). Cities against states? Hopes, dreams and shortcomings of the European municipal movement, 1900-1960. *Contemporary European History, 11*, 597–622.

Gee, J. P. (1996). *Social linguistics and literacies: Ideology in discourses* (2nd cd.). London, UK: Taylor & Francis.

Gee, J. P. (2000). New people in new worlds: Networks, the new capitalism, and schools. In B. Cope & M. Kalantzis (eds), *Multiliteracies: Literacy learning and the design of social futures* (pp. 43–68). London, UK: Routledge & Kegan Paul.

Gee, J. P. (2004). Discourse analysis: What makes it critical? In R. Rogers (ed.), *An introduction to critical discourse analysis in education* (pp. 19–50). Mahwah, NJ: Lawrence Erlbaum.

Ghahremani-Ghajar, S. & Mirhosseini, S. A. (2005). English class or speaking about everything in class? Dialogue journal writing as a critical EFL literacy practice in an Iranian high school. *Language, Culture and Curriculum, 18*(3), 286–299.

Gibson-Graham, J. K. (2006). *A post-capitalist politics.* Minneapolis, MN: University of Minnesota Press.

Giddens, A. (1990). *The consequences of modernity.* Stanford, CA: Stanford University Press.

Gilchrist, R. & Jeffs, T. (eds). (2001). *Settlements, social change, and community action.* London, UK: Jessica Kingsley.

Giroux, H. A. (1981). *Ideology, culture and the process of schooling,* Lewes, UK: Falmer Press.

Giroux, H. A. (1983). *Theory and resistance in education: A pedagogy for the opposition.* South Hadley, MA: Bergin & Garvey.

Gomes, F. de M. (1988). Peace and language learning. *TESOL Newsletter, 22*(4), 16.

Gore, J. M. (1993). *The struggle for pedagogies: Critical and feminist discourses as regimes of truth.* New York: Routledge.

Gorham, D. (2005). Dora and Bertrand Russell and Beacon Hill School. *Russell: The journal of Bertrand Russell Studies, 25*, 39–76.

Gramsci, A. (1971). *Selections from the prison notebooks* (Q. Hoare & G. Nowell Smith, trans., eds). London, UK: Lawrence and Wishart.

Granville, S. (1993). *Language, advertising and power.* Witwatersrand, South Africa: Hodder & Stoughton/ Witwatersrand University Press.

Gray, J. (2002). The global coursebook in English Language Teaching. In D. Block & D. Cameron (eds), *Globalization and language teaching* (pp. 151–167). London, UK: Routledge.

Gray, J. (2010). The branding of English and the culture of the new capitalism: Representations of the world of work in English language textbooks. *Applied Linguistics, 31*(5), 714–733.

Grotlüschen, A. (2005). Expansive learning: Benefits and limitations of subject-scientific learning theory. *European Journal of Vocational Training, 36,* 15–20.

Gudeman, S. (2008). *Economy's tension.* New York: Berghahn Books.

Guilherme, M. (2002). *Critical citizens for an intercultural world: Foreign language education as cultural politics.* Clevedon, UK. Multilingual Matters.

Gumbel, P. (2006). *On achève bien les ecoliers.* Paris, France: Editions Grasset.

Gunn, C & Gunn, H. D. (1991). *Reclaiming capital: Democratic initiatives and community development.* Ithaca, NY: Cornell University Press.

Gutek, G. L. (2007). George S. Counts and social issues. In S. Totten & J. E. Pedersen (eds), *Addressing social issues in the classroom and beyond: The pedagogical efforts of pioneers in the field* (pp. 31–48). New York: Information Age Publishers.

Haber, H. F. (1994). *Beyond postmodern politics.* New York: Routledge.

Habermas, J. (1984). *The theory of communicative action* (vol. 1). London, UK: Heinemann.

Hahn, C. L. (1998). *Becoming political: Comparative perspectives on citizenship education.* Albany, NY: SUNY Press.

Halliday, M. A. K. (1961). Categories of the theory of grammar. In G. R. Kress (ed.), *System and function in language* (pp. 52–72). Oxford, UK: Oxford University Press.

Halliday, M. A. K. (1973). *Explorations in the functions of language.* London, UK: Edward Arnold.

Halliday, M. A. K. (1990). New ways of meaning: A challenge to applied linguistics. *Journal of Applied Linguistics* [Greece] *6,* 7–36.

Halliday, M. A. K. (2002). Michael Halliday. In K. Brown and V. Law (eds), *Linguistics in Britain: Personal histories* (pp. 116–126). Oxford, UK: Blackwell.

Halpin, D. D. (2003). *Hope and education: The role of the utopian imagination.* London, UK: RoutledgeFalmer.

Hammond, K. (2006). More than a game: A critical discourse analysis of a racial inequality exercise in Japan. *TESOL Quarterly, 40*(3), 546–571.

Hardy, T. (2007). MEXT-authorized English textbooks: Designing a junior high school text series. *Second Language Acquisition—Theory and Pedagogy: Proceedings of the 6th Annual JALT Pan-SIG Conference* (pp. 12–20). Sendai, Japan: Tohoku Bunka Gakuen University.

Hare, W. (1985). Open-mindedness in the classroom. *Journal of Philosophy of Education 19*(2), 251–259.

Hare, W. (2007). Ideological indoctrination and teacher education. *The Journal of Educational Controversy, 2*(2). Retrieved November 2010 from www.wce.wwu.edu/Resources/CEP/eJournal/v002n002/a006.shtml

Harklau, L. (2000). From the "good kids" to the "worst": Representations of English language learners across educational settings. *TESOL Quarterly, 34*(1), 35–67.

Harris, I. (1988). *Peace education.* Jefferson, NC: McFarland.

Harris, I. (2004). Peace education theory. *Journal of Peace Education, 1,* 5–20.

Harris, I. & Morrison, M. L. (2003). *Peace education* (2nd. edn.). Jefferson, NC: McFarland.

Hart, C. & Lukes, D. (eds). (2007). *Cognitive linguistics in Critical Discourse Analysis: Application and theory.* Newcastle, UK: Cambridge Scholars Publishing.

Hartley, D. (2007). The emergence of distributed leadership in education: Why now? *British Journal of Educational Studies, 55*(2), 202–214.

Hartshorne, K. (1992). *Crisis and challenge: Black education 1910–1990.* Cape Town, South Africa: Oxford University Press.

Harvey, D. (1990). *Postmodernity: An enquiry into the origins of cultural change.* London, UK: Blackwell.

Hatch, S. & Moyland, S. (1972). The role of the community school. In J. Raynor & J. Harden (eds), *Equality and City Schools: Readings in Urban Education* (vol. 2, pp. 218–223). London, UK: Routledge and KeganPaul.

Haymes, S. N. (2002). Race, pedagogy, and Paulo Freire. In S. Fletcher (ed.), *Philosophy of Education Yearbook 2002* (pp. 151–159). Urbana, IL: Philosophy of Education Society.

Hazareesingh, S. (1997). Defining the Republican good life: Second empire municipalism and the emergences of the third republic. *French History, 11*(3), 310–337.

Hazareesingh, S. (2001). *Intellectual founders of the Republic: Five studies in nineteenth-century French republican political thought.* Oxford, UK: Oxford University Press.

Hazen, B. S. (1983). *Tight times.* New York: Penguin Putnam Books.

Heater, D. (2004). *A history of education for citizenship.* London, UK: Routledge.

Heath, S. B. (1983). *Ways with words: Language, life, and work in communities and classrooms.* Cambridge, UK: Cambridge University Press.

Hebbert, M. (2007). Municipalism, urbanism and international action. *Universidad Autonoma de Madrid, Departamento de Ciencia Política y Relaciones Internacionales, Working Paper 81.* Retrieved July 1, 201 from http://www.uam.es/centros/derecho/cpolitica/papers.htm

Heller, M. (1982). *Language, ethnicity, and politics in Quebec.* (Unpublished doctoral dissertation.) University of California, Berkeley, CA.

Heller, M. (1987). The role of language in the formation of ethnic identity. In J. Phinney & M. Rotheram (eds), *Children's ethnic socialization* (pp. 180–200). Newbury Park, CA: Sage.

Heller, M. (1995). Language choice, social institutions, and symbolic domination. *Language in Society, 24*, 373–405.

Hodgson, G. (2008). Editorial. *Views & Reviews: The newsletter of the Critical Literacy Special Interest Group* [IATEFL] *1*, 2–3. Retrieved August 2010, from www.teachingenglish.org.uk/sites/teacheng/files/Views%20&%20Reviews_Issue%201.pdf

Hodson, D. (1999). Going beyond cultural pluralism: Science education for sociopolitical action. *Science Education, 83*(6), 775–796.

Holt, J. (1976). *Instead of education: Ways to help people do things better.* New York: Dutton.

Holst, J. D. (2006). Paulo Freire in Chile, 1964–1969: *Pedagogy of the Oppressed* in its sociopolitical economic context. *Harvard Educational Review, 76*(2), 243–270.

Hoover, R. L. & Kindsvatter, R. (1997). *Democratic discipline: Foundation and practice.* Upper Saddle River, NJ: Merrill/ PrenticeHall.

Horton, M. & Freire, P. (1990). *We make the road by walking.* Philadelphia, PA: Temple University Press.

Howatt, A. P. R. (1984). *A history of English Language Teaching.* Oxford, UK: Oxford University Press.

Humphries, S. (1981). *Hooligans or rebels?: An oral history of working-class childhood and youth 1889–1939.* Oxford, UK: Basil Blackwell.

Hutchinson, T. & Torres, E. (1994). The textbook as an agent of change. *English Language Teaching Journal, 48*, 315–328.

Huttunen, R. (2003). Habermas and the problem of indoctrination. In M. Peters, P. Ghiraldelli, B. Žarnić, A. Gibbons (eds), *Encyclopaedia of Philosophy of Education*. Retrieved 19 June, 2012 from http://www.ffst.hr/ENCYCLOPAEDIA/doku.php?id=habermas_ and_the_problem_of_indoctrination

Hyslop-Margison, E. J. & Dale, J. (2011). *Paulo Freire: Teaching for freedom and transformation: The philosophical influences on the work of Paulo Freire*. New York: Springer.

Hytten, K. (2008). Education for critical democracy and compassionate globalization. In R. D. Glass (ed.), *Philosophy of Education Yearbook 2008* (pp. 333–341). Retrieved June 15, 2011 from http://ojs.ed.uiuc.edu/index.php/pes/issue/view/10

Islam, C. & Mares, C. (2003). Adapting classroom materials. In Tomlinson, B. (ed.), *Developing materials for language teaching* (pp. 86–100). New York: Continuum.

Izadina, M. & Abednia, A. (2010). Dynamics of an EFL reading course with a critical literacy orientation. *Journal of Language and Literacy Education, 6*(2), 51–67.

Jacobs, G. M., Gan, S. L. & Ball, J. (1997). *Learning cooperative learning via cooperative learning: A sourcebook of lesson plans for teacher education*. San Clemente, CA: Kagan Publications.

Jacobs, G., Kumarasamy, P. M., Nopparat, P. & Amy, S. (1998). *Linking language and the environment*. Toronto, Canada: Pippin Publishing.

Jacobs, G. M., Power, M. A. & Inn, L. W. (2002). *The teacher's sourcebook for cooperative learning*. Thousand Oaks, CA: Corwin Press.

Janks, H. (October, 1989). Critical linguistics: A starting point for oppositional reading. Unpublished paper presented at the 14th Annual Boston University Conference on Language Development, Boston, MA (ED314942).

Janks, H. (1991). A critical approach to the teaching of language. *Educational Review 43*(2), 191–199.

Janks, H. (1993a). *Language and position*. Witwatersrand, SA: Hodder & Stoughton/ Witwatersrand University Press.

Janks, H. (1993b). *Language, identity and power*. Witwatersrand, SA: Hodder & Stoughton/ Witwatersrand University Press.

Janks, H. (1995). *The research and development of Critical Language Awareness materials for use in South African schools*. (Unpublished doctoral dissertation). The University of Lancaster, Lancaster, UK.

Janks, H. & Sethole, M. P. (2006). Reaching out and reaching in: "We had to develop ourselves before we could be developed". In K. Cooper & R. White (eds), *The practical critical educator* (pp. 165–178). Dordrecht, The Netherlands: Springer.

Jasso-Aguilar, R. (1999). Sources, methods and triangulation in needs analysis: A critical perspective in a case study of Waikiki hotel maids. *English for Specific Purposes, 18*(1), 27–46.

Jasso-Aguilar, R. (2005). Sources, methods and triangulation in needs analysis: A critical perspective in a case study of Waikiki hotel maids. In M. H. Long (ed.), *Second language needs analysis* (pp. 127–158). Cambridge, UK: Cambridge University Press.

Jenkins, H. (2006). *Convergence culture: Where old and new media collide*. New York: New York University Press.

Jocuns, A. (2005). *Knowledge and discourse: Mediated discourse and distributed cognition in two Balinese gamelan orchestras in the United States*. (Unpublished doctoral dissertation). Georgetown University, Washington, DC.

Johnson, S. & McCauslan, M. (1999). Is there still room for negotiating the curriculum? *English in Australia, 124*, 92–98.

Jones, L. (2008). *Let's talk 2*. Cambridge, UK: Cambridge University Press.

Jorge, M. (March, 2009). Critical EFL in Brazil. Unpublished paper presented at the American Association for Applied Linguistics conference, Denver, CO.

Kalantzis, M. & Cope, B. (1999). Multicultural education: Transforming the mainstream. In S. May (ed.), *Critical multiculturalism: Rethinking multicultural and antiracist education* (pp. 245–274). Philadelphia, PA: Falmer Press.

Kalantzis, M., Cope, B., Noble, G. & Poynting, S. (1990). *Cultures of schooling: Pedagogies for cultural difference and social access*. London, UK: Falmer Press.

Kanno, Y. & Norton, B. (eds). (2003). Imagined communities and educational possibilities [special issue]. *Journal of Language, Identity, and Education, 2*(4).

Kanpol, B. (1999). *Critical pedagogy: An introduction* (2nd. edn.). Westport, CT: Bergin & Garvey.

Kanpol, B. & McLaren, P. (1995). Resistance multiculturalism and the politics of difference. In B. Kanpol & P. McLaren (eds), *Critical multiculturalism* (pp. 1–17). Westport, CN: Bergin & Garvey.

Kanpol, B., Yeo, F. & SooHoo, S. (1997). A critical pedagogy for principals: Necessary conditions for moral leadership. In B. Kanpol (ed.), *Issues and trends in critical pedagogy* (pp. 79–91). Cresskill, NJ: Hampton Press.

Karusa. (1995). *The streets are free*. Willowdale, Canada: Annick Press.

Kato, R. (2010). *Teachers' resistance: Japanese teachers stories from the 1960s*. (Doctoral dissertation.) University of Massachusetts at Amherst. *Open Access Dissertations,* Paper 286. Retrieved October 1, 2011 from http://scholarworks.umass.edu/open_access_dissertations/286

Keesing-Styles, L. (2003). The relationship between critical pedagogy and assessment in teacher education. *Radical Pedagogy, 5*(1), 1–21.

Kempner, K. (1991). Getting into the castle of administration. *Peabody Journal of Education, 66*(3), 104–123.

Kenway, J. & Modra, H. (1992). Feminist pedagogy and emancipatory possibilities. In C. Luke & J. Gore (eds), *Feminisms and critical pedagogy* (pp. 138–166). New York: Routledge, Chapman & Hall.

Kilpatrick, W. H. (ed.), with Bode, B. H., Childs, J. L., Hullfish, H. G., Dewey, J., Raup, R. B. & Thayer, V. T. (1933). *The Educational Frontier*. New York: The Century Co.

Kim, Y. (2002). A critical approach to culture education in EFL. *Foreign Language Education, 9*(3), 243–264.

Kimber, M. & Ehrich, L. C. (2011). The democratic deficit and school-based management in Australia. *Journal of Educational Administration, 49*(2), 179–199.

King, C. & Osborne, L. B. (1997). *Oh, Freedom! Kids talk about the Civil Rights Movement with the people who made it happen*. New York: Scholastic.

Klamath County YMCA Preschool Staff (1993). *Land of many colors*. New York: Scholastic.

Knox, A. B. (1993). *Strengthening adult and continuing education*. San Francisco, CA: Jossey-Bass.

Kobayashi, T. (1997). *Thinking of Japanese education*. Tokyo, Japan: Eichosha.

Kobayashi, Y. (2002). The role of gender in foreign language learning attitudes: Japanese female students' attitudes towards English learning. *Gender and Education, 14*(2), 181–197.

Köhler, E. (1936). *Aktivitetspedagogik*. Stockholm, Sweden: Bokforlaget Natur och Kultur.

Kohn, A. (1996). *Beyond discipline: From compliance to community*. Alexandria, VA: ASCD.

Konoeda, K. & Watanabe, Y. (2008). Task-based critical pedagogy in Japanese EFL classrooms. In M. Montero, P. C. Miller & J. L. Watzke (eds), *Readings in language studies* (vol. 1; pp. 45–61). St. Louis, MO: International Society for Language Studies.

Kozol, J. (1978). *Children of the revolution: A yankee teacher in the Cuban schools.* New York: Delacorte Press.

Kozulin, A. & Rand, Y. (2000). *Experience of mediated learning: An impact of Feuerstein's theory in education and psychology.* New York: Pergamon.

Kramer-Dahl, A. (2001). Importing critical literacy pedagogy: Does it have to fail? *Language and Education, 15*(1), 14–32.

Kridel, C. A., Bullough, R. V. & Goodlad, J. I. (2007). *Stories of the eight-year study: Reexamining secondary education in America.* Albany, NY: SUNY Press.

Kubota, R. (1999). Japanese culture constructed by discourses: Implications for applied linguistics research and ELT. *TESOL Quarterly, 33*(1), 9–35.

Kubota, R. (2003). Critical approaches to culture and pedagogy in foreign language contexts. In J. Sharkey & K. Johnson (eds), *The TESOL Quarterly dialogues: Rethinking issues of language, culture and power* (pp. 114–121). Alexandria, VA: TESOL.

Kubota, R. (2004). Critical multiculturalism and second language education. In B. Norton & K. Toohey (eds), *Critical pedagogies and language learning* (pp. 30–52). Cambridge, UK: Cambridge University Press.

Kubota, R. (2010). Critical multicultural education and second/foreign language teaching. In S. May & C. E. Sleeter (eds), *Critical multiculturalism: Theory and praxis* (pp. 99–112). New York: Routledge.

Kubota, R. & Lin, A. (2006a). Race and TESOL: Introduction to concepts and theories. *TESOL Quarterly, 40*(3), 471–493.

Kubota, R. & Lin, A. (eds). (2006b). Race and TESOL [special issue]. *TESOL Quarterly, 40*(3).

Kumagai, Y. (2007). Tension in a Japanese language classroom: An opportunity for critical literacy? *Critical Inquiry in Language Studies, 4*(2–3), 85–116.

Kumaravadivelu, K. (2006). TESOL methods: Changing tracks, challenging trends. *TESOL Quarterly, 40*(1), 59–81.

Kuo, J.-M. (2009.) Critical literacy and a picture-book-based dialogue activity in Taiwan. *Asia Pacific Education Review, 10*(4), 483–494.

Kuroyanagi, T. (1982). *Totto-chan: The little girl at the window.* Tokyo, Japan: Kodansha.

Kurth-Schai, R., &, Green, C. R. 2006. *Re-envisioning education and democracy.* New York, NY: IAP Books.

Kwek, D., Albright, J. & Kramer-Dahl, A. (2007). Building teachers' creative capacities in Singapore's English classrooms: A way of contesting pedagogical instrumentality. *Literacy, 41*(2), 71–79.

Kwon, O. (2001). Teaching English as a global language in the Asian context. Unpublished paper presented at the 2001 summer conference of the Korean Association of Teachers of English, Seoul, Korea.

Laclau, E. (1991). Community and its paradoxes: Richard Rorty's liberal utopia. In The Miami Theory Collective (ed.), *Community at Loose Ends* (pp. 83–98). Minneapolis, MN: University of Minnesota Press.

Laclau, E. & Mouffe, C. (1985). *Hegemony and socialist strategy.* London, UK: Verso.

Lakomski, G. (2005). *Managing without leadership: Towards a theory of organizational functioning.* Amsterdam, the Netherlands: Elsevier.

Lam, W. & Wong, J. (2000). The effects of strategy training on developing discussion skills in an ESL classroom. *ELT Journal, 54*(3), 245–255.

Lamey, D. S. (2009). The impact of teachers' beliefs and practices on students' learning: A participant observation. In P. Wachob (ed.), *Power in the EFL classroom* (pp. 217–236). Newcastle upon Tyne, UK: Cambridge Scholars Publishing.

Lankshear, C. (1994). *Critical literacy (Occasional paper no. 3)*. Canberra: Australian Curriculum Studies Association.

Lantolf, J. P. & Pavlenko, A. (2001). (S)econd (L)anguage (A)ctivity: Understanding learners as people. In M. Breen (ed.), *Learner contributions to language learning: New directions in research* (pp. 141–158). London, UK: Pearson.

Lantolf, J. P. & Thorne, S. L. (2006). *Sociocultural theory and the genesis of second language development*. Oxford, UK: Oxford University Press.

Lasswell, H. (1936). *Politics: Who gets what, when, how*. New York: McGraw Hill.

Lave, J. (1997). On learning. *Forum Kritische Psychologie* (Lernen Holzkamp-Colloquium) *38*, 120–135.

Lave, J. & Wenger, E. (1991). *Situated learning: Legitimate peripheral participation*. Cambridge, UK: Cambridge University Press.

Lea, V. (2010). Empowering preservice teachers, students, and families through critical multiculturalism: Interweaving social foundations of education and community action projects. In S. May & C. E. Sleeter (eds). 2010. *Critical multiculturalism: Theory and praxis* (pp. 33–46). New York: Routledge.

Leland, C. H. & Harste, J. C. (2002). Critical literacy. In A. A. McLure & J. V. Kristo (eds), *Adventuring with books* (pp. 465–488). Washington, DC: National Council of Teachers of English.

Lennon, J. (1971). Imagine. On *Imagine*. London, UK: Apple/EMI.

Leonardo, Z. (2005). *Critical pedagogy and race*. New York: Blackwell.

Leont'ev, A. N. (1959). *Problems of the development of the mind* (1st edn.). Moscow: Progress.

Leont'ev, A. N. (1981). *Problems of the development of the mind* (4th edn.). Moscow: Progress.

Levine, E. (1995). *I hate English!* New York: Scholastic.

Levine, J. (1981). Developing pedagogies for multilingual classes. *English in Education, 15*(3), 25–33.

Levine, J. & Bleach, J. (1990). Mainstreaming, partnership teaching, teachers' action research. In J. Levine & J. Bleach (eds), *Bilingual learners and the mainstream curriculum: Integrated approaches to learning and the teaching and learning of English as a second language in mainstream classrooms* (pp. 29–53). London, UK: Routledge.

Lewis, B. A. (1991). *The kid's guide to social action*. Minneapolis, MN: Free Spirit Publishing.

Licht, E., Maher, B. & Webber, A. A. (2004). Teaching workers: Learner-centered instruction for English acquisition and social change. *The CATESOL Journal, 16*(1), 1–18

Lincicombe, M. E. (1995). *Principles, praxis, and the politics of educational reform in Meiji Japan*. Honolulu, HI: University of Hawaii Press.

Little, A. & Lloyd, M. (2009). *The politics of radical democracy*. Edinburgh, UK: Edinburgh University Press.

Littlejohn, A. P. (1982). *A procedural guide for teacherless language learning groups*. (Unpublished M.A. dissertation.) The University of Lancaster, Lancaster, UK.

Littlejohn, A. P. (1983). Increasing learner involvement in course management. *TESOL Quarterly, 17*(4), 595–608.

Liu, J., Sakamoto, A. & Su, K.-H. (2010). Exploitation in contemporary capitalism: An empirical analysis of the case of Taiwan. *Sociological Focus, 43*(3), 259–281.

Locke, T. (2010). Critical multiculturalism and subject English. In S. May (ed.), *Critical multiculturalism: Theory and praxis* (pp. 87–97). New York: Routledge.

Long, E. (2003). *Book clubs: Women and the use of reading in everyday life.* Chicago, IL: University of Chicago Press.

Long, M. H. (ed.). (2005). *Second language needs analysis.* Cambridge, UK: Cambridge University Press.

Lopez, A. E. A., Santamaria, C. M. & Aponte, R. M. V. (1993). Producing an ecology-based textbook. *English Teaching Forum, 31*(4), 11–15.

Louis, R. (2005). Performing English, performing bodies: A case for critical performative language pedagogy. *Text and Performance Quarterly, 25*, 334–353.

Luke, A. (1994). On reading and the sexual division of literacy. *Journal of Curriculum Studies, 26*(4), 361–81.

Luke, A. (2000). Critical literacy in Australia: A matter of context and standpoint. *Journal of Adolescent & Adult Literacy, 43*(5), 448–461.

Mackie, R. (1981a). Introduction. In R. Mackie (ed.), *Literacy and revolution: The pedagogy of Paulo Freire* (pp. 1–11). New York: Continuum.

Mackie, R. (1981b). Contributions to the thought of Paulo Freire. In R. Mackie (ed.), *Literacy and revolution: The pedagogy of Paulo Freire* (pp. 93–119). New York: Continuum.

MacIntyre, A. (1981). *After virtue: A study in moral theory.* Notre Dame, IN: University of Notre Dame Press

Magnusson, W. (2005). Urbanism, cities and local self-government. *Canadian Public Administration, 48*(1), 96–123.

Maher, F. (1985). Classroom pedagogy and the new scholarship of women. In M. Culley & C. Portuges (eds), *Gendered subjects* (pp. 29–48). London, UK: Routledge & Kegan Paul.

Maher, F. A, & Tetreault, M. K. T. (eds). (1994). *The feminist classroom: An inside look at how professors and students are transmuting higher education for a diverse society.* New York: Basic Books.

Mahiri, J. (1998). *Shooting for excellence: African American and youth culture in new century schools.* New York: Teachers College Press.

Marcos, S. (1999). *The story of colors = La historia de los colores.* El Paso, TX: Cinco Puntos Press.

Marshall, C. (1997). Dismantling and reconstructing policy analysis. In C. Marshall (ed.), *Feminist critical policy analysis* (pp. 1–40). London, UK: Falmer Press.

Marshall, C. & Oliva, M. (2006). *Leadership for social justice: Making revolutions in education.* Boston, MA: Pearson Education.

Martens, M. (2011). Transmedia teens: Affect, immaterial labor, and user-generated content. *Convergence: The international journal of research into new media technologies, 17*(1), 49–68.

Martín-Baró, I. (1994). *Writings for a liberation psychology.* Cambridge, MA: Harvard University Press.

Martin, J. R. & Rose, D. (2007). *Working with discourse: Meaning beyond the clause.* New York: Continuum.

Mason, R. & Rennie, F. (2008). *E-learning and social networking handbook: Resources for higher education.* New York: Routledge.

Matsui, M. (1995). Gender role perceptions of Japanese and Chinese female students in American universities. *Comparative Education Review, 39,* 356–378.

May, S. (1994). Review: The case for antiracist education. *British Journal of Sociology of Education, 15*(3), 412–428.

May, S. (ed.). (1999). *Critical multiculturalism: Rethinking multicultural and antiracist education.* Philadelphia, PA: Falmer Press.

May, S. & Sleeter, C. E. (eds). 2010. *Critical multiculturalism: Theory and praxis.* New York: Routledge.

Mayo, P. (1995). Critical literacy and emancipatory politics: The work of Paulo Freire. *International Journal of Educational Development, 15*(4), 363–379.

Mayo, P. (1999). *Liberating praxis: Paulo Freire's legacy for radical education and politics.* Westport, CT: Praeger.

McCowan, T. (2003). Participation and education in the Landless People's Movement of Brazil. *Journal for Critical Education Policy Studies, 1*(1). Retrieved January 2011 from http://www.jceps.com

McGovern, A. (1997). *The lady in the box.* New York: Turtle Books.

McGrath, I. (2002). *Materials evaluation and design for language teachers.* Edinburgh, UK: Edinburgh University Press.

McGroarty, M. (1998). *Partnerships with linguistic minority communities* (TESOL Occasional Paper #4). Washington, DC: TESOL.

McLaren, P. (1995). *Critical pedagogy and predatory culture.* New York: Routledge.

McLaren, P. (2005a). Critical pedagogy and class struggle in the age of neoliberal globalization. *Journal of Inclusive Democracy, 2*(1).

McLaren, P. (2005b). Critical pedagogy in the age of terror. In I. Gur-Ze'ev (ed.), *Critical theory and critical pedagogy today* (pp. 70–94). Haifa, Israel: Faculty of Education, University of Haifa.

McLaren, P. & Jaramillo, N. (2009). *Pedagogy and praxis in the age of empire: Towards a new humanism.* New York: Sense Publishers.

McLaughlin, M. & DeVoogd, G. L. (2004). *Critical literacy: Enhancing students' comprehension of text.* New York: Scholastic.

McMahill, C. (1997). Communities of resistance: A case study of two feminist English classes in Japan. *TESOL Quarterly, 31*(3), 612–621

McMahill, C. (2001). Self-expression, gender, and community: A Japanese feminist English class. In A. Pavlenko, A. Blackledge, I. Piller & M. Teutsch-Dwyer (eds), *Multilingualism, second language learning, and gender* (pp. 307–244). Berlin, Germany: Mouton.

McMahill, C. & Reekie, K. (1996). Forging alliances: Grassroots feminist language education in the Tokyo area. In C. Casanave & A. D. Yamashiro (eds), *Gender issues in language education* (pp. 15–30). Fujisawa, Japan: Keio University SFC. (ED 425652)

McNamara, T. (1998). Policy and social considerations in language assessment. *Annual Review of Applied Linguistics, 18,* 304–319.

McNamara, T. & Roever, C. (2006). *Language testing: The social dimension.* Malden, MA: Blackwell.

McShay, J. C. (2010). Digital stories for critical multicultural education: A Freirean approach. In S. May & C. E. Sleeter (eds). 2010. *Critical multiculturalism: Theory and praxis* (pp. 139–150). New York: Routledge.

McVeigh, B. J. (2002). *Japanese higher education as myth.* Armonk, NY: M. E. Sharpe.

Mercogliano, C. (1998). *Making it up as we go along: The story of the Albany Free School.* Portsmouth, NH: Heinemann.

Merchant, B. M. & Shoho, A. R. (2006). Bridge people; Civic and educational leaders for social justice. In C. Marshall & M. Oliva (eds), *Leadership for social justice: Making revolutions in education* (pp. 85–109). Boston, MA: Pearson Education.

Miettinen, R. (1990, May). Transcending the traditional school learning: Teachers' work and the networks of learning. Unpublished paper presented at the 2nd International Congress for Research on Activity Theory, Lahti, Finland.

Miller, D. (1987). *The Blackwell encyclopedia of political thought*. Oxford, UK: Basil Blackwell.

Mills, S. (1997). *Discourse*. London, UK: Routledge.

Mitchell, R. & Myles, F. (2004). *Second language learning theories* (2nd. edn.). London, UK: Hodder Arnold.

Moffatt, L. & Norton, B. (2005). Popular culture and the reading teacher: A case for feminist pedagogy. *Critical Inquiry in Language Studies, 2*(1), 1–12.

Moll, L.C. & Greenberg. J. (1990). Creating zones of possibilities: Combining social contexts for instruction. In L.C. Moll (ed.), *Vygotsky and education* (pp. 319–348). Cambridge. UK: Cambridge University Press.

Montero, A. P. & Samuels, D. (eds). (2004). *Decentralization and democracy in Latin America*. Notre Dame, IN: University of Notre Dame Press.

Montessori, M. (1972). *Education and peace*. Chicago, IL: Regency.

Moodley, K. (1999). Antiracist education through political literacy: The case of Canada. In May, S. (ed.). 1999. *Critical multiculturalism: Rethinking multicultural and antiracist education* (pp. 138–152). Philadelphia, PA: Falmer Press.

Morgan, B. (1998). *The ESL classroom: Teaching, practice, and community development.* Toronto, Canada: University of Toronto Press.

Morgan, B. (2004). Modals and memories: A grammar lesson on the Quebec referendum on sovereignty. In B. Norton & K. Toohey (eds), *Critical pedagogies and language learning* (pp. 158–178). Cambridge, UK: Cambridge University Press.

Morgan, B. (2009). Fostering transformative practitioners for critical EAP: Possibilities and challenges. *Journal of English for Academic Purposes, 8*, 86–99.

Morrell, E. (2003, March). Writing the word and the world; Critical literacy as critical text production. Unpublished paper presented at the 54th annual Conference on College Composition and Communication, New York (ED 475208).

Morrison, T. & Morrison, S. (1999). *The big box.* New York: Hyperion.

Morss, J. R. (1996). *Growing critical: Alternatives to developmental psychology.* London, UK: Routledge.

Moss, P. (1996). Enlarging the dialogue in educational measurement: Voices from interpretive research traditions. *Educational Researcher, 25*, 20–28.

Mouffe, C. (1988). Radical democracy: Modern or postmodern? In A. Ross (ed.), *Universal abandon? The politics of postmodernism* (pp. 52–45). Minneapolis, MN: University of Minnesota Press.

Mouffe, C. (1992). Democratic politics today. In C. Mouffe (ed.), *Dimensions of radical democracy: Pluralism, citizenship, community* (pp. 1–14). London, UK: Verso.

Mouffe, C. (2000). *The democratic paradox.* London, UK: Verso.

Mouffe, C. (2005). *On the political.* London, UK: Routledge.

Mphahlele, E. (1959). *Down Second Avenue.* London, UK: Faber and Faber.

Murdoch, K. & Le Mescam, N. (2009). Negotiating the curriculum with students: A conversation worth having. *Education Quarterly Australia.* Retrieved March 2012 from www.eqa.edu.au/site/negotiatingthecurriculum.html

Murphey, T. (2010). *The tale that wags.* Tokyo, Japan: Perceptia Press.

Na, Y. & Kim, S. (2003). Critical literacy in the EFL classroom. *English Teaching 58*(3), 143–163.

Nagai, M. (1976). *Education and indoctrination: The sociological and philosophical bases.* Tokyo, Japan: University of Tokyo Press. (Originally published 1952.)

Nagata, Y. (2007). *Alternative education: Global perspectives relevant to the Asia-Pacific region.* Dordrecht, Netherlands: Springer.

Nardi, B. A. (1996). Activity theory and human-computer interaction. In B. A. Nardi (ed.), *Context and consciousness: Activity theory and human-computer interaction* (pp. 7–16). Cambridge, MA: MIT Press.

Nash, A., Cason, A., Rhum, M., McGrail, L. & Gomez-Sanford, R. (1992). *Talking shop: A curriculum sourcebook for participatory adult ESL.* Washington, DC: Center for Applied Linguistics/Delta Systems.

National Education Crisis Committee (1987). NECC press release: 1986. In University of the Western Cape & National Education Coordinating Committee (South Africa), *People's education for teachers.* Bellville, South Africa: University of the Western Cape.

Neill, A. S. (1937). *That dreadful school.* London, UK: Jenkins.

Nelson, C. (1999). Sexual identities in ESL: Queer Theory and classroom inquiry. *TESOL Quarterly, 33*(3), 371–391.

Nelson, C. A. (2010). A gay immigrant student's perspective: Unspeakable acts in the language class *TESOL Quarterly, 44*(3), 441–464.

Newfield, D. (1993). *Words and pictures.* Witwatersrand, South Africa: Hodder & Stoughton/ Witwatersrand University Press.

Nguyen, H. T. & Kellogg, G. (2005). Emergent identities in on-line discussions for second language learning. *The Canadian Modern Language Review, 62,* 111–136.

Nicholls, J. G. & Hazzard, S. P. (1995). Students as collaborators in curriculum construction. In J. G. Nicholls & T. A. Thorkildsen (eds), *Reasons for learning: Expanding the conversation on student–teacher collaboration* (pp. 114–136). New York: Teachers College Press.

Nieto, S. (1999). Critical multicultural education and students' perspectives. In May, S. (ed.). 1999. *Critical multiculturalism: Rethinking multicultural and antiracist education* (pp. 191–215). Philadelphia, PA: Falmer Press.

Norton, B. (1995). Social identity, investment, and language learning. *TESOL Quarterly, 29,* 9–31.

Norton, B. (ed.) (1997a). Language and identity [special issue]. *TESOL Quarterly, 31*(3).

Norton, B. (1997b). Language, identity, and the ownership of English. *TESOL Quarterly, 31,* 409–429.

Norton, B. (2000). *Identity and language learning: Gender, ethnicity, and educational change.* Harlow, UK: Pearson Education.

Norton, B. & Pavlenko, A. (2004a). *Gender and English language learners.* Washington, DC: TESOL.

Norton, B. & Pavlenko, A. (2004b). Addressing gender in the ESL/EFL classroom. *TESOL Quarterly, 38*(4), 504–514.

Norton, B. & Toohey, K. (eds). (2004). *Critical pedagogies and language learning.* Cambridge, UK: Cambridge University Press.

Nozaki, Y. (2000). Essentializing dilemma and multiculturalist pedagogy: An ethnographic study of Japanese children in a U.S. school. *Anthropology & Education Quarterly, 31*(3), 355–80.

Numrich, C. (2003). *Consider the issues.* New York: Pearson.

Nunan, D. (1985). *Language teaching course design*. Adelaide, Australia: National Curriculum Resource Centre.

O'Cadiz, M. del P., Wong, P. L. & Torres, C. A. (1998). *Education and democracy: Paulo Freire, social movements, and educational reform in Sao Paulo*. Boulder, CO: Westview Press.

Ogawa, R. T. (1994). The institutional sources of educational reform: The case of school-based management. *American Educational Research Journal, 31*(3), 519–548.

O'Halloran, K. (2003). *Critical discourse analysis and language cognition*. Edinburgh, UK: Edinburgh University Press.

Ohara, Y., S. Saft & G. Crookes. (2001). Toward a feminist critical pedagogy in a beginning Japanese as a foreign language class. *Japanese Language and Literature: Journal of the Association of Teachers of Japanese, 35*(2), 105–133.

O'Mochain, R. (2006). Discussing gender and sexuality in a context-appropriate way; queer narratives in an EFL college classroom in Japan. *Journal of Language, Identity, and Education, 5*(1), 51–66.

Orlek, J. (1993). *Languages in South Africa*. Witwatersrand, South Africa: Hodder & Stoughton/Witwatersrand University Press.

Osborn, T. (2006). *Teaching world languages for social justice*. Mahwah, NJ: Lawrence Erlbaum.

O'Sullivan, E. (ed.). (1999). *Transformative learning: Building educational vision in the 21st century*. London, UK: Zed Books.

Oyler, C. (2011). *Actions speak louder than words; Community activism as curriculum*. New York: Routledge.

Nussbaum, M. (1995). *Poetic justice: The literary imagination and public life*. Boston, MA: Beacon Press.

Palmer, R. R. (1985). *The improvement of humanity: Education and the French revolution*. Princeton, NJ: Princeton University Press.

Panofsky, C. P. (2003). The relations of learning and student social class: Toward "re-socializing" Sociocultural Learning Theory. In A. Kozulin, B. Gindis, V. S. Ageyev & S. M. Miller (eds), *Vygotsky's educational theory in cultural context* (pp. 411–431). New York: Cambridge University Press.

Parker, F. W. (1937). *Talks on pedagogics*. New York: John Day for Progressive Education Association. (Originally published 1891.)

Parkinson & O'Sullivan, K. (1990). Negotiating the learner-centered curriculum. In G. Brindley (ed.), *The second language curriculum in action* (pp. 112–127). Macquarie University: National Centre for Language Teaching and Research.

Parr, T. (2004). *The peace book*. New York: Little, Brown.

Pavlenko, A. (2000). Access to linguistic resources: Key variable in second language learning. *Estudios de Sociolingüística, 1*(2), 85–105.

Pavlenko, A. & Blackledge, A. (eds). (2004). *Negotiation of identities in multilingual contexts*. Clevedon, UK: Multilingual Matters.

Pecheux, M. (1982). *Language, semantics and ideology: Stating the obvious*. London, UK: Macmillan.

Pennycook, A. (1994). *The cultural politics of English as an international language*. New York: Longman.

Pennycook, A. (2001). *Critical applied linguistics*. Mahwah, NJ: Lawrence Erlbaum.

Pennycook, A. (2004). Critical moments in a TESOL praxicum. In B. Norton & K. Toohey (eds), *Critical pedagogies and language learning* (pp. 327–346). Cambridge, UK: Cambridge University Press.

Pestalozzi, J. H. (1910). *Leonard and Gertrude* (E. Channing, trans., ed.). Boston, MA: D. C. Heath. (Originally published 1781.)

Pestalozzi, J. H. (1898). *How Gertrude teaches her children.* Syracuse, NY: E. W. Bardeen. (Originally published 1801.)

Peters, M. (1995). Radical democracy, the politics of difference, and education In B. Kanpol & P. McLaren (eds), *Critical multiculturalism* (pp. 39–57). Westport, CT: Bergin & Garvey.

Peterson, B. (1994). The complexities of encouraging social action. In B. Bigelow, L. Christensen, S. Karp, B. Miner & B. Peterson (eds). *Rethinking our classrooms* (vol. 1, pp. 40–41). Milwaukee, WI: Rethinking Schools.

Petrie, B. M. (1985). ESL through issues in the women's movement. *TESL CANADA Journal, 3*(1), 59–69.

Pierce, B. N. (1989). Toward a pedagogy of possibility in the teaching of English internationally: People's English in South Africa. *TESOL Quarterly, 23*(3), 401–420.

Pike, G. & Selby, D. (1988). *Global teacher, global learner.* London, UK: Hodder & Stoughton.

Pittenger, B. F. (1941). *Indoctrination for American democracy.* New York: Macmillan.

Placzek, B. (ed.). (1982). *Record of a friendship: The correspondence of Wilhelm Reich and A. S. Neill.* New York: Farrar, Strauss & Giroux.

Popkewitz, T. S. (ed.) (2005). *Inventing the modern self and John Dewey.* New York: Palgrave Macmillan.

Porter, P. A. & Grant, M. (1992). *Communicating effectively in English: Oral communication for non-native speakers.* Belmont, CA: Wadsworth.

Prilleltensky, I. & Nelson, G. (2002). *Doing psychology critically: Making difference in diverse settings.* New York: Palgrave Macmillan.

Prilleltensky, I. & Prilleltensky, O. (2006). *Promoting well-being: Linking personal, organizational, and community change.* Hoboken, NJ: John Wiley.

Purcell-Gates, V. & Waterman, R. (2000). *Now we read, we see, we speak: Portrait of literacy development in an adult Freirean-based class.* Mahwah, NJ: Erlbaum.

Radunsky, V. (2004). *What does peace feel like?* New York: Simon & Schuster.

Rajagopalan, K. (2004). TESOL and the question of learners' cultural identity: Towards a critical approach. *ITL, Review of Applied Linguistics, 145–146,* 167–179.

Ratner, C. (2000). Agency and culture. *Journal for The Theory of Social Behaviour, 30,* 413–434.

Ravitch, D. (2010). *The death and life of the great American school system.* New York: Basic Books.

Reardon, B. (1988). *Comprehensive peace education.* New York: Teachers College Press.

Reeve, A. (1987). *Modern theories of exploitation.* London, UK: Sage.

Renner, C. E. (1991, June). Using the language of justice and peace: Integrating peace education into EFL curriculum. Unpublished paper presented at the 4th International Conference of Teachers for Peace, Paris, France (ED 375610).

Rhodes, F. H. T. (ed.). (1997). *Successful fund raising for higher education.* Phoenix, AZ: American Council on Education/ Oryx Press.

Ricento, T. (2005). Considerations of identity in L2 learning. In E. Hinkel (ed.), *Handbook of research on second language teaching and learning* (pp. 895–910). New York: Routledge.

Richards, K. (2008). Making the break: Establishing a new school. In S. Garton & K. Richards (eds), *Professional encounters in TESOL* (pp. 173–191). London, UK: Palgrave Macmillan.

Riley, K. L. & Stern, B. S. (2002). "A Bootlegged Curriculum": The American Legion versus Harold Rugg. Unpublished paper (ED 465674).

Rivers, W. (1968). Teaching foreign language skills. Chicago, IL: University of Chicago Press.

Roberts, P. (1996). Rethinking conscientization. Journal of Philosophy of Education, 30(2), 179–196.

Robin, P. (1869–1872). De l'enseignement intégrale. Revue de Philosophie Positive, 5, 7 & 9.

Rodall, C. A. S. & Martin, C. J. (2009). School-based management and citizen participation: Lessons for public education from local educational projects. Journal of Education Policy, 24(3), 317–333.

Rofes, E. & Stulberg, L. M. (eds). (2004). The emancipatory promise of charter schools. Albany, NY: SUNY Press.

Rogers, J. (1982). The world for sick proper. ELT Journal, 36(3), 144–151.

Rogers, R. (2004). An introduction to Critical Discourse Analysis in education. In R. Rogers (ed.), An introduction to critical discourse analysis in education (pp. 1–18). Mahwah, NJ: Erlbaum.

Rogoff, B. & Lave, J. (eds). (1984). Everyday cognition: Its development in social context. Cambridge, MA: Harvard University Press.

Röhrs, H. & Lenhart, V. (1995). Progressive education across the continents. Berlin, Germany: Peter Lang.

Rosenblum, S. (1996). Union-sponsored workplace ESL instruction. ERIC Digest (ED392317).

Rousseau, J.-J., (1979). Emile or on education (trans. A. Bloom). New York: Basic Books.

Rugg, H. (1931). An introduction to problems of American culture. Boston, MA: Ginn & Co.

Rule, P. (1993). Language and the news. Witwatersrand, South Africa: Hodder & Stoughton/ Witwatersrand University Press.

Russell, B. (1926). On education. London, UK: Unwin.

Sadeghi, S. (2009). Critical pedagogy in an EFL teaching context: Ignis fatuus or an alternative approach? In L. J. Zhang, R. Rubdy & L. Alsagoff (eds), Englishes and literatures-in-English in a globalised world: Proceedings of the 13th International Conference on English in Southeast Asia (pp. 349–362). Singapore: National Institute of Education, Nanyang Technological University.

Sakui, K. (2007). Classroom management in Japanese EFL classrooms. JALT Journal, 29(1), 41–58.

Samuda, V. & Bygate, M. (2008). Tasks in second language learning. Basingstoke, UK: Palgrave Macmillan.

Santos, T. (2001). The place of politics in second language writing. In T. Silva & P. Matsuda (eds), On second language writing (pp. 173–190). Mahwah, NJ: Erlbaum.

Sartre, J.-P. (2004). The imaginary: A phenomenological psychology of the imagination. New York: Routledge. (Originally published 1940.)

Sarup, M. (1991). Education and the ideologies of racism. Stoke-on-Trent, UK: Trentham.

Sattler, C. L. (1997). Talking about a revolution: The politics and practice of feminist teaching. Cresskill, NJ: Hampton Press.

Sawchuk, P. H., Duarte, N. & El Hammoumi, M. (eds). (2006). Critical perspectives on activity: Explorations across education, work, and everyday life. Cambridge, UK: Cambridge University Press.

Sawchuk, P. H. (2006). Activity and power: Everyday life and development of working-class groups. In P. H. Sawchuk, N. Duarte & M. El Hammoumi, (eds), Critical perspectives on activity: Explorations across education, work, and everyday life (pp. 238–268). Cambridge, UK: Cambridge University Press.

Scarcella, R. (1976). Socio-drama for social interaction. *TESOL Quarterly, 12*, 41–46.

Schecter, D. (2005). *Beyond hegemony: Towards a new philosophy of political hegemony.* Manchester, UK: Manchester University Press.

Schenke, A. (1996). Not just a "social issue": Teaching feminist in ESL. *TESOL Quarterly, 30*, 155–159.

Schleppegrell, M. S. & Bowman, B. (1995). Problem-posing: A tool for curriculum renewal. *ELT Journal*, 49, 297–307.

Schneiter, P. H. & Nelson, D. T. (1982). *The thirteen most common fund-raising mistakes.* Washington, DC: Taft Corporation.

Schniedewind, N. (1975a). *A model integrating personal and social change in teacher education; its implementation in a racism and sexism training program.* (Unpublished doctoral dissertation.) University of Massachusetts, MA.

Schniedewind, N. (1975b). A model integrating personal and social change in teacher education: A project report (ED 150095).

Schniedewind, N. (1987). Feminist values: Guidelines for teaching methodology in Women's Studies. In I. Shor (ed.), *Freire in the classroom* (pp. 171–179). Portsmouth, NH: Boynton/Cook. (Originally published 1978.)

Schniedewind, N. (1993). Teaching feminist process in the 1990s. *Women's Studies Quarterly*, 21(3 & 4), 17–30.

Scollon, R & Scollon, S. B. K. (1981). *Narrative, literacy, and face in interethnic communication.* Norwood, NJ: Ablex.

Schrag, F. (2006). The school is the problem, not the solution. *Theory and Research in Education, 6*, 283–307.

Schraube, E. (2000). Reflecting on who we are in a technological world. In T. Sloan (ed.), *Critical psychology.* London, UK: Macmillan.

Schumann, J. H. (1978). The acculturation model for second-language acquisition. In R. C. Gingras (ed.), *Second language acquisition and foreign language teaching* (pp. 27–50). Washington, DC: Center for Applied Linguistics.

Schutz, A. (2001). John Dewey's conundrum; Can democratic schools empower? *Teachers College Record, 103*(2), 267–302.

Seedhouse, P., Walsh, S. & Jenks, C. (2010). *Conceptualising "learning" in applied linguistics.* London, UK: Palgrave Macmillan.

Seuss, Dr. (1984). *The butter battle book.* New York: Random House.

Shannon, P. (1990). *Struggle to continue.* Portsmouth, NH: Heinemann.

Shapiro, S. (ed.). (2009). *Education and hope in troubled times.* New York: Routledge.

Shatkin, G. & Gershberg, A. I. (2007). Empowering parents and building communities: The role of school-based councils in educational governance and accountability. *Urban Education, 42*(6), 582–615.

Shin, J. K. (2004). The use of Freirean pedagogy in teaching English as an international language: Raising the critical consciousness of EFL teachers in Korea. *LLC Review*, 4(1), 64–84. [University of Maryland Baltimore County, Language, Literacy and Culture Department.] Retrieved June 2008 from http://www.umbc.edu/llc/llcreview/2004/llcreview2004.html

Shin, H. & Crookes, G. (2005a). Indigenous critical traditions for TEFL?—A historical and comparative perspective in the case of Korea. *Critical Inquiry in Language Studies, 2*(2), 95–112.

Shin, H. & Crookes, G. (2005b). Exploring the possibilities for EFL critical pedagogy in Korea – a two-part case study. *Critical Inquiry in Language Studies, 2*(2), 113–138.

Shirley, D. (1997). *Community organizing for urban school reform.* Austin, TX: University of Texas Press.

Shohamy, E. (2001a). Democratic assessment as an alternative. *Language Testing, 18*(4), 373–391.

Shohamy, E. (2001b). *The power of tests: A critical perspective on the uses of language tests.* Harlow, UK: Pearson.

Shor, I. (1980). *Critical teaching and everyday life.* Boston, MA: South End Press.

Shor, I. (ed.). (1987). *Freire for the classroom.* Portsmouth, NH: Boynton/Cook.

Shor, I. (1992). *Empowering Education: Critical teaching for social change.* Chicago, IL: University of Chicago Press.

Shor, I. (1996). *When students have power.* Chicago, IL: University of Chicago Press.

Shor, I. & Freire, P. (1987). *A pedagogy for liberation: Dialogues on transforming education.* New York: Bergin & Garvey.

Shulman, M. (1988). *Cultures in contrast.* Ann Arbor, MI: University of Michigan Press.

Shulman, M. (2004). *Thinking critically: World issues for reading, writing and research.* Ann Arbor, MI: University of Michigan Press.

Simon, R. (1987). Empowerment as a pedagogy of possibility. *Language Arts, 64,* 370–382.

Simon, R. (1992). *Teaching against the grain: Texts for a pedagogy of possibility.* New York: Bergin & Garvey.

Simon-Maeda, A. (2004). Transforming emerging feminist identities: A course on gender and language issues. In B. Norton & A. Pavlenko (eds), *Gender and English Language Learners* (pp. 127–143). Washington DC: TESOL.

Skutnabb-Kangas, T. (2000). *Linguistic genocide in education--or worldwide diversity and human rights?* Mahwah, NJ: Lawrence Erlbaum.

Small, R. (2005). *Marx and education.* Aldershot, UK: Ashgate.

Smith, L. C. & Mare, N. N. (1990). *Issues for today: An effective reading skills text.* New York: Newbury House.

Smith, M. P. (1983). *The libertarians and education.* London, UK: George Allen & Unwin.

Smith, P. B. (2009). Reflections on aspects of Marxist anti-utopianism. *Critique: Journal of Socialist Theory, 37*(1), 99–120.

Smith, W. (1976). *The meaning of conscientizacao: The goal of Paulo Freire's pedagogy.* Amherst, MA: Center for International Education, University of Massachusetts (ED 171651).

Smyth, J. (1987). *Rationale for teachers' critical pedagogy: A handbook.* Geelong, Australia: Deakin University Press.

Smyth, J. (ed.). (1989). *Critical perspectives on educational leadership.* London, UK: Falmer Press.

Snook, I. A. (1972a). *Indoctrination and education.* London, UK: Routledge & Kegan Paul.

Snook, I. A. (ed.). (1972b). *Concepts of indoctrination: Philosophical essays.* Boston, MA: Routledge & Kegan Paul.

South African Council of Higher Education (1988). *Down Second Avenue: The Comic.* Johannesburg, South Africa: Ravan Press/Sached Trust.

Spivak, G. (1987). *In other worlds: Essays in cultural politics.* London, UK: Taylor and Francis.

Stanley, W. B. (1992). *Curriculum for utopia: Social reconstructionism and critical pedagogy in the postmodern era.* New York: SUNY Press.

Stapp, W. B., Bennet, D., Bryan, W., Fulton, J., Swan, J. & Wall, R. (1969). The concept of environmental education. *Journal of Environmental Education, 1*(1), 30–31.

Starkey, H. (1988). Foreign languages. In G. Pike & D. Selby (eds), *Global teacher, global learner* (pp. 239–241). London, UK: Hodder & Stoughton.

Steger, W. & Bowermaster, J. (1990). *Saving the Earth: A citizen's guide to environmental action*. New York: Harper & Row.

Steig, W. (1984). *Rotten island*. New York: David R. Godine.

Stempleski, S. (1993). From the classroom to the world: The environment and EFL. *English Teaching Forum, 31*(4), 2–11.

Stevens, V. (2006). *Second Life* in education and language learning. *TESL-EJ, 10*(3). Retrieved from www.tesl-ej.org/wordpress/

Stevick, E. (1986). *Images and options in the language classroom*. Cambridge, UK: Cambridge University Press.

Stomfay-Stitz, A. (1993). *Peace education in America: 1828–1990: Sourcebook for education and research*. Metuchen, NJ: Scarecrow Press.

Stone, M. K. (1999). The Francis W. Parker school: Chicago's Progressive Education legacy. In S. F. Semel & A. R. Sadovnik (eds), *"Schools of tomorrow, schools of today": What happened to progressive education* (pp. 23–66). New York: Peter Lang.

Sullivan, E. V. (1984). *A critical psychology: Interpretation of the personal world*. New York: Plenum Press.

Sullivan, E. V. (1990). *Critical psychology and critical pedagogy*. New York: Bergin & Garvey.

Sung, K. W. (2001). Changing the terrain of English teaching: An inquiry approach using multimedia. *Multimedia-assisted Language Learning, 4*(1), 57–85.

Sung, K. W. (2002). Critical theory and pedagogy: Remapping English teaching in Korea. *English Teaching, 57*(2), 65–89.

Sung, K. W. (2006). A critical analysis of current discursive practices in ELT in Korea. *Foreign Language Education, 13*(3), 80–104.

Sung, K. (2007). In P. McLaren & J. L. Kincheloe (eds), *Critical pedagogy: Where are we now?* (pp. 163–182). Berlin, Germany: Peter Lang.

Surat, M. (1990). *Angel child, dragon child*. New York: Scholastic.

Swain, A. (ed.). (2005). *Education as social action, knowledge, identity and power*. New York: Palgrave Macmillan.

Swan, J.A. (1969). The challenge of environmental education. *Phi Delta Kappan, 51*, 26–28.

Swing, E. S. (2000). *Problems and prospects in European education*. New York: Greenwood.

Sworowski, J. (1995). Condorcet's education: Haunted by the ghost of Rousseau. *International Journal of Lifelong Education, 14*(3), 320–330.

Takayama, K. (2009). Progressive struggle and critical education scholarship in Japan: Toward the democratization of critical education studies. In M. W. Apple, W. Au & L. A. Gandin (eds), *The Routledge international handbook of critical education* (pp. 354–367). New York: Routledge.

Tajfel, H. (1982). Social psychology of intergroup relations. *Annual Review of Psychology, 33, 1–39.*

Taylor, L. (2006). Wrestling with race: The implications of integrative antiracism education for immigrant ESL youth. *TESOL Quarterly, 40*(3), 519–544.

Taylor, P. V. (1993). *The texts of Paulo Freire*. Buckingham, UK: Open University Press.

Templer, B. (2009). Graphic novels in the ESL classroom. *Humanising Language Teaching, 11*(3). Retrieved from http://www.hltmag.co.uk/jun09/mart03.htm

Theoharis, G. (2007). Social justice educational leaders and resistance: Toward a theory of social justice leadership. *Educational Administration Quarterly, 43*, 221–258.

Thorne, S. L. (2004). Cultural historical activity theory and the object of innovation. In K. van Esch & Oliver St. John (eds), *New insights into foreign language learning and teaching* (pp. 51–68). Berlin, Germany: Peter Lang.

Thorne, S. L. (2005). Epistemology, politics, and ethics in sociocultural theory. *Modern Language Journal, 89*(3), 393–409.

Thorne, S. L. & Lantolf, J. P. (2006). A linguistics of communicative activity. In S. Makoni & A. Pennycook (eds), *Disinventing and reconstituting languages* (pp. 170–195). Clevedon, UK: Multilingual Matters.

Tilly, C. (2003). When do (and don't) social movements promote democratization? In P. Ibarra (ed.), *Social movements and democracy* (pp. 21–45). New York: Palgrave Macmillan.

Tilly, C. (2004). *Social movements, 1768–2004*, Boulder, CO: Paradigm Publishers.

Tolman, C. W. (1994). *Psychology, society, and subjectivity: An introduction to German critical psychology.* London, UK: Routledge.

Tonkiss, F. (2008). Postcapitalist politics? *Economy and Society, 37*(2), 304–312.

Torres, C. A. (1994). Popular education: Building from experience. In A. Brooks & K. E. Watkins (eds), *The emerging power of action inquiry technologies* (pp. 81–92; New Directions for Adult and Continuing Education, no. 63). San Francisco, CA: Jossey-Bass.

Tyler, M. H. C., Bretherton, D., Halfoff, A. & Yung, N. (2008). Developing a peace education curriculum for Vietnamese primary schools. *Journal of Research in International Education, 7*(3), 346–368.

Tyler, R. W. (1949). *Basic principles of curriculum and instruction.* Chicago, IL: University of Chicago Press.

Van Allsburg, C. (1990). *Just a dream.* New York: Houghton Mifflin.

Vandrick, S. (1994). Feminist pedagogy and ESL. *College ESL, 1*(2), 69–92.

Vandrick, S. (1995). Teaching and practicing feminism in the university ESL Class. *TESOL Journal, 1*(3), 4–6.

Vandrick, S. (1999). Who's afraid of critical feminist pedagogies? *TESOL Matters 9*, 9.

Vandrick, S. (2000). Selected resources on critical and feminist ESL/EFL pedagogies. *TESOLers for Social Responsibility Newsletter, 1*(2), 9–10.

Vandrick, S. (2001, March). Teaching sexual identity issues in ESL classes. Unpublished paper presented at the 35th annual TESOL convention, St Louis, MO (ED 474464).

Vandrick, S. (2005a). Feminist pedagogy and TESOL in a "postfeminist" age. *TESOLers for Social Responsibility Newsletter, 5*(1).

Vandrick, S. (2005b, March). ESL, feminist pedagogy, and social class. Unpublished paper presented at TESOL Conference, San Antonio, TX.

Vandrick, S. (2009). *Interrogating privilege: Reflections of a second language educator.* Ann Arbor, MI: University of Michigan Press.

Van Duinen, D. V. (2005). Authentic assessment: Praxis with power. *International Journal of Learning, 12*(6), 141–148.

van Lier, L. (2004). *The ecology and semiotics of language learning: A sociocultural perspective.* Boston, MA: Kluwer.

Vavrus, M. J. (2002). *Transforming the multicultural education of teachers: Theory, research and practice.* New York, NY: Teachers College Press.

Vygotsky, L. (1997). *Educational psychology.* Boca Raton, FL: CRC Press. (Originally published 1926.)

Wallace, C. (1992). Critical literacy in the EFL classroom. In N. Fairclough (ed.), *Critical language awareness* (pp. 59–92). London, UK: Longman.

Wallace, C. (1999). Critical Language Awareness: Key principles for a course in Critical Reading. *Language Awareness, 8*(2), 98–110.

Wallace, C. (2003). *Critical reading in language education.* London, UK: Macmillan.

Wallace, J. M. (1995). The origins and development of Progressive Education in the United States of America: New world progressives in the old world. In H. Röhrs & V. Lenhart (eds), *Progressive education across the continents* (pp. 133–146). Berlin, Germany: Peter Lang.

Wallerstein, N. (1983a). *Language and culture in conflict: Problem-posing in the ESL classroom.* New York: Addison Wesley.

Wallerstein, N. (1983b). The teaching approach of Paulo Freire. In J. W. Oller & P. A. Richard-Amato (eds), *Methods that work* (pp. 190–204). Rowley, MA: Newbury House.

Wallerstein, N. (1983c). Problem posing can help students learn: From refugee camps to resettlement country classrooms. *TESOL Newsletter, 17*(5), 1–2, 5.

Wallerstein, N. & Auerbach, E. (2004). *Problem-posing at work: Popular educator's guide.* Edmonton, Canada: Grass Roots Press.

Wang, W. & Zhang, K. (2007). Tao Xingzhi and the emergence of public education in China. In D. T. Hansen (ed.), *Ethical visions of education* (pp. 95–110). New York: Teachers College Press.

Washburne, C. & Stearns, M. (1926). *New schools in the old world.* New York: John Day.

Waters, A. (2009). Managing innovation in English language education. *Language Teaching, 42*(4), 421–458.

Watras, J. (2003). Relativism and indoctrination: The critical reception of the Commission on the Social Studies, 1926–1941. *International Journal of Social Education, 18*(2), 47–57.

Watts, R. J., Griffiths, D. M. & Abdul-Adil, J. (1999). Sociopolitical development as an antidote for oppression—theory and action. *American Journal of Community Psychology, 27*(2), 255–272.

Watts, R. J., Williams, N. C. & Jagers, R. J. (2003). Sociopolitical development. *American Journal of Community Psychology, 31*(1/2), 185–194.

Weil, D. K. (1998). *Towards a critical multicultural literacy.* New York: Peter Lang.

Weinstein, C. S., Tomlinson-Clarke, S. & Curran, M. (2006). Toward a conception of culturally responsive classroom management. *Journal of Teacher Education, 55*(1), 25–38.

Wenger, E. (1998). *Communities of practice: Learning, meaning and identity.* Cambridge, UK: Cambridge University Press.

Wenman, M. A. (2003). Laclau or Mouffe? Splitting the difference. *Philosophy & Social Criticism, 29*(5), 581–606.

Wertsch, J. V., del Rio, P. & Alvarez, A. (eds). 1995. *Sociocultural studies of mind.* Cambridge, UK: Cambridge University Press.

West, G. (2010). My fruitless efforts to change national education. *Grenoble Life.* Retrieved March 2012 from http://www.grenoblelife.com/my-fruitless-efforts-to-change-national-education/

White, R., Hockley, A., Jansen, J. van deer H. & Laughner, M. S. (2008). *From teacher to manager: Managing language teaching organizations.* Cambridge, UK: Cambridge University Press.

Whitty, G., Gewirtz, S. & Edwards, T. (2000). New schools for new times? Notes toward a sociology of recent education reform. In T. S. Popkewitz (ed.), *Educational knowledge: Changing relationships between the state, civil society, and the educational community* (pp. 111–130). Albany, NY: SUNY Press.

Wieder, A. (ed.). (2003). *Voices from Cape Town classrooms.* New York: Peter Lang.

Wilkins, D. (1976). *Notional syllabuses.* Oxford, UK: Oxford University Press.

Williams, M. R. (1989). *Neighborhood organizing for school reform.* New York: Teachers College Press.

Williams, W. & Robins, W. (1980). Observations on the California case. In C. Fletcher & N. Thompson (eds), *Issues in Community Education* (pp. 55–62). Barcombe, UK: Falmer Press.

Willis, P. E. (1977). *Learning to labor: How working class kids get working class jobs.* New York: Columbia University Press.

Wink, J. (1997). *Critical pedagogy: Notes from the real world.* New York: Longman.

Wolfe-Quintero, K. & Okazaki, T. (2004, Feb.). Analyzing input: Content-based grammar teaching. Unpublished paper presented at the Hawaii TESOL conference, Honolulu, HI.

Wong, S. (2006). *Dialogic approaches to TESOL: Where the ginkgo tree grows.* New York: Routledge.

Wong, P-Y. C., Chan, C-W. & Firkins, A. (2006). School-based critical literacy programme in a Hong Kong secondary school. *Hong Kong Teachers' Centre Journal, 5,* 129–139.

Woods, P. A. & Woods, G. J. (eds). (2009). *Alternative education for the 21st century.* London, UK: Palgrave Macmillan.

World Bank (2007). *What do we know about school-based management?* Washington, DC: International Bank for Reconstruction and Development/The World Bank.

Wright, N. (1989). *Assessing radical education: A critical review of the radical movement in English schooling, 1960–1980.* Milton Keynes, UK: Open University Press.

Wright, T. (2005). *Classroom management in language education.* New York: Palgrave Macmillan.

Xu, Z. (2002). An overview of private education development in modern China. *Education Policy Analysis Archives, 10*(47). Retrieved from epaa.asu.edu

Yamada, M. (2011). Awareness of racial and ethnic diversity in Japanese junior high schools' English language textbooks. *Critical Inquiry in Language Studies, 8*(3), 289–312.

Yang, A. & Cheung, C. P. (2003). Adapting textbook activities for communicative teaching and cooperative learning. *English Teaching Forum, 41*(3). http://exchanges.state.gov/forum/vols/voI41/n03/pI6.htm.

Yasnitsky, A. (2009). *Vygotsky circle during the decade of 1931–1941: Toward an integrative science of mind, brain, and education.* (Unpublished doctoral dissertation.) Toronto, Canada: Ontario Institute for Studies in Education, University of Toronto.

Young, I. M. (1990). *Justice and the politics of difference.* Princeton, NJ: Princeton University Press.

Young, I. M. (2000). *Inclusion and democracy.* Oxford, UK: Oxford University Press.

Young, K. S., Wood, J. T., Phillips, G. M. & Pedersen, D. J. (2001). *Group discussion: A practical guide to participation and leadership* (3rd edn.). Prospect Heights, IL: Waveland Press.

Zhang, L. & Adamson, B. (2011). The new Independent higher education institutions in China: Dilemmas and challenges. *Higher Education Quarterly, 65*(3), 251–266.

Zinchenko, V. P. (1995). Cultural-historical psychology and the psychological theory of activity: Retrospect and prospect. In J. V. Wertsch, P. del Rio, and A. Alvarez (eds), *Sociocultural Studies of Mind* (pp. 37–55). Cambridge, UK: Cambridge University Press.

Zuengler, J. & Miller, E. R. (2006). Cognitive and sociocultural perspectives: Two parallel SLA worlds? *TESOL Quarterly, 40*(1), 35–59.

INDEX

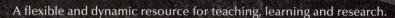